GOVERNMENTAL FINANCIAL RESILIENCE: INTERNATIONAL PERSPECTIVES ON HOW LOCAL GOVERNMENTS FACE AUSTERITY

PUBLIC POLICY AND GOVERNANCE

Series Editor: Evan Berman

Previously published as Research in Public Policy Analysis and Management

Recent Volumes:

PUBLIC POLICY AND GOVERNANCE   VOLUME 27

GOVERNMENTAL FINANCIAL RESILIENCE: INTERNATIONAL PERSPECTIVES ON HOW LOCAL GOVERNMENTS FACE AUSTERITY

EDITED BY

ILEANA STECCOLINI
Newcastle University London, UK

MARTIN JONES
Nottingham Business School, UK

IRIS SALITERER
Albert-Ludwigs University Freiburg, Germany

emerald
PUBLISHING

United Kingdom – North America – Japan
India – Malaysia – China

Emerald Publishing Limited
Howard House, Wagon Lane, Bingley BD16 1WA, UK

First edition 2017

British Library Cataloguing in Publication Data
A catalogue record for this book is available from the British Library

ISBN: 978-1-78714-263-3 (Print)
ISBN: 978-1-78714-262-6 (Online)
ISBN: 978-1-78714-915-1 (Epub)
ISBN: 978-1-83867-927-9 (Paperback)

ISSN: 2053-7697 (Series)

INVESTOR IN PEOPLE

CONTENTS

LIST OF CONTRIBUTORS

Nora Albrecht	Albert-Ludwigs University Freiburg, Germany
Roland Almqvist	Stockholm University, Sweden
Carmela Barbera	Department of Economics and Business Management Sciences, Catholic University of the Sacred Heart, Milan, Italy
Ricardo Lopes Cardoso	Brazilian School of Public and Business Administration, Getulio Vargas Foundation, Brazil; School of Business and Finance, State University of Rio de Janeiro Rio de Janeiro, Brazil
Sandra Cohen	Athens University of Economics and Business, Greece
André C. B. de Aquino	Accounting Department, School of Economics, Business Administration and Accounting at Ribeirao Preto, University of Sao Paulo, Ribeirão Preto, Brazil
Joseph Drew	University of Technology Sydney, Australia
Céline du Boys	Aix-Marseille University, France
Nikolaos Hlepas	National and Kapodistrian University of Athens, Greece
Martin Jones	Department of Accounting and Finance, Nottingham Business School, Nottingham Trent University, England, UK
Sanja Korac	Alpen-Adria University Klagenfurt, Austria
Tom Overmans	Utrecht University School of Governance, The Netherlands
Ulf Papenfuß	University of Leipzig, Germany
Iris Saliterer	Albert-Ludwigs University Freiburg, Germany

Eric Scorsone	Michigan State University, USA
Ileana Steccolini	Newcastle University London, UK
Niklas Wällstedt	Stockholm University, Sweden

CHAPTER 1

INTRODUCTION: GOVERNMENTS AND CRISES

Iris Saliterer, Martin Jones and Ileana Steccolini

ABSTRACT

Governments are no strangers to dealing with crises. On the contrary, a central role of any government is to absorb, navigate and mitigate them. However, crises themselves are unpredictable and represent a significant challenge to governments at both the national and local level. Despite such uncertainty, studying how governments in different countries respond to crises offers a great opportunity to learn from the past and to understand the nature of resilience in the face of significant shocks and disruption.

This book charts how local governments in 11 countries, covering Europe, the United States, South America and Australia, responded to the recent crises and austerity period by shedding new light on the role of contextual- and policy-related conditions as well as the internal capacities and conditions that may influence responses and, ultimately, performance.

This chapter sets the scene for the book, by highlighting the relevance of examining financial crises and austerity and the ways in which governments, and more specifically, local governments, are facing the related shocks. In doing so, it proposes a preliminary framework for exploring governmental financial resilience at the local level. In such a framework, financial resilience is seen as the dynamic combination of internal and external dimensions,

Governmental Financial Resilience: International Perspectives on how Local Governments Face Austerity
Public Policy and Governance, Volume 27, 1–16
ISSN: 2053-7697/doi:10.1108/S2053-769720170000027001

including the external environment, financial shocks, vulnerability, anticipatory capacity and coping capacity.

Keywords: Local government; austerity; financial resilience

Governments are no strangers to dealing with crises. On the contrary, it could be said that one of central roles of any government is to absorb, navigate and mitigate them. However, crises are not straightforward to solve, as they do not respect timescales, are unexpected and disruptive and tend to be dynamic and chaotic in nature (Boin & 't Hart, 2003). Indeed, they are a challenge to governments, which may even make mistakes along the way in their attempts to deal with them (Peters, 2011).

While crises and shocks are often described as one-shot, unique events, it has been observed that they are increasingly becoming 'routine', requiring governments to be constantly ready to tackle with them, as they are left with the ultimate responsibility to manage and cope with them. As such, there have been increasing claims for studying how governments face crises so as to learn important lessons for the future (Boin & Lodge, 2016). There have also been calls to ensure that the wider complexities and nuances of responses to crises are explored, not only focusing on political and policy perspectives, but also allowing a greater understanding of institutional effects and organisational practices, together with how these are changed and implemented and the outcomes they deliver (Boin, 't Hart, & McConnell, 2009; Lodge & Hood, 2012; Peters, 2011). As such, a multidisciplinary approach may be required to give a fuller understanding of crisis responses within and across governments (Grossi & Cepiku, 2014).

The recent global financial crises, and the ensuing context of austerity, representing another important and contemporary crisis that governments have had to face, can provide an interesting opportunity for learning lessons of general relevance on how governments cope with difficulties and unexpected events. Whereas much of the preceding empirical literature on crisis responses has been focused on discrete events (such as natural disasters or terrorist attacks), and is therefore very localised and not necessarily generalisable, the global financial crisis and austerity period offer the opportunity to examine responses from a large population of essentially similar organisations from a wide range of countries, all facing a similar (though not identical) set of circumstances.

This book shows how local governments in 11 countries responded to the recent crises and austerity by shedding new light on the role of contextual and policy-related conditions as well as the internal capacities and conditions that may influence such responses and, ultimately, performance. In spite of national governments having attracted most scholarly attention (Kickert, 2012; Lodge & Hood, 2012; Peters, 2011; Peters, Pierre, & Randma-Liiv, 2011; and Raudla, Savi, & Randma-Liiv, 2013), local governments are often the residual bearer of the impacts of crises and shocks, and have been significantly affected by recent crises and austerity (Barbera, Guarini, & Steccolini, 2016; Steccolini, Barbera, & Jones, 2015). Moreover, while traditional literature on crises, austerity, fiscal stress, cutback management and financial difficulties has focused on the contextual conditions and the organisational actions and reactions to difficulties, this book considers the role of internal preexisting conditions and organisational capacities in affecting such responses. In doing so, it adopts the conceptual perspective of financial resilience. The concept of resilience, which can be defined more generally as the ability to 'learn how to do better through adversity' (Wildavsky, 1988, p. 2), can contribute to the adoption of a long-term and lifelong perspective on organisational ability to cope with difficult times. Moreover, a resilience perspective can help overcome the traditional focus of management approaches to efficiency, stability and control (Leach, 2008; Shaw, 2012) and point to the likely importance of flexibility and adaptation, or the enduring capacity to absorb shocks (Dalziell & McManus, 2004; Hood, 1991; Martin-Breen & Anderies, 2011; Pain & Levine, 2012; Scotti-Petrillo & Prosperi, 2011).

This chapter sets the scene for the book and in so doing it introduces and explores a number of issues relevant to understanding the following chapters. The remainder of this chapter considers the need to examine the financial crises and austerity period and introduces the concept of financial resilience. It proposes a first framework, where financial resilience is viewed as a dynamic combination of interrelated dimensions which are seen as being at the same time the antecedents and the results of their interactions with the external context and shocks. The possible dimensions of resilience from the literature (in terms of robustness, recovery ability, awareness and flexibility) are identified and translated into a first conceptualization of financial resilience. This seeks to show how local authorities' capacity to anticipate, absorb and react to shocks, which affect their finances over time, can be considered to be a dynamic combination of interrelated dimensions, namely financial shocks, vulnerability, anticipatory capacity and coping capacity. Finally, we discuss the importance of the global financial crisis and associated austerity to the study of resilience before focusing on the impact that each has had on local government.

STUDYING CRISES AND AUSTERITY IN THE PUBLIC SECTOR

Crises have been the subject of enduring interest in public administration and public policy research. While a variety of approaches and standpoints have been adopted in the study of governmental responses to crises, at least three different streams of research can be identified from the literature that are considered below.

The first stream has developed at the intersection of public management and organisation theory (e.g. Andrews, Boyne, & Walker 2012; Boyne & Meier, 2009; Meier & O' Toole, 2009; Meier, O'Toole, & Hicklin, 2010; O' Toole & Meier, 2010), and focuses on organisational reactions to shocks, threats, uncertainties and turbulences. This predominantly quantitative research stream highlights the role of the overall management capacity in coping with shocks, and has pointed to the need to further explore such capacity and its dynamic properties over time (Boyne & Meier, 2009).

The second stream of literature has developed at the intersection of public policy and organisational studies and has been more traditionally focused on understanding how policy makers respond to major crises (such as natural and man-made disasters and terrorist acts) and the effectiveness with which they link to the administrative processes that underpin crisis management and disaster recovery systems (Boin & 't Hart, 2010). More recently, this literature has focused on changing societal conditions that give crises transboundary characteristics, allowing them, as with the financial crisis, to wickedly cut across geographic boundaries and policy sectors (Boin & Lodge, 2016).

The third stream of literature is more focused on financial management and accounting. There is a long-standing academic interest in financial crises and fiscal stress in public sector financial management literature (Behn, 1980; Greenwood, 1981; Hood & Wright, 1981; Levine & Posner, 1981; Levine, 1978, 1979; Schick, 1980). Building on this literature, studies of how governments tackled the fiscal crisis and austerity worldwide have been developed (Baker, 2011; Cepiku & Bonomi Savignon, 2012; Dougherty & Klase, 2009; Klase, 2011; Raudla et al., 2013; Sacco, Stalebrink, & Posner, 2011; Scorsone & Plerhoples, 2010; West & Condrey, 2011), providing detailed accounts and classifications of reactions to the crisis and austerity, therefore ensuring an accumulation of contextual and descriptive knowledge on response strategies. Less attention appears to have been devoted to austerity and crises in the accounting literature, with a few notable exceptions (see Bracci, Humphrey, Moll, & Steccolini, 2015; Hodges & Lapsley, 2016).

These streams of research offer a mix of empirical and theory building approaches and while each stream is valuable in its own right, they do not on their own capture the dynamic and interrelated nature of crises responses, and tend to underplay the complex and interrelated nature of capacities that underpin strategic responses, something which a resilience view can help in understanding.

AN ALTERNATIVE CONCEPTUAL LENS: RESILIENCE

Since its origins in the field of physics and ecology (see Davoudi & Porter, 2012), the concept of resilience has been adopted and extended to other disciplines, including public policy, urban planning and disaster and crisis management (Boin & Van Eeten, 2013; Comfort, 2002; Pain & Levine, 2012; Reid & Botterill, 2013; Vale & Campanella, 2005; Wildavsky, 1988; Wukich, 2013). In the next sections, we advance the case for conceptualising financial resilience.

Organisational Resilience: Definitions and Dimensions

The concept of resilience refers to both organisational capacity to recover from crises and reduce risks (Boin & Van Eeten, 2013; Holling, 1973; Pickett, Cadenasso, & Grove, 2004; Shaw, 2012; Sutcliffe & Vogus, 2003; Vickers & Kouzmin, 2001; Wukich, 2013) as well as the ability to 'keep operating even in adverse "worst case" conditions and to adapt rapidly in a crisis' (Hood, 1991, 14). The former view focuses on recovery and bouncing back to equilibrium (Altintas & Royer, 2009; Boin & McConnell, 2007; Coutu, 2002; Davoudi, 2012). In this perception of resilience, organisations build slack that cushions and absorbs shocks (Huy & Mintzberg, 2003; Meyer, 1982), presumably with the aim to resist and survive. The latter, i.e., the evolutionary approach to resilience (Davoudi, 2012; Hamel & Välikangas, 2003; Pike, Dawley, & Tomaney, 2010), draws more on anticipatory responses (Martin & Sunley, 2006). This view interprets resilience as a continually changing process and goal, and as a case of becoming rather than being, interpreting it as part of a path-dependent trajectory. In this view, organisations become resilient not despite of distress or decline, but in anticipation or because of it (Sutcliffe & Vogues, 2003). Such organisations see disruptions as opportunities for change and take preemptive action before the need arises (Gunderson & Holling, 2002; Hamel & Välikangas, 2003; Holling, 1986).

Resilience can work across organisations in a number of ways including (1) situation awareness, the extent to which an organisation and/or relevant actors have a clear understanding of the organisational operating environment, including opportunities and potential crises as well as their trigger factors, (2) the management of key vulnerabilities, to reduce the susceptibility of the organisation to disturbances and (3) adaptive capacity, the set of available resources and competencies that give the ability to adapt to disturbances (McManus et al., 2007; Nelson, Adger, & Brown, 2007). In general, these are discussed in broad terms, with a variety of meanings and there have been calls in the public administration literature to give more depth on these facets of resilience (Boin & Van Eeten, 2013). Based on a recent empirical studies (e.g. (Barbera, Jones, Korac, Saliterer, & Steccolini, 2015), this book seeks to add to this clarification.

Resilience literature has tended to adopt a predominantly prescriptive and normative stance, highlighting the need for more empirical research (see, e.g. Boin & Van Eeten, 2013, p. 430; Wukich, 2013) as well as for the development of measures to assist in the operationalization of resilience

(Dalziell & McManus, 2004; Reid & Botterill, 2013). The literature on resilience in the public sector has often focused on public policy issues (Bailey & Berkeley 2012; Maguire & Cartwright, 2008; Reid & Botterill, 2013; Seville, 2009; Shaw, 2012; Walker, Walker, & Salt, 2006) or crisis management (Boin, 2009; Boin & Van Eeten, 2013; Comfort, 2002; Rosenthal, Michael, & Hart, 1989, 2001; Vale & Campanella, 2005; Wukich, 2013). However, much less attention has been devoted in this literature to how governments face and absorb external shocks affecting public finances, i.e., financial resilience.

A FRAMEWORK FOR EXPLORING FINANCIAL RESILIENCE

This section presents a framework for exploring financial resilience that emerged from a recent study (Barbera et al., 2015), and which is used to guide the analysis of the subsequent chapters. Building on this framework, the dimensions generally identified in the literature are considered in a finer grained way and in terms of their dynamic evolution over time. Financial resilience of local governments, i.e., their capacity to anticipate, absorb and react to shocks affecting their finances over time, can be considered to be a dynamic combination of four interrelated dimensions, namely *financial shocks, vulnerability, anticipatory capacity and coping capacity*.

Financial Shocks

These represent any unexpected external or internal events that have significant and long-lasting impacts on the finances of an organisation, negatively affecting its financial position and possibly ultimately threatening its survival. Shocks could have a direct financial impact, such as a reduction in transfer payments from central government or the failure of a PPP/PFI contract, or could have a more indirect relationship in the case of demographic changes, natural disasters or emergencies, or changes in government policy, the consequences of which may lead to a financial impact in terms of increased demands for expenditure or reduced income.

Vulnerability

From a resilience perspective, vulnerability is interpreted as the level of exposure to a specific shock. A range of external and internal factors could contribute to this including dependence on uncertain revenue bases, rigidity of expenditure, uncertain or reducing resource transfers from higher governmental levels and the degree of diversification of sources of income. Furthermore, high levels of debt, or a reliance on PPP/PFI schemes, may lead to non-controllable liabilities or financial risks. The general level of vulnerability can be compared before and after a crisis event by identifying where action has been taken to reduce or mitigate exposure, something which the authors consider in relation to the countries considered in each chapter.

Anticipatory and Coping Capacities

Anticipatory capacities refer to the availability of tools and capabilities in place, or built up over time, that enable organisations to better identify and manage their vulnerabilities and to recognise potential financial shocks before they arise, as well as their nature, likelihood, timing, scale and potential impacts. These tools and capabilities could include internal and external monitoring processes and might occur within a medium-term financial planning framework or be built up incrementally over time.

Coping capacities refer to resources and abilities that allow shocks to be faced and vulnerabilities to be managed. Dealing with shocks may require reliance on different coping capacities, namely *buffering capacity* (i.e. the ability for absorbing shocks), *adaptive capacity* (i.e. the ability for implementing incremental changes) and *transformative capacity* (i.e. the ability for taking paths of more radical changes) (see also Béné, Wood, Newsham, & Davies, 2012; Darnhofer, 2014; Davoudi, Brooks, & Mehmood, 2013; Keck & Skadapolrak, 2013). *Buffering capacity* represents more traditional budget management techniques such as the use of reserves, virement and slack resources (contingencies) to absorb short-term, one-off and minor financial shocks. It may also include increases in tax revenues or short-term reductions in programme expenditures or deferring expenditures to later periods. A*daptive capacity* represents latent competences and experiences that can be drawn on for adjusting organisational activities, while not jeopardising the overall status quo. These include capacities that promote the ability to innovate around the edges or find new ways of doing the same or similar things. *Transformative capacity,* enabling more radical fiscal or organisational changes, represents a higher order capacity and may not be present at the start of a crisis, but become a feature afterwards.

THE CONTEXT OF THE BOOK: GLOBAL FINANCIAL CRISIS AND AUSTERITY

The global financial crisis, which began with the collapse of the sub-prime banking sector in the United States in 2007, reverberated around the financial markets of the world, leading to an international economic crisis and ultimately resulting in significant fiscal crisis for national governments (Kickert, 2012). The impact of the crises were severe. Wolman (2014) reported that in OECD countries, for example, the average annual rate of GDP real output growth was 3.4% between 2000 and 2007, but only 0.9% in 2007/2008. Between 2007 and 2011, this dropped to 0.5%, with some countries experiencing negative growth rates during this period. This was accompanied by increases in unemployment rates (from 5.6% for OECD countries as a whole in 2007 to 8.1% in 2009) as well as initial fiscal stimulation policies and bailout packages for the banking sector, all of which put additional strain on national budget deficits and borrowing positions. For example, there was a fiscal deficit of 7.9% of GDP in 2009 across OECD countries, with the OECD predicting that in 2011, as the crises unwound, gross government debt would exceed 100% of GDP (OECD-SBO, 2011). The dire economic and fiscal consequences that followed triggered a period of fiscal and economic policy making that has come to be generally referred to as the era of austerity.

Despite its global reach, however, the impact of the global financial crisis was not felt equally by countries across the world, with some such as the PIIGS countries of Portugal, Italy, Ireland, Greece and Spain being significantly affected, while others such as Sweden experiencing very little impact (OECD-SBO, 2011). Similarly, austerity as a policy response has taken on different forms in different countries, whether this be fiscal consolidation through reduced expenditure and increased taxation, an opportunity to shrink the size of the state itself, or through some intermediate approach (Heald & Hodges, 2015). For some countries such as the United Kingdom, austerity was adopted voluntarily, whereas for others such as Greece austerity was an external requirement of supra-national bodies such as the International Monetary Fund (IMF) and the European Union (EU). For EU states in the European Monetary Fund (EMU), responding to the crisis was further complicated through the ongoing enforcement of the growth and stability pact that preceded the onset of the financial crisis. Drawing on crisis management literature, Peters (2011) observes a range of responses in play across countries in response to the financial crisis, including the centralisation and politicisation of decision making (although for some countries such as Slovenia a more consultative approach was introduced), as well as governments using the crisis as an opportunity to drive through changes that would previously have been impossible (austerity in the United Kingdom, for example) or to reinforce their approaches to policy and governance.

The global financial crisis, and the ensuing era of austerity, bears all the hallmarks of a crisis as we have described them in this chapter. As such it is a highly suitable situation around which to frame a study of resilience, and financial resilience in particular. The international yet disparate reach of the crises and the lack of uniformity of the subsequent policy responses mean that an international comparison of the impact and reactions to austerity are timely.

THE CRISIS, AUSTERITY AND LOCAL GOVERNMENTS

Within the national context, sublevels of government, such as states, regions, municipalities and local governments, provide an interesting lens through which to view austerity for a variety of reasons. The scale, scope and reach of such organisations tend to be significant in most countries and as such the impact on them of the consequences of the financial crisis is also large. Across OECD countries, such sublevels of government account for about 31% of total government spending and 22% of tax revenues (Blochliger, Charbit, Pinero Campos, & Vammalle, 2010, p. 5). At the same time, administrative arrangements at this level differ across countries and it is therefore useful to explore whether similar or different reactions have occurred in response to the crisis and austerity period.

The detailed composition of 'local government' varies across countries and is largely dependent upon the federal or unitary nature of the country in question. There is also a wide difference in the numbers and sizes of local governments both within and across nation states. For example, Austria is a federal state consisting of 9 regions (*Länder*) and 2,100 local governments that enjoy relatively high political and functional autonomy and have an average population of around 3,000 inhabitants. England, on the other hand, is part of the unitary state of the United Kingdom and has no regions and only 353 local governments (excluding parish councils). English local governments have considerably higher populations than their Austrian counterparts (around 155,000 based on the current population estimates). Such differences provide interesting points of comparison between the chapters of this book. Table 1 shows the main features of local governments in each of the included countries, in terms of number of local governments and their average/median population size, local government debt, revenues and expenditures, as well as their role in public investment. Moreover, the expenditure and revenue structure of local governments are shown giving first insights into their intergovernmental fiscal relationships and autonomy.

Notwithstanding the differences across countries in the size and composition of their local governments, it is fair to say that in each case, local governments have a direct impact on the lives of local people, the functioning of local economies and the delivery of national governments' policies. They are often the focal point for local economic development, public health and wellbeing, security and education.

They are also the beneficiaries of large-scale transfer payments form national/higher levels of governments, something which they usually have little control over but are often reliant on. Austerity responses at the national level have filtered down to the local level in various degrees, impacting upon the resources available to deliver services and subsequently impacting on the availability of services to local communities.

Table 1. Country Table.

	Australia	Austria	Brazil[a]	France	Germany	Greece	Italy	Netherlands	Sweden	UK	US
Unitary/Federal Countries	Federal	Federal	Federal	Unitary	Federal	Unitary	Unitary	Unitary	Unitary	Unitary	Federal
Population in thousands (OECD, 2014)	23,639	8,544	202,769	66,169	80,983	10,927	60,795	16,864	9,696	64,597	319,173
GDP per capita (USD) (OECD, 2014)	46,973	47,693	11,921	39,357	46,394	2.5950	35,459	48,256	45,298	40,210	54,353
General debt level in % of GDP, 2014	62.7	102.2	63.3	119.2	82.2	179.8	156.2	81	62.5	116.6	126.7
General budget balance as % of GDP, 2014	−2.6	−2.7	−4.3	−3.9	0.3	−3.6	−3.0	−2.4	−1.7	−5.7	−4.9
No. of local governments, 2014	571	2,100	5,570	35,885	11,092	325	8,047	390	290	324/389	35,879
Average LG size (OECD)	41,005	4,090	34,361	1,855	7,320	33,410	7,545	43,540	33,890	166,060	8,990
Median LG size (OECD, 2014)	12,605	1,790	n.a.	435	1,710	n.a.	2,430	26,515	15,435	132,240	n.a.
LG Debt in % of total public debt, 2014	n.a.	4.8	n.a.	9.3	6.3	0.6	7.7	14.3	24.2	8.1	n.a.
LG revenues in % of total government revenues, 2014	n.a.	17.3	21.9	21.6	17.50	7.90	30.80	31.00	49.90	28.80	n.a.
Own tax revenues of LG as % of total tax revenue	3.59	4.5	n.a.	19.4	13.1	3.4	21.8	6.3	33.7	5.9	n.a.
LG revenues by type in %, 2014											
Taxes	n.a.	14.7	23.13	48.5	38.20	24.00	44.40	10.30	53.70	14.30	n.a.
Grants and subsidies	n.a.	65	60.33	34.3	40.40	66.80	42.40	70.90	31.70	68.80	n.a.
Tariffs and fees	n.a.	15.1	n.a.	15.7	17.50	8.30	11.60	14.20	10.30	13.10	n.a.
Property income	n.a.	2.3	n.a.	1.1	2.40	0.80	1.1	2.70	1.80	1.10	n.a.
Social contributions	n.a.	2.9	8.08	0.3	1.5	0.0	0.5	1.8	2.6	2.7	n.a.
LG expenditure in % of total government expenditure, 2014	n.a.	16.4	n.a.	20.5	17.8	6.6	28.7	30.1	49.1	25.2	n.a.

LG expenditure by function in %, 2014[b]

General public services	n.a.	16.0	n.a.	19.1	18.1	28.0	13.0	7.7	11.8	7.8	n.a.
Public order and safety	n.a.	1.8	n.a.	2.9	3.3	0.7	1.7	2.7	0.8	8.9	n.a.
Economic affairs	n.a.	12.2	n.a.	18.4	14.5	18.3	13.5	14.8	6.0	8.5	n.a.
Environmental protection	n.a.	2.2	n.a.	7.5	4.3	17.3	5.9	10.1	0.7	4.1	n.a.
Housing and community ammenities	n.a.	2.3	n.a.	8.6	3.6	4.1	3.9	2.5	2.9	4.7	n.a.
Health	n.a.	22.3	n.a.	0.7	2.1	0.0	47.7	1.9	26.8	1.5	n.a.
Recreation. culture. and religion	n.a.	5.7	n.a.	9.9	6.2	8.3	2.4	8.5	3.4	2.2	n.a.
Education	n.a.	16.4	n.a.	14.5	15.2	10.0	6.7	31.3	19.9	27.8	n.a.
Social protection	n.a.	21.2	n.a.	18.5	32.8	13.2	5.2	20.5	27.6	34.4	n.a.
Local government investment in % of total government investment, 2014	n.a.	29.6	n.a.	58.8	35.7	17.9	54.9	51.5	48.4	35.3	n.a.

Notes: OECD (2016). Subnational governments in OECD countries: Key data (brochure). OECD. Paris, www.oecd.org/regional/regional-policy Database: http://dx.doi.org/10.1787/05fb4b56-en.
[a]Data for Brazil taken from IMF Country Outlook (2014) and Brazil National Statistics Office (2013).
[b]EUROSTAT.

In parallel with this, local governments are usually able to raise their own resources through local taxation and other revenue in the form of fees and charges. The proportion of these resources and the degree of autonomy over these own sources of income vary across nation states, and over time, and represents an interesting juxtaposition from which to compare the ways in which responses to the crisis were managed at a local level.

THE STRUCTURE OF THE BOOK

The remaining chapters of the book are structured as follows. In Chapters 2–12, the experiences of 11 countries during the austerity period are examined. These chapters cover Europe, the United States, South America and Australia. The countries covered by the respective chapters are as follows:

- Australia
- Austria
- Brazil
- England
- France
- Germany
- Greece
- Italy
- The Netherlands
- Sweden
- The United States

As such, they cover a range of different structural forms, legislative requirements and cultural differences. They also reveal differences in the timings and impact of the crisis and austerity period, as well as the range of responses at both the national and local levels. Each chapter has been written by experienced academics in this field within their respective country and follows a similar structure, except where the national context requires a different approach (e.g., Australia). Generally speaking, within each chapter, the context of local government is explored in relation to the impact the financial crisis and austerity had within each country. There is an overview provided of the methodology employed in each case that while similar, again varies sometimes due to individual country circumstances. Most of the country chapters focus on the fortunes of four local government cases that are summarised within each chapter before a discussion of their similarities and differences and their capacities. Where applicable, each country chapter concludes by classifying types of resilience patterns that were evident within the cases.

Finally, we summarise the position across all the chapters and draw conclusions regarding the nature of financial resilience in an international context in response to austerity. In the final chapter, a synthesis and interpretation of the case studies are presented, which assist in (1) further developing and operationalizing the concept of governmental financial resilience, its components, as well as the different approaches to resilience and (2) capturing the related contextual and organisational explanatory variables. The identification of similar patterns and perceptions of resilience within different national contexts and, at the same time, the recognition of distinct configurations point to the role of economic, institutional and organisational circumstances in affecting the relative effectiveness of approaches to resilience as well as models to measure it. Moreover, they highlight the boundaries of a universalistic approach in the description of responses to a global crisis.

REFERENCES

Altintas, G., & Royer, I. (2009). Renforcement de la résilience par un apprentissage post-crise: une étude longitudinale sur deux périodes de turbulence. *Management, 12*(4), 266–293.

Andrews, R., Boyne, G. A., & Walker, R. M. (2012). Overspending in public organizations: Does strategic management matter? *International Public Management Journal, 15*(1), 39–61.

Bailey, D., & Berkeley, N. (2012). *Regional responses to recession: The role of the West Midlands regional taskforce.* SURGE Working Paper Series – Working Paper No. 4, pp. 1–32.

Baker, D. L. (2011). Local government cutback budgeting. *The Public Manager, 40*(1), 9–11.

Barbera, C., Guarini, E., & Steccolini, I. (2016). Italian Municipalities and the fiscal crisis: Four strategies for muddling through. *Financial Accountability and Management, 32*(3), 335–361.

Behn, R. D. (1980). Leadership for cut-back management: The use of corporate strategy. *Public Administration Review, 40*(6), 613–620.

Barbera, C., Jones, M., Korac, S., Saliterer, I., & Steccolini, I. (2015). Bouncing back and bouncing-forward – Applying an alternative perspective on European municipalities' responses to financial shocks. EGPA annual conference, Toulouse, France, PSG VI: Governance of Public Sector Organizations, August 26–28.

Béné, C., Wood, R. G., Newsham, A., & Davies, M. (2012). *Resilience: New Utopia or New Tyranny? Reflection about the potentials and limits of the concept of resilience in relation to vulnerability reduction programmes.* IDS Working Paper No. 405. Institute of Development Studies, Brighton, UK.

Blochliger, H., Charbit, C., Pinero Campos, J. M., & Vammalle, C. (2010). Sub-central governments and the economic crisis. OECD Economics Department Working Papers No. 752, Paris.

Boin, A. (2009). The new world of crises and crisis management: Implications for policymaking and research. *Review of Policy Research, 26*(4), 367–377.

Boin, A., & Lodge, M. (2016). Designing resilient institutions for transboundary crisis management: A time for public administration. *Public Administration, 94*(2), 289–298.

Boin, A., & McConnel, A. (2007). Preparing for critical infrastructure breakdowns: The limits of crisis management and the need for resilience. *Journal of Contingencies and Crisis Management, 15*(1), 50–59.

Boin, A., & 't Hart, P. (2003). Public leadership in times of crisis: Mission impossible? *Public Administration Review, 63*(5), 544–553.

Boin, A., & 't Hart, P. (2010). Organising for effective emergency management: Lessons from research. *The Australian Journal of Public Administration, 69*(4), 357–371.

Boin, A., 't Hart, P., & McConnell, A. (2009). Crisis exploitation: Political and policy impacts of framing contests. *Journal of European Public Policy, 16*(1), 81–106.

Boin, A., & Van Eeten, M. J. G. (2013). The resilient organization. *Public Management Review*, *15*(3), 429–445.

Boyne, G. A., & Meier, K. J. (2009). Environmental change, human resources and organizational turnaround. *Journal of Management Studies*, *46*(5), 835–863.

Bracci, E., Humphrey, C., Moll, J., & Steccolini, I. (2015). Public sector accounting, accountability and austerity: More than balancing the books? *Accounting, Auditing & Accountability Journal*, *28*(6), 878–908.

Cepiku, D., & Bonomi Savignon, A. (2012). Governing cutback management: Is there a global strategy for public administrations? *International Journal of Public Sector Management*, *25*(6/7), 428–436.

Comfort, L. K. (2002). Managing intergovernmental responses to terrorism and other extreme events. *Publius*, *32*(4), 29–40.

Coutu, D. L. (2002). How Resilience Works. *Harvard Business Review*, 46–55. Retrieved from https://www.boyden.pt/mediafiles/attachments/7030.pdf

Dalziell, E. P., & McManus, S. T. (2004). Resilience, vulnerability and adaptive capacity; Implications for systems performance. International Forum for Engineering Decision Making (IFED), Switzerland. Retrieved from http://ir.canterbury.ac.nz/bitstream/10092/2809/1/12593870_ResOrgs_IFED_dec04_EDSM.pdf. Accessed on March 10, 2013.

Darnhofer, I. (2014). Resilience and why it matters for farm management. *European Review of Agricultural Economics*, *41*(3), 461–484. doi:10.1093/erae/jbu012

Davoudi, S. (2012). Resilience: A bridging concept or a dead end? *Planning Theory and Practice*, *13*(2), 299–333.

Davoudi, S., Brooks, E., & Mehmood, A. (2013). Evolutionary resilience and strategies for climate adaptation. *Planning Practice and Research*, *28*(3), 307–322.

Davoudi, S., & Porter, L. (Eds.). (2012). Applying the resilience perspective to planning: Critical thoughts from theory and practice. interface. *Planning Theory & Practice*, 13(2), 299–333.

Dougherty, M. J., & Klase, K. A. (2009). Fiscal retrenchment in state budgeting: Revisiting cutback management in a new era. *International Journal of Public Administration*, *32*(7), 593–619.

Greenwood, R. (1981). Fiscal pressure and local government in England and Wales. In C. Hood & M. Wright (Eds.), *Big government in hard times* (pp. 77–99). Oxford: Wiley-Blackwell.

Grossi, G., & Cepiku, D. (2014). Editorial. *Public Money & Management*, *34*(2), 79–81.

Gunderson, L. H., & Holling, C. S. (Eds.). (2002). *Panarchy: Understanding transformations in human and natural systems*. Washington, DC: Island Press.

Hamel, G. V., & Valikangas, L. (2003). The quest for resilience. *Harvard Business Review*, *81*(9), 52–63. Retrieved from http://rhesilience.com/blog/wp-content/uploads/2012/07/23HBRQuestforResilience-gary-hamel.pdf

Heald, D., & Hodges, R. (2015). Will 'austerity' be a critical juncture in European public sector financial reporting? *Accounting, Auditing and Accountability Journal*, *28*(6), 1–31.

Hodges, R., & Lapsley, I. (2016). A private sector failure, a public sector crisis – Reflections on the great recession. *Financial Accountability and Management*, *32*(3), 265–280.

Holling, C. S. (1973). Resilience and stability of ecological systems. *Annual Review of Ecology and Systematics*, *4*, 1–23. doi:10.1146/annurev.es.04.110173.000245

Holling, C. S. (1986). The resilience of terrestrial ecosystems: Local surprise and global change. In W. C. Clark & R. E. Munn (Eds.), *Sustainable development of the biosphere* (pp. 292–320). Cambridge: Cambridge University Press.

Hood, C. (1991). A public management for all seasons? *Public Administration*, *69*, 3–19.

Hood, C., & Wright, M. (1981). From decrementalism to quantum cuts? In C. Hood & W. Maurice (Eds.), *Big government in hard times* (pp. 199–227). Oxford: Wiley-Blackwell.

Huy, Q. N., & Mintzberg, H. (2003). The rhythm of change. *MIT Sloan Management Review*, *44*(4), 79–84. Retrieved from http://vdonnell.pbworks.com/f/Rhythm+of+Change.pdf

Keck, M., & Skadapolrak, P. (2013). What is social resilience? Lessons learned and ways forward. *Erdkunde*, *67*, 5–19.

Kickert, W. (2012). State responses to the fiscal crisis in Britain, Germany and the Netherlands. *Public Management Review, 14*(3), 299–309.

Klase, K. A. (2011). The intersection of flexible budgeting and cutback management: Factors affecting the responses of selected states to recent economic recessions. *Public Finance and Management, 11*(2), 197–230.

Leach, M. (2008). *Re-framing resilience: A symposium Report*. STEPS Centre, Brighton.

Levine, C. H. (1978). Organizational decline and cutback management. *Public Administration Review, 38*(4), 316–325.

Levine, C. H. (1979). More on cutback management: Hard questions for hard times. *Public Administration Review, 39*(2), 179–183.

Levine, C. H., & Posner, P. L. (1981). Centralizing effects of austerity on the intergovernmental system. *Political Science Quarterly, 96*(1), 67–85.

Lodge, M., & Hood, C. (2012). Into an age of multiple austerities? Public management and public service bargains across OECD countries. *Governance: An International Journal of Policy, Administration, and Institutions, 25*(1), 79–101.

Maguire, B., & Cartwright, S. (2008). *Assessing a community's capacity to manage change: A resilience approach to social assessment*. Social Sciences Program, Bureau of Rural Sciences, Australia. Retrieved from http://www.tba.co.nz/tba-eq/Resilience_approach.pdf. Accessed on March 9, 2013.

Martin, R., & Sunley, P. (2006). Path dependence and regional economic evolution. *Journal of Economic Geography, 6*, 395–437.

McManus, S., Seville, E., Brunsdon, D., & Vargo, J. (2007). *Resilience management. A framework for assessing and improving the resilience of organizations.*

Meier, K. J., & O'Toole, L. J. Jr. (2009). The dog that didn't bark: How public managers handle environmental shocks. *Public Administration, 87*(3), 485–502.

Meier, K. J., O'Toole, L. J. Jr., & Hicklin, A. (2010). I've seen fire and I've seen rain: Public management and performance after a natural disaster. *Administration and Society, 20*(10), 1–25.

Meyer, A. D. (1982). Adapting to environmental jolts. *Administrative Science Quarterly, 27*(4), 515–537.

Nelson, D. R., Adger, W. N., & Brown, K. (2007). Adaptation to environmental change: Contributions of a resilience framework. *Annual Review of Environment and Resources, 32*, 395–419.

O'Toole, L. J., & Kenneth, J. M. (2010). In defense of bureaucracy. public managerial capacity, slack and the dampening of environmental shocks. *Public Management Review, 12*(3), 341–361.

OECD-SBO. (2011). *Restoring public finances*. Paris: OECD Publishing.

Pain, A., & Levine, S. (2012). *A conceptual analysis of livelihoods and resilience: Addressing the 'insecurity of agency'*. HPG Working Paper. Retrieved from http://www.odi.org.uk/sites/odi.org.uk/files/odi-assets/publications-opinion-files/7928.pdf. Accessed on March 25, 2013.

Peters, B. G. (2011). Governance responses to the fiscal crisis—Comparative perspectives. *Public Money & Management, 31*(1), 75–80.

Peters, B. G., Pierre, J., & Randma-Liiv, T. (2011). Global financial crisis, public administration and governance. Do new problems require new solutions? *Public Organization Review, 11*(1), 13–28.

Pickett, S. T. A., Cadenasso, M. L., & Grove, J. M. (2004). Resilient cities: Meaning, models, and metaphor for integrating the ecological, socio-economic, and planning realms. *Landscape and Urban Planning, 69*(4), 369–384.

Pike, A., Dawley, S., & Tomaney, J. (2010). Resilience, adaptation and adaptability. *Cambridge Journal of Regions, Economy and Society, 3*, 59–70. doi:10.1093/cjres/rsq001

Raudla, R., Savi, R., & Randma-Liiv, T. (2013). *Literature review on cutback management, COCOPS deliverable 7.1*. Retrieved from: http://www.cocops.eu/wp-content/uploads/2013/03/COCOPS_Deliverable_7_1.pdf

Reid, R., & Botterill, L. C. (2013). The multiple meanings of 'Resilience': An overview of the literature. *Australian Journal of Public Administration*, *72*(1), 31–40. doi:10.1111/1467-8500.12009

Rosenthal, U., Boin, A., Louise, & Comfort, K. (2001). The changing world of crises and crisis management. In U. Rosenthal, A. Boin, & L. K. Comfort (Eds.), *Managing crises — Threats, dilemmas, opportunities* (pp. 5–27). Springfield, IL: Charles C. Thomas.

Rosenthal, U., Michael, T. C., & Hart, P. T. (1989). *Coping with crises: The management of disasters, riots, and terrorism, hardcover*. Springfield, IL: Charles C. Thomas.

Sacco, J. F., Stalebrink, O., & Posner, P. L. (2011). Introduction to the symposium on flexible budgeting. *Public Finance and Management*, *11*(2), 86–92.

Schick, A. (1980). *Congress and money. Budgeting, spending, and taxing*. Washington, DC: Urban Institute.

Scorsone, E. A., & Plerhoples, C. (2010). Fiscal stress and cutback management amongst state and local governments: What have we learned and what remains to be learned? *State and Local Government Review*, *42*(2), 176–187.

Scotti-Petrillo, A., & Prosperi, D. C. (2011). Metaphors from the resilience literature: Guidance for planners. In M. Schrenk, V. V. Popovich, P. Zeile, & P. Elisei (Eds.), *REAL CORP 2011. Re-mixing the city. Towards sustainability and resilience* (pp. 601–611). Tagungsband. Retrieved from http://www.corp.at/archive/CORP2011_99.pdf. Accessed on June 25, 2013.

Seville, E. (2009). Resilience: Great concept ... but what does it mean for organisations? *Community resilience: Research, planning and civil defence emergency management* (Vol. 22). New Zealand: Ministry of Civil Defence & Emergency Management.

Steccolini, I., Barbera, C., & Jones, M. (2015). Governmental financial resilience under austerity: The case of English local authorities. *CIMA Executive Summary Report*, *11*(3), 1–13.

Sutcliffe, K. M., & Vogus, T. J. (2003). Organizing for resilience. In K. S. Cameron, J. E. Dutton, & R. E. Quinn (Eds.), *Positive organizational scholarship: Foundations of a new discipline* (pp. 94–121). San Francisco, CA: Berrett-Koehler.

Vickers, M. H., & Kouzmin, A. (2001). 'Resilience' in organizational actors and rearticulating 'voice': Towards a humanistic critique of new public management. *Public Management Review*, *3*(1), 95–119.

Walker, V. R., Walker, B., & Salt, D. (2006). *Resilience thinking: Sustaining ecosystems and people in a changing world*. Washington, DC: Island Press.

West, J. P., & Condrey, S. E. (2011). Municipal government strategies for controlling personnel costs during the fiscal storm. *Journal of Public Budgeting, Accounting and Financial Management*, *23*(3), 395–426.

Wildavsky, A. B. (1988). *The new politics of the budgetary process*. Glenwiew, IL: Scott, Foresman.

Wolman, H. (2014). *National fiscal policy and local government during the economic crisis*. Urban Policy Paper Series, The German Marshall Fund of the United States, Washington, DC.

Wukich, C. (2013). Searching for resilience. *Journal of Public Administration Research and Theory Advance*, *23*(4), 1013–1019.

CHAPTER 2

AUSTRIA – BUILDING CAPACITIES VERSUS RESTING ON LAURELS

Sanja Korac

ABSTRACT

Unfolding almost a decade ago, the global financial crisis still affects governments all over the world. Austria has been hit only moderately, showing one of the lowest debt and unemployment levels in the European Union throughout the crisis years. However, the crisis' aftermath affected the financial situation of Austrian local governments significantly. Although they are self-administered and exert high political and functional autonomy, local governments rely heavily on shared tax revenues with the federal level. These shared revenues as well as local governments' own tax revenues declined, mirroring the economic turmoil following the financial crisis. This chapter aims to explore how Austrian local governments responded to these challenges. It does so by investigating the contextual conditions as well as internal capacities through the lens of financial resilience. All four cases included in the analysis highlighted that institutional conditions and general trends, e.g. tasks devolved from upper levels of government without sufficient compensation, limit their ability to cope with financial shocks. In this context, different patterns of financial resilience can be observed. While two cases initially showed low anticipatory and coping capacities, awareness of decision-makers resulted in building internal capacities and in making necessary changes early or as a response to the shock. The other two, however, seem to rest on their

Governmental Financial Resilience: International Perspectives on how Local Governments Face Austerity
Public Policy and Governance, Volume 27, 17–33
ISSN: 2053-7697/doi:10.1108/S2053-769720170000027002

laurels of strong capacities in the past, and to rely mainly on their buffering
capacities in reacting to shocks, thus increasing their vulnerability in the
future.

Keywords: Financial resilience; Austria; local government; financial crisis;
financial autonomy

Thanks to its good economic situation before the global financial crisis,
Austria seemed to have weathered the storm better than most other countries
in Europe, and in particular its partners in the Eurozone (see, e.g. Famira-
Mühlberger & Leoni, 2013). Austria succeeded in retaining its relatively low
unemployment rate (4.9% in 2007) during the crisis years (5.3% in 2009;
4.8% in 2010; 4.6% in 2011). Although the unemployment rate has been
slightly increasing since 2011, Austria still shows one of the lowest within
the European Union (see Eurostat, 2016b). As in other countries of the
Eurozone, the crisis years led to a breach of the Maastricht criteria, with a
deficit of 5.3 (2009) and 4.5% (2010) of GDP and the debt level exceeding the
threshold significantly (Statistik Austria, 2016c, 2016d). While in 2007,
Austria showed a slightly higher national debt level than the EU average
(64.8% of GDP), it rose by 23% during the peak of the financial crisis in
2009. Although it incurred new debt in the following years, the debt to GDP
ratio in 2015 was around the EU-28 average (86.2% and 85.2%, respectively)
(Statistik Austria, 2016c, 2016d).

When the crisis hit and the central government experienced diminishing
(income and sales) tax revenues, revenue shares for local governments
decreased by 6.6% between 2008 and 2010. This was a turning point for local
governments that experienced a longer phase of constantly increasing revenue
shares prior to the crisis. However, this was only one side of the coin. The situation for local governments additionally worsened as municipal taxes, the local
governments' most important own taxes, were hit due to lay-offs and temporary employment with lower wages in the businesses sector. In general, local
government finances mirrored the economic turmoil stemming from the financial crisis. Their surplus dropped by almost 60% in 2008 compared to 2007,
their debt level increased (2.4% in 2009, 1.7% in 2010) and they generated a
total deficit of 387.6 mio. Euro in 2009 and 127.8 mio. Euro in 2010. Although
the budgets were balanced again in 2011 (226 mio. Euro surplus), investments
at the local level which dropped by 18% in 2010 were still declining strongly
(by 9% in 2011).[1]

LOCAL GOVERNMENTS IN AUSTRIA – CONTEXT AND CONDITIONS

Austria is a federal state consisting of 9 regions (*Länder*) and 2,100 local governments that are organised based on the principle of self-administration and thus exert relatively high political and functional autonomy. In this regard, the country has often been compared to its larger neighbour Germany, as both share the administrative tradition of the Continental European federal model (Kuhlmann & Wollmann, 2014, p. 17). Considering Austria's total population (8.6 mio in 2015, see Statistik Austria, 2016a), the local government level is dominated by small municipalities; excluding the capital Vienna, the average population is 3,268 and overall, only 62 cities have more than 10,000 inhabitants (Statistik Austria, 2016b). Austrian municipalities are characterised by the 'strong mayor' form of government (see Mouritzen & Svara, 2002), which translates into strong mayoral authority not only in policy, but also in administrative terms. However, the budget and policy decisions have to be approved by the council. Most local governments have a city manager or chief executive officer who directs the administrative affairs and implements local policies. The local level has a multiplicity of competencies and carries out complex, tangible services, ranging from water and sewer to libraries, public works, recreational facilities, kindergartens, and elderly homes. Over the past years, an increasing number of tasks have been devolved to the local level. This has been subject to strong criticism by local government associations and interest groups. The compensation by upper levels of government has been regarded as disproportionately low, which inhibited investments and increased the local government debt level (Biwald & Rossmann, 2012; KDZ, 2011).

Austrian local governments rely heavily on shared tax revenues (mainly based on sales and income taxes) from the federal level, which account for about 40% of total local revenues. This system of shared tax revenues is a vertical redistribution of tax revenues, but it also aims to ensure horizontal equalisation between local governments in general based on their population figures. Apart from service fees and charges, local governments can collect local taxes like property tax (a land value tax that however does not mirror the actual market value) and the municipal tax (a payroll tax paid by businesses based on the number of employees and the wages). These account for about 21% of revenues in larger local governments and 14% on average (see Österreichischer Städtebund, 2015; OECD 2014), which is why the financial autonomy is often described as limited (see also Kuhlmann, 2010; Proeller, 2006; Saliterer & Korac, 2014). The average annual budget of a local government is about 9.2 mio. Euro,[2] and most expenditures are made in the field of health (22.1%) and social protection (21.1%), followed by education, general public services, and economic affairs (16.1%, 16.5% and 12.5%, respectively).[3]

ACCOUNTING REFORMS AND INSTITUTIONAL CHANGES AT THE LOCAL LEVEL

In Austria, the so-called Stability Pact ensures that the budgetary rules of the Economic and Monetary Union are met. This regulation determines each governmental level's (federal, regional and local) responsibility in achieving a balanced budget. During the crisis years, deficits and debt levels were rising, proving the intergovernmental arrangements in the Pact insufficient. Thus the Pact was renegotiated in 2011 and 2012, tightening the limits of deficit for the federal and the regional level (a balanced budget is mandatory for the local level), regulating liabilities, introducing a brake on debt and a brake on expenditures (BGBl. I 2011 Nr. 117; BGBl. I 2013 Nr. 30). At the same time, local governments experienced a phase of uncertainty in preparing for substantial changes that would be implemented in 2015. First, structural reforms in one region (*Steiermark*) led to a reduction of the total number of Austrian local governments from 2,352 to 2,100. Second, in 2013 and 2014, new budgeting and accounting regulations for the subnational level were negotiated. The respective legal framework was enacted in 2015 and will come into full effect in 2020. It will alter the current commitment-based budgeting and accounting systems and introduce accrual budgeting and accounting principles to regional and local governments (Meszarits & Saliterer, 2013, Saliterer, 2013a, 2013b). The system follows IPSAS (International Public Sector Accounting Standards) and aims towards providing transparent and comparable financial reporting. Thus, it also regulates the valuation and depreciation of assets and visualises different types of liabilities in a comprehensive way – aspects that have not been integrated in local governments' balance sheets so far (Rauskala & Saliterer, 2015).

The next sections present the results of an investigation of financial resilience of Austrian local governments. The research builds on the financial resilience concept described in the introduction. Accordingly, financial resilience consists of different dimensions: financial shocks; the filtering of the latter by local government decision-makers; perceived vulnerability; anticipatory capacity; and coping capacities, namely buffering, adapting and transforming. The dynamic interplay of those dimensions shapes different patterns of financial resilience, which characterize how local governments anticipate, absorb and react to shocks that affect their finances.

METHOD

Following the general research design reflected in the book, a purposive sampling approach has been applied (see Patton, 2015). In the first step of the sampling process, local governments that are seats of district authorities have been selected for the investigation. The latter have comparable functions and administrative responsibilities, and are subject to similar institutional pressures. Second, the criteria of (1) the average financial performance or budgetary position and (2) its volatility over 10 years have been calculated for all 72 district authorities. Considering the still predominant commitment-based accounting system in Austrian local governments, budgetary position is represented by the variation in the commitment-based surplus/deficit position over 10 years (2002–2011). Volatility of the budgetary position, or the extent of variation of the budgetary position, has been calculated as its standard deviation over the same 10-year period. Subsequently, all cases have been classified according to the combination of the normalised average budgetary position and volatility. The most common combinations were (1) low volatility and a budgetary position around zero, (2) high volatility and a budgetary position around zero, (3) high volatility with a negative budgetary position, or (4) medium volatility with a positive budgetary position. This reflects cases that are polar, but at the same time also well represented, i.e. occur frequently (see Barbera, Jones, Korac, Saliterer, & Steccolini, 2015).

No cases of low volatility and a positive budgetary position or low volatility and a negative budgetary position were found in the Austrian seats of district authorities. In the next step, one case representing each of the four most common but polar combinations of budgetary position and its volatility has been randomly selected for the qualitative analysis. Table 1 shows the respective financial position of the four selected cases.

COLLECTION OF DATA AND ANALYSIS

A total of seven semistructured interviews (Bailey 2007) have been carried out, two in each of the four local governments. To ensure triangulation of data and views, different respondents were interviewed: Chief Executive Officers (CEOs) as the administrative apex of local government (see Mouritzen & Svara, 2002) and Chief Finance Officers (CFOs) as heads of the financial department, responsible for the preparation of the budget and financial statements/reports,

Table 1. Financial Position of the Selected Cases.

Volatility	Budgetary Position		
	Negative	Around Zero	Positive
Low		A	
Medium			C
High	B	D	

and for the legality of transactions. Considering their positions, responsibilities, as well as formal power, these actors play a crucial role in influencing local government responses and coping strategies in the context of crises with a financial character. Two researchers conducted the interviews between May and November 2014. They lasted between 45 and 90 minutes, were recorded, and full transcripts of the interviews also covering manifest as well as latent content (e.g. silence, sighs) (Holsti 1969) were created. The interviews included open-ended questions regarding the financial health of the local government, the main financial and non-financial goals, the main risks and shocks that the local government experienced over a 10-year period, how the latter had been identified and how the local government responded to them. The interviews served as the cornerstone of the case study (Yin 2009), but triangulation with quantitative data and document analysis was used to validate statements. Data were analysed using a sequential process (Stewart 2012). Within-case analyses were used to identify general themes and categories, and an across-case analysis was applied to trace out differences and detailed characteristics of resilience dimensions. During the analysis, an iterative approach (see Eisenhardt and Graebner 2007) has been applied where preliminary findings have been blended, reflected and verified with the extant literature in the field.

RESULTS

The Austrian cases revealed different patterns of resilience that were partly dependent on the external socioeconomic and the institutional context of the respective local governments (Table 2). More importantly, however, their financial resilience seems to be influenced by their internal capacities to anticipate and cope with financial shocks. This section begins with a description of the results by case, highlighting the local government's characteristics in terms of perceived financial shocks, the impact on the local governments and its filtering, the local government's financial vulnerability and the anticipatory and coping capacities. Subsequently, a discussion of recurring themes across the cases is provided, and findings distinguishing the local governments in this analysis are highlighted.

A

A is the second-largest city in its region, and although the population in the metropolitan area is stagnating, the local government succeeded in using its industrial past and present, as well as positioning itself as an educational and cultural community. Its budgetary position over the last 10 years was around zero, and it showed low volatility. The general financial condition is perceived

Table 2. Resilience Patterns of the Austrian Cases.

	A	B	C	D
Shock/impact	Decrease in shared tax revenues and own taxes	Decrease in shared tax revenues and own taxes	Delayed decrease in shared tax revenues, difficulties to balancing the budget	Decrease in shared tax revenues
Filtering	Threat/Opportunity	Threat/Trigger	Threat/Opportunity	Threat/Threat
		Economic crisis as a shock/struggle, not foreseeable,	No substantial political promises possible in election year 2009 due to the crisis	Financial crisis as risk, financial crisis as chance as interest rates dropped
Perceived vulnerability levels before the shock /their evolution over time	Initially low/ stable over time	Initially high/ decreasing over time	Low/increasing	Low/increasing
Level of anticipatory capacity before the shock /their evolution over time	Initially high/ stable over time	Initially high/ decreasing over time	Low/increasing	Low/increasing
Levels of coping capacity[a]	Comprehensive	Selective	Limited	Limited

[a]Level of coping capacity: selective – several coping actions of buffering and adapting indicate selective coping capacities; comprehensive – the full use of the spectrum of coping actions in buffering, adapting, and transforming indicates comprehensive coping capacities.

as very good and the debt level as low. This is supported by the financial data, which is why the local government's financial vulnerability can be considered as low. A was able to invest in infrastructure constantly, and even during the crisis, did not have to defer maintenance or investments.

> In fact, very, very good. Very good. We ensured that our roads, our truck fleet, is in good shape. This is why we managed the crisis well. Our principle was always: 'waste not, want not'. (CEO, A)

A did not foresee the crisis, although in hindsight it was acknowledged that there have been some signals. The local government experienced the impact of the crisis in 2008/2009, with revenue shares dropping by 25%. However, cutting costs, deferring some of the bigger investments, and especially using its financial reserves, the local government was able to weather the storm well.

> During the last crisis, in 2008, we lost revenue shares, but we handled the situation well. As it seems to be getting better now, we have to start building up a financial buffer again. (CEO, A)

During the past years, service quality has been enhanced constantly while costs and thus service fees have partly decreased. Anticipatory capacities both before and after the crisis can be considered as high. In particular, medium-term financial planning, monitoring and control processes, cautious planning, and spending reviews helped in keeping potential risks under control. The overall attitude towards financial shocks is that a local government cannot prevent a large crisis, but that it can be prepared by having enough rainy day funds. This is mirrored in A's reliance on a careful operation and the reliance on reserves.

> We have mindful financial management. And mindful political decision-makers – this goes hand in hand. (CEO, A)

One of the local government's strategic aims is to obtain more financial wiggle room and relative independence from the regional government.

> I know other local governments, they did not care about this, they are indifferent about raising the debt level. We took a different path, we tried to have a large share of own funding. (CFO, A)

This orientation is shown in the local government's ability to develop new sources of revenue, e.g. by mastering applications for EU funding, utilising synergies, as well as in infrastructure projects of the local government. A couple of years ago, A had invested in the erection of a shopping mall and despite an uncertain economic situation succeeded in winning private partners for the project. In 2014, the local government sold its shares and thereby generated a considerable surplus.

> One has to be able to find partners who are willing to invest in a stagnating region, to invest about 35 mio. Euro into a shopping mall. And to create about 350 jobs. (CEO, A)

As the local government was successful in developing and using coping capacities that addressed its vulnerabilities in a rather unfavourable environment, A represents a case of *self-regulatory/proactive* resilience. Some years ago, the local government has re-municipalized waste collection and has managed to offer highly competitive service quality and prices. A has attempted to offer waste collection services also for neighbouring local governments, which was not successful but led business firms servicing those local governments to offer significant price reductions as a reaction to the emergence of a new competitor. The local government invested in building adaptive capacities by implementing collegiate planning, hiring people with professional knowledge and thereby enhancing internal competencies, but also transformative capacities, like restructuring certain local government services and developing alternative income sources to strengthen the local government's self-sufficiency.

B

B is an industrial community located in a non-metropolitan border area. The local government had a very wealthy history, where the largest employer not only ensured relatively high municipal tax revenues, but also provided child care facilities, organised public transport and supported local clubs financially. When this firm experienced severe financial stress and had to downsize, the local government suffered a double hit: a severe drop in revenues on the one hand, and the pressure to provide and pay for the mentioned services itself on the other hand.This tense financial situation is mirrored in its negative budgetary position over the last 10 years, of which the volatility during that time was medium.

The local government's dependence on few relatively large industrial businesses makes it vulnerable to changes in the national, but also the global economic situation. Another source of vulnerability is seen in the institutional framework and the level of control by the regional government, leaving local governments in this region more often in a financial deadlock than in comparable regions. The sphere of influence is seen pessimistically, and heavily dependent on external factors like political decisions at the regional level.

The financial crisis was perceived as a shock that had a massive impact on the local government — in the years 2009 and 2010, revenue shares dropped and the local businesses cut personnel which caused a dip in the municipal tax revenues. After the crisis, B experienced budget deficits for three years due to unstable and undiversified revenues sources, high debt financing and strong reliance on grants. At the time the crisis unfolded, local government decision-makers did not see it coming, which they look back to in a self-critical way.

> Looking back, one has to ask oneself, how did you not see this coming? The local govern-
> ment reacted too late – the political decision-makers, but also the administration. I do not
> want to make an exempt here. (CEO, B)

The interviewees recognised a virtual absence of anticipatory capacities
which is also supported by the fact that the local government was not able to
build up financial reserves before the crisis. It seems that with any surplus,
political demand for additional infrastructure projects increased, while the
future need for maintenance was neglected.

As a first reaction to cope with the crisis and to consolidate the budget, B
stopped investment projects, deferred maintenance, sold assets after a needs
assessment, cut personnel costs, and increased fees and charges where possible. When the local government experienced political turmoil and its long-
term mayor resigned in 2010, B installed a parity-based structural committee
that is endowed with setting strategic goals and preparing policy decisions
before they are taken to the council. During the financial crisis, this committee decided on long-term structural adaptations that would add to a financial
recovery.

> We developed a plan, looked at the infrastructure, assessed the condition and identified the
> investment demand. [...] We focused very much on attracting businesses, despite the eco-
> nomic crisis, and we also succeeded in attracting some employers. [...] This has helped a lot
> with municipal taxes, we have counteracted the negative development. (CEO, B)

The financial situation of the local government during the crisis years
seemed to have awakened the attention and awareness of political decision-
makers. Perceiving its financial situation as critical, B adopted measures such
as the implementation of a long-term investment plan and scenario analysis,
as well as the build-up and deployment of coping capacities. Acknowledging
its limited ability of positioning as a touristic community and embracing its
character as an industrial municipality, B reached out to businesses and successfully attracted new business to settle in its area. As a result, much of the
municipal taxes recovered and the local government was able to improve core
services like kindergartens and sports and recreational facilities, and to contain cuts in the area of non-mandatory services, e.g. financial support of local
sports clubs.

> We have just developed a future profile - we want to grow as a city, but moderately. [...] the
> focus is certainly on our identity as an industrial community, which we want to keep.
> (CEO, B)

While the crisis has magnified B's vulnerability, it also appears to have triggered strengthening of both anticipatory as well as coping capacities and thus a
path of *reactive adaptation*. Notwithstanding its challenging institutional and
economic environment and the impact of the shock, the interviewees felt they
were in the position to address their vulnerabilities. Moreover, they perceived

the crisis as the trigger to bring about changes as well as an opportunity to (re-) gain control over their financial vulnerabilities.

C

C is a wealthy touristic community with a local economy that is characterised by small and medium sized commercial enterprises. It experienced two natural disasters in the past, which it managed well thanks to its preparedness and not least due to the help by the central government. Initially, it was not perceived as particularly vulnerable, mainly considering its high, stable, and diversified own-revenue base.

> The revenue situation in C certainly is a good one. (CEO, C)

Over the last 10 years, C's budgetary position was positive and its volatility medium. The local government's debt level was generally low and the budget was balanced even during the crisis years. There is a strong political will to maintain a high quality of services in order to stay an attractive residential community. Municipal tax revenues, however, were described as stagnating and several growing businesses had left the landlocked local government in the past when C was unable to provide larger business space. When the financial crisis hit, C experienced a decrease of revenue shares and the local government had to incur new debt for upcoming investment projects.

Administrators perceived the crisis, however, also as an opportunity, since politicians during the local government elections in the midst of the crisis in 2009 could not make generous but unfunded promises of future investments. Long-term trends like the population stagnation seemed, however, to be an important challenge that could potentially cause a financial shock for the local government. While anticipatory capacities in C were initially weak as they were not seen as necessary, the crisis years highlighted the need for an improved monitoring of the financial situation. The local government invested in its anticipatory capacities and implemented anticipated approval of supplementary budget, as well as quarterly information of the council on the city's financial condition.

> The supplementary budget is passed in July. Not in autumn when I cannot steer anymore, but in summer, where we can intervene, in a positive or a negative way. And this works relatively well. (CFO, C)

In coping with decreasing revenue shares during the financial crisis, C responded mainly by buffering – cutting costs, deferring investments and larger expenses, and following the regional government's instruction to increase fees and charges. While this seemed to be sufficient in order to balance the budget and C currently is lowering fees and charges again, it showed only limited success in developing the required coping capacities in order to address emerging vulnerabilities. On the one hand, the local government strengthened its urban planning – C proactively offered real estate consulting and intermediary services for owners of commercial property in order to address the increasing vulnerability of deteriorating buildings as businesses were leaving the municipality. On the other hand, the city's strategies in approaching the long-term issue of being a well-known tourist destination but not having appropriate accommodation capacity were not successful. Similarly, although the local government cooperated with neighbouring municipalities in public works and sewer infrastructure in the past, attempts to implement intercommunal land use planning to address its vulnerability of being landlocked failed due to the partners' concerns of sharing of property and municipal taxes.

> Our problem is, we do not have enough space. (Mountain 1) and (Mountain 2) also count to the area of our local government, but the biggest part of the lots of course are non-buildable. C's city area is restricted, but the neighbouring local governments have space [...] and our mayor repeatedly tried to cooperate with them. But of course, the others do not want to share their revenues with us. (CEO, C)

The municipality struggled to address its most important vulnerability source of an ageing and stagnating population, as respondents perceived that they can influence the population-related distribution of funds by the central government only marginally.

> That the population has been stagnating over the last years, [...] we are rather declining. That hurts us since revenue shares are related to the population. [...] To the state government, you are a solicitor. (CFO, C)

C seems to lack real strategies to tackle the most important issues for the local government's future. While some ideas were developed in the past years, it seems that the present anticipatory and coping capacities are insufficient for addressing long-term challenges and emerging vulnerability sources. The favourable conditions of its environment and the modest results that were achieved through adaptive capacity allow the local government to muddle through for the next years to come. Still, this pattern of resilience is likely to call for an increased investment in building anticipatory and coping capacities once the economic environment worsens or socio-demographic developments display their full impact on the local government's budget.

D

D is a wealthy local government where population numbers increased and the local economy had grown constantly over the last years. This accounted for a good revenue base and low financial vulnerability of the municipality. Thanks to its favourable conditions and stable revenue base, D invested in several large infrastructure projects. However, those were financed by selling assets and substantially increasing its debt level. This is shown also in the high volatility of its budgetary position that was around zero over the period of 10 years. Subsequently, the respondents described the local government's financial situation also as quite diverse. The CEO perceives D's financial capacity in terms of its revenues as very good and its financial health compared to similar local governments as good, though he acknowledges that the situation worsened during the last 10 years. In contrast, the CFO perceives the financial situation as tense and estimates that the local government could not cope with an additional financial challenge.

> Considering our size, our financial capacity is very good. [...] Compared to the past, our financial situation worsened. Compared to other local governments in the state, it is good, no need to worry. (CEO, D)

> The debt level, this is very...bad. (CFO, D)

This asymmetry was also present in the perception of financial shocks. While the CEO did not identify any financial shock within the last 10 years, the CFO pointed to the financial crisis in 2008. As with the other local governments that were part of the analysis, D experienced a decrease in revenue shares during that time. D, however, was able to compensate this by the relatively high municipal tax revenues from high-tech businesses — an industry that was only marginally sensitive to the national and global economic turmoil. Although the budget was balanced throughout the last 10 years, the crisis seems to have magnified issues on the local government's expenditure side and reduced its financial wiggle room to a minimum.

> Our problem is rather the expenditure side. We invested in infrastructure heavily, and we created value for generations within the short period of the last 10 years. (CFO, D)

However, the financial crisis is perceived not only as a threat to the local government's finances, but also as an opportunity: given that interest rates dropped, D benefited from more favourable conditions in debt service. There is a clear vision for the near future, positioning D as a livable, green, cultural and research and development oriented city. Interestingly, while the local government uses medium-term financial planning, there is no framework that connects the vision and the strategic goals with the funds or necessary investments.

> Well, there is no strategic plan, something where we say: 'we align our budget to performance indicators and want to achieve this and that'...this does not exist. (CFO, D)

With regard to anticipating developments, D seems to rely very much on the experience and intuition of its public servants of setting priorities. When certain circumstances occur and a crisis is unfolding, a so-called crisis management team consisting of the mayor, the CEO, the CFO and the council member responsible for finance comes into action. The implementation of this crisis management team was the answer to prior experience that actual costs repeatedly exceeded the budgeted expenses in large infrastructure projects.

However, the team does not carry out comprehensive risk management including prevention and preparation. Although the respondents seem to be aware of the local government's sources of vulnerability, there are no risk management processes in place to anticipate negative developments.

> We know about our specific vulnerability. Now you might ask whether we take any precautionary measures? Well, at this time, this is not possible, as our financial wiggle room is still limited. (CEO, D)

Within the past years, the local government increased the level of services and constantly was looking for areas where services could even be expanded. Although prior investments and therefore accumulated debt account for a tense financial situation, service cuts are rejected on principle.

> Of course, you can always build roads in a better, nicer, bigger way! Maybe we also exaggerated in the past, and we are back to reality now. (CFO, D)

> Service cuts? You see, this is a political problem. As a public servant, I am not the right addressee in this regard. [...] We have to, it is our duty, to answer to the demand by political decision-makers as good as we can, and to achieve the best possible outcome with the minimum of financial input – that is our task. (CEO, D)

As a response to the decreased shared tax revenues, D centralised purchasing in order to cut cost, deferred investments and negotiated a moratorium on debt service. These measures represent buffering capacities which seemed sufficient in coping with the only marginally experienced impact of the financial crisis. However, D's favourable environmental conditions, and in particular its steadily growing population, may have encouraged the local government to downplay increasing vulnerabilities, e.g. very low financial reserves, high debt level and maintenance requirements of infrastructure that has been built during the last 10 years. As a consequence, D appears as *contended* somewhat neglecting the importance of building and strengthening necessary anticipatory and coping capacities.

CONCLUSION

In all four cases, respondents repeatedly related to institutional conditions and general trends that impact their ability to cope with emerging financial challenges or arising financial shocks. First, they pointed to the low financial autonomy of local governments. On the one hand, Austrian municipalities are able to control the revenue side of the budget only to a limited extent. They are highly dependent on shared tax revenues and grants, which they receive from the central and the respective regional government. The distribution of these funds often discriminates against municipalities that are neither small nor large enough, meaning that the mechanisms that equalise limited opportunity to collect municipal taxes or the need to provide a larger variety of services do not come into effect. On the other hand, the Austrian government has increasingly devolved tasks and service responsibility to the local level during the past years, and the compensations for the increased expenditures seem to be insufficient. One of the most recent examples is the decision of the Austrian central government to offer free kindergartens for five-year-olds in 2009. Some regional governments (*Länder*) expanded the service to all ages and hence made kindergarten free of charge in general. The late and insufficient compensation paid to the local governments created annual shortfalls of several hundred thousand Euros for some municipalities. At the same time, the transfer payments that local governments have to pay to their regional governments for the provision of social services and health care have increased continuously. In sum, the funding system of local governments was perceived as unsatisfactory and demanding reforms, which was pointed out illustratively by one respondent:

> The system of transfer payments... it is like giving my son 100 Euro and then I say: 'you have to pay me 50 Euro rent, and then 10 Euro for this, 10 for that' and so on, so that he has only 10 Euro left. (CFO; C)

Other institutional conditions that were perceived as restraining in all of the analysed local governments were the Maastricht criteria, or in fact the Austrian Stability Pact mentioned above. This mechanism limited the local governments' possibilities of incurring debt or operating with deficits. Other topics that dominated the public debate on the financial situation of local governments in Austria, derivative financial instruments and foreign currency loans, seem to be less relevant in the selected municipalities. None of the four cases that were analysed used derivative financial instruments, which basically were perceived as speculation with tax money. Only one case showed debt in foreign currency loans. At the time of the analysis, this caused an extensive burden of debt service; however, the local government did not opt to convert its debt in Euro yet.

The Austrian cases support one general finding on financial resilience that has emerged throughout the book. Financial resilience in Austrian local governments exists in different patterns, which are not necessarily related to, or dependent on, measures of financial performance, namely budgetary position and its volatility over time. Taking a closer look at the dimensions of financial resilience, it turns out that strong anticipatory capacities were expressed by high awareness of the local government's particular sources of vulnerability or potential risks and cautious planning of both the political as well as administrative decision-makers. Instruments like embedded medium-term financial planning, i.e. with an actual impact on planning processes and annual budgets, long-term investment plans, monitoring and control processes, or scenario analyses, supported the capacity to anticipate developments and to be prepared for and able to cope with potential financial shocks. Those different anticipatory capacities in turn supported the capacity to buffer financial shocks, adapt to moderate changes in the local government's vulnerability, or transform in case of more challenging long-term goals. Where those anticipatory and coping capacities were initially low, it was the awareness and consciousness of decision-makers, administrators and politicians that led to the impact of a financial shock being recognised and appreciated as a trigger to undergo necessary changes, and build up or strengthen the local government's internal capacities.

Interestingly, C and D appear to have had strong coping capacities in the past, which translated into wealthy conditions (i.e. stable and diversified revenue base, image of the local government). Resting on their laurels however, they did not anticipate the crisis, and hoped to weather the storm relying merely on their buffering capacities. In the long term, however, this pattern of resilience bears the risk of increased vulnerability, and the local governments need to take stronger actions in further developing their anticipatory and coping capacities in order to be able to sustain their service level and be prepared for future challenges.

NOTES

1. Data obtained from the series on local government finances, Kommunalkredit Austria (2009, 2010, 2011, 2012).
2. Mean local government revenues 2014, excluding the capital Vienna due to its size and special administrative functions. Data based on the Austrian Municipal Association 2015 (Gemeindebund, 2015).
3. Data for 2013, based on Eurostat (2016a).

REFERENCES

Bailey, K. (2007). *Methods of Social Research*. (4th ed.) New York, NY: Free Press.
Barbera, C., Jones, M., Korac, S., Saliterer, I., & Steccolini, I. (2015). Bouncing back and bouncing forward - Applying an alternative perspective on European municipalities' responses to financial shocks. EGPA Annual Conference, PSG VI: Governance of Public Sector Organizations. Toulouse, France, August 26-28.
BGBl. I (2011). Nr. 117. Vereinbarung zwischen Bund, den Ländern und den Gemeinden über eine Weiterführung der stabilitätsorientierten Budgetpolitik (Österreichischer Stabilitätspakt 2011). Ausgegeben am 12. 12. 2011.
BGBl. I (2013). Nr. 30. Vereinbarung zwischen Bund, den Ländern und den Gemeinden über einen Österreichischen Stabilitätspakt 2012 – ÖstP 2012. Ausgegeben am 23. 1. 2013.
Biwald, P., & Rossmann, B. (2012). Gemeindefinanzen im Korsett der europäischen Steuerungsarchitektur. *Wirtschaft und Gesellschaft*, *38*(3), 505–548.
Eisenhardt, K. M., & Graebner, M. E. (2007). Theory building from cases: Opportunities and challenges. *Academy of Management Journal*, *50*(1), 25–32.
Eurostat. (2016a). GDP per capita in PPS. Data from 1st of June 2016. Retrieved from http://ec.europa.eu/eurostat/tgm/table.do?tab=table&init=1&language=en&pcode=tec00114&plugin=1
Eurostat. (2016b). Unemployment by sex and age – Annual average. Data from Eurostat last update 29.07.2016.

Famira-Mühlberger, U., & Leoni, T. (2013). *The economic and social situation in Austria*. Österreichisches Institut für Wirtschaftsforschung and European Economic and Social Committee. Retrieved from http://www.eesc.europa.eu/resources/docs/qe-02-13-551-en-c.pdf

Gemeindebund. (2015). Gemeindefinanzbericht 2015. Wien. Retrieved from http://gemeindebund.at/images/uploads/downloads/2015/Publikationen/Gemeindefinanzbericht/Gemeindefinanzbericht_2015_klein.pdf

Holsti, O. R. (1969). *Content analysis for the social sciences and humanities*. Reading, MA: Addison-Wesley.

KDZ. (2011). Pressemitteilung. Investitionskraft der Städte stark gebremst. Wien, 22, 11.2011.

Kuhlmann, S. (2010). Vergleichende Verwaltungswissenschaft: Verwaltungssysteme, Verwaltungskulturen und Verwaltungsreformen in internationaler Perspektive. In H.-J. Lauth (Ed.), *Vergleichende Regierungslehre. Eine Einführung* (Vol. 3). Berlin: Aktualisierte und erweiterte Auflage. Springer.

Kuhlmann, S., & Wollmann, H. (2014). *Introduction to comparative public administration, administrative systems and reforms in Europe*. Cheltenham: Edward Elgar.

Meszarits, V., & Saliterer, I. (2013). Die Bundeshaushaltsrechtsreform - Ausgangspunkt für eine neue Voranschlags- und Rechnungsabschlussverordnung für Länder und Gemeinden. *RWZ, 2013*(7/8), 43–59.

Mouritzen, P., & Svara, J. (2002). *Leadership at the apex. Politicians and administrators in Western local governments*. Pittsburgh, PA: Pittsburgh University Press.

Österreichischer Städtebund. (2015). Österreichische Gemeindefinanzen 2015 – Entwicklungen 2004 bis 2018. Wien.

Patton, M. Q. (2015). *Qualitative research & evaluation methods* (4th ed.). Thousand Oaks, CA: Sage.

Proeller, I. (2006). Trends in local government in Europe. *Public Management Review, 8*(1), 7–29.

Rauskala, I., & Saliterer, I. (2015). Public sector accounting and auditing in Europe. In I. Brusca, E. Caperchione, S. Cohen, & F. Manes Rossi (Eds.), *Public sector accounting and auditing in Europe. The challenge of Harmonization*. Basingstoke: Palgrave MacMillan.

Saliterer, I. (2013a). Einheitliche Weiterentwicklung des Haushalts- und Rechnungswesens der Länder und Gemeinden Implikationen und Vorschläge für eine VRV Neu (Teil I). *Öffentliches Haushaltswesen, 53*(1), 1–14.

Saliterer, I. (2013b). Einheitliche Weiterentwicklung des Haushalts- und Rechnungswesens der Länder und Gemeinden Implikationen und Vorschläge für eine VRV Neu (Teil II). *Öffentliches Haushaltswesen, 53*(4).

Saliterer, I., & Korac, S. (2014). The discretionary use of performance information by different local government actors – Analysing and comparing the predictive power of three factor sets. *International Review of Administrative Sciences, 80*(3), 637–658.

Statistik Austria. (2016a). Bevölkerungsstand und –struktur 17.08.2016. Retrieved from http://www.statistik.at/web_de/statistiken/menschen_und_gesellschaft/bevoelkerung/index.html

Statistik Austria. (2016b). Gemeindegrößenklassen mit Einwohnerzahl 30.06.2016. Statistik Austria Wien.

Statistik Austria. (2016c). Öffentlicher Schuldenstand 1995-2015. 31.3.2016. Wien.

Statistik Austria. (2016d). Öffentliches Defizit 1995-2015. 31.3.2016. Wien.

Stewart, J. (2012). Multiple-case study methods in governance-related research. *Public Management Review, 14*(1), 67–82.

Yin, R. K. (2009). *Case study research: Design and methods* (4th ed.). Thousand Oaks, CA: Sage.

CHAPTER 3

A TALE OF TWO JURISDICTIONS: A FOCUS ON THE EFFECT OF REGULATORY CONSTRAINTS ON MUNICIPAL RESILIENCE IN AUSTRALIA

Joseph Drew

ABSTRACT

Australia notably was one of the few developed nations to avoid a technical recession subsequent to the Global Financial Crisis (GFC). However, the fact that the nation escaped a technical recession doesn't mean that citizens and local governments were not subject to some of the measures associated with post-GFC austerity. In particular, intergovernmental grants – an important source of revenue for Australian local governments – were frozen by the federal government seeking to mitigate large deficits over the forward estimates. This chapter compares and contrasts the budgetary outcomes for the local governments of Australia's two most populous states – New South Wales and Victoria. We find that the disparate regulatory controls in the two municipal jurisdictions were strongly associated with the budgetary outcomes of the individual municipalities: In particular, we present evidence which suggests that taxation limitations and lax investment guidelines in New South Wales can be associated with relatively inferior budgetary positions and higher budgetary volatility. By way of contrast, Victorian councils had the flexibility to vary rates of taxation to the changing conditions and

Governmental Financial Resilience: International Perspectives on how Local Governments Face Austerity
Public Policy and Governance, Volume 27, 35–52
Copyright © 2017 by Emerald Publishing Limited
ISSN: 2053-7697/doi:10.1108/S2053-769720170000027003

largely avoided investment losses associated with the financial failure of Lehman Brothers. In New South Wales the regulatory response to deteriorating municipal budgets (subsequent to the GFC) has been to execute a radical programme of forced amalgamations. Somewhat ironically, the Victorian state government has recently imposed taxation limitations on its municipalities. In summary, this chapter demonstrates the saliency of regulatory constraints on municipal resilience, in the context of post-GFC economic challenges.

Keywords: Australia; municipal resilience; regulatory constraints; Victoria; New South Wales

INTRODUCTION

Australia has long been lauded as one of the few advanced economies to escape recession subsequent to the Global Financial Crisis (GFC). Credit for Australia's uninterrupted growth since the GFC has been variously ascribed to its strong banking system and robust regulatory agencies which existed prior to the GFC as well as the Commonwealth Government stimulus and bank deposit guarantee schemes initiated after the onset of the crisis (the fiscal stimulus ceased some time ago, however, the bank guarantee scheme has no expiry date – see, for instance Fenna, 2013; Wittenhall, 2011). However, Australia was also the beneficiary of a steep rise in demand for commodities from its largest and fourth largest trading partners (China and India, respectively) in the post-GFC period. Indeed, Day (2011, p. 23) has conducted empirical analysis to show that 'had growth in export volumes to China been commensurate with pre-stimulus rates, Australia would have experienced three consecutive quarters of negative real GDP growth'. Less well recognised is the contribution of net migration to the country – a comparison of the average net migration for the seven years either side of the GFC reveals an increase of 169% peaking at 300 million in 2009 (Australian Bureau of Statistics (ABS), 2014). An indication of the pervasive effect of migration on national growth is illustrated by the GDP per capita recording three consecutive quarters of negative growth between September 2008 and March 2009 (ABS, 2014). Thus, while the nation may have escaped a 'technical recession' it would be incorrect to conclude that individuals have not experienced fiscal stress. Moreover, an aggressive fiscal stimulus programme, combined with the introduction of a number of unfunded social programmes and falling tax receipts associated with a sudden drop-off in commodity prices, means that the federal government is now grappling with large deficits over the forward estimates (Commonwealth of Australia, 2015).

This in turn has prompted the federal government to reduce intergovernmental transfers, thereby placing stress on state and municipal budgets.

Australia is a federation comprising six independent states (Queensland, New South Wales, Victoria, Tasmania, South Australia and Western Australia) and two Commonwealth-controlled territories (the Northern Territory and the Australian Capital Territory). There have been two failed attempts to have local government recognised in the federal constitution. As a result, local government remains a 'creature of statute' exercising a limited remit of services according to the delegated powers of the six states and one territory which regulate municipal entities (the Australian Capital Territory, ACT) – which is the seat of the Australian federal parliament – does not have a system of local government; (Twomey, 2012). Historically, local government in Australia has been responsible for roads, rates (local government taxes based on property value) and rubbish. In more recent times the local government remit has been expanded to include addressing market failure (for instance, in providing aged care, child care and medical services in rural locations), recreation services and development planning, as well as limited welfare and law and order functions. Most of the expanded remit has gone unfunded by higher tiers of government (Dollery, Grant, & Crase, 2011). State government is responsible for operating *inter alia* schools, police and fire fighting and providing most of the rail infrastructure. The Commonwealth Government is responsible for public goods such as defence, tertiary education and social security (Drew & Dollery, 2015a). In common with most federalist systems, Australia is characterised by a high degree of vertical fiscal imbalance, with the Commonwealth collecting 81% of tax revenues, compared with just 3.4% attributed to local government (ABS, 2015). Intergovernmental grants are therefore an important source of income for Australian municipalities.

This chapter differs from others in this book by placing a particular emphasis on the effect of regulatory constraints on municipal resilience. The polar approaches of regulators in Australia's two largest jurisdictions – New South Wales (NSW), which regulates 152 municipalities covering a third of the nation's population and Victoria, which regulates 79 municipalities encompassing a quarter of the nation's population – present the ideal institution milieu for such an investigation. For instance, Victorian local government is subject to central auditing (including a thorough system of performance monitoring and performance analysis), has narrowly defined roles for elected representatives (by legislation), was subject to an almost two-thirds reduction in the number of councils in 1994 and has no extant taxation limitations. By way of contrast NSW currently has no system of central auditing (and has only recently introduced an (inadequate) system of performance monitoring), has widely defined roles for elected representatives, is presently in the throes of a forced amalgamation programme and has had a system of taxation limitations since 1977. In general, it is probably fair to say that (with the exception of taxation limitations) the Victorian local governments have been subject to heavier regulation and intervention than their NSW peers. This is neither good nor bad, just different – the focus of this chapter is to determine whether the different approaches (particularly taxation limitations) manifest as different budget outcomes over the period of study. To facilitate our investigation of the effect of regulatory constraints on municipal resilience we draw on two case studies from each of the jurisdictions. One council from each jurisdiction has been selected from two polar budgetary positions – councils with low-volatility negative budget outcomes and councils with highly volatile positive budgetary positions – to expediently highlight the importance of regulatory constraint on municipal resilience.

The section 'Context' describes the context and, in particular, the features of the two jurisdictions. The section 'Methods' details the methodology used to construct a budgetary position and volatility matrix and inter-temporal analysis of mean budgetary position and volatility over the period spanning 1 July 2008 to 30 June 2014. The results of the analysis are presented in the section 'Results', with a particular emphasis on the effect of regulatory constraints on the financial resilience of four exemplar municipalities. The chapter ends with some observations on the importance of regulatory constraints for municipal resilience.

CONTEXT

Local government in Australia has a more limited remit than many of the other countries discussed in other chapters, focussing on providing roads, rubbish removal, development planning and health inspections, and maintaining parks and recreation facilities. In rural areas there is often a demand for local government to provide important services which may not be commercially viable – such as aged care, home and community care, child care and infrastructure to attract and retain medical practitioners. In contrast, metropolitan municipalities often play a complementary role in welfare (for instance, setting up homeless shelters or 'safe' drug injecting sites) and security (e.g. setting up a system of video surveillance in entertainment precincts). Road maintenance is the single largest item of municipal expenditure – accounting for approximately a quarter of local government budgets (PwC, 2006). It should be noted that Australian municipalities are responsible for over 80% of the national road infrastructure (Chakrabarti, Kodikara, & Pardo, 2002).

The Australian Accounting Standards Board is the Commonwealth statutory body for prescribing accounting standards. Since 1 January 2005 *all* Australian entities have reported on a full accruals basis according to AASB equivalent International Financial Reporting Standards (IFRS). Local governments experienced difficulty setting up asset registers and have subsequently adopted inconsistent approaches to reporting depreciation accruals, which account for approximately a quarter of the quantum of expenditure (see, for instance, Drew & Dollery, 2015b; Pilcher, 2002; Pilcher & Van de Zahn, 2010). Auditing and assurance practices differ for the two jurisdictions, as do a number of other contextual features:

New South Wales Local Government

The New South Wales local government sector comprises 152 general-purpose municipalities. In addition to the functions detailed above, many rural municipalities are also responsible for water and sewerage services (unlike their Victorian peers). The average population size of NSW municipalities in 2013 was 48,026, although individual municipalities had populations ranging from 1,180 to 317,598. Length of municipal roads maintained by individual municipalities ranged from 65 km to 3,982 km, with a state mean of 1,090 km. In terms of fiscal responsibilities, the average operating expenditure in 2014 was A $39.07 million (minimum A$7.3 million, maximum A$266.4 million).

NSW municipalities are not recognised in the state or federal constitution and so they govern under delegated powers conferred via the Local Government Act (1993). The State Local Government Minister has virtually unlimited powers over NSW local government, including the ability to reconstitute boundaries and dismiss elected representatives. In the first decade of the millennium 23 municipalities were forcibly amalgamated, and NSW local government faces imminent amalgamation of approximately a quarter of the extant entities (Drew & Dollery, 2015c). Elections are held for representatives every four years with compulsory voting applying to all citizens. Municipalities have between 6 and 15 representatives, including the Mayor, who is directly elected in only 34 instances. Councillors elect the Mayor (who has both additional ceremonial and executive functions) for the other 118 municipalities on a one-year term. The General Manager of each council is appointed by the elected representatives on a maximum five-year term and the enabling legislation requires that the elected council be consulted on the appointment and dismissal of all senior staff (ILGRP, 2013). There is no statutory requirement for municipalities to have an audit committee and only around one half of municipalities do so (Independent Local Government Review Panel, ILGRP, 2013).

NSW municipalities extract about 70% of their revenues through taxes and fees. Taxes are calculated on the unimproved value of land and increases to total taxation take are capped according to a single rate set for the entire state by the Independent Pricing and Regulatory Tribunal (IPART). This tax limitation regime has existed for almost four decades and has resulted in both uneven revenue effort across the state and significant budget constraints (see Drew & Dollery, 2015d). Intergovernmental grants are an important source of income for NSW municipalities. The bulk of the grants emanate from the Commonwealth Government but are allocated by state government grants commissions due to constitutional constraints (see Drew & Dollery, 2015a). Grants may be tied to specific purposes or untied. The major untied grants are the Financial Assistance Grants (FAGs), which had a quantum of A$711.5 million for NSW in 2015/2016 (Department of Infrastructure and Regional Development, 2015). The Commonwealth Government has recently frozen FAGs for three years in order to help repair the federal budget deficits.

Victorian Local Government

The Victorian local government sector comprises 79 municipalities and had an average population size of 71,245 in 2013 (minimum 3,099, maximum 267,892). Thus, Victoria has fewer and larger (on average) local government entities than NSW. Length of municipal roads maintained by individual municipalities ranged from 42 km to 11,234 km, with a state mean of 1,659 km. In terms of fiscal responsibilities, the average expenditure in 2014 was A$91 million (minimum A$9.55 million, maximum A$364 million).

Victorian municipalities are recognised in the state constitution, although the Minister still has wide discretion, which has recently been employed to establish proscribed development application fees, performance monitoring metrics and contentious tax limitations starting in the 2016/2017 financial year. In 1994 the state government forcibly reduced the number of municipalities from 210 to just 78. The subsequent de-amalgamation of Delatite Council in 2002, due to a sustained popular de-amalgamation campaign, increased the number of municipalities to 79. Elections are held for representatives every four years, with compulsory voting applying to all citizens (Drew & Dollery, 2015e). Owners of property who do not reside in the council area also have statutory voting rights, as do corporations occupying property (one representative of each corporation is entitled to vote in elections). Municipalities have between 5 and 12 representatives, including the Mayor, who is directly elected in only two instances. Councillors in the other 77 municipalities elect the Mayor for a one-year term (Economou, 2010). The General Manager of each council is the sole appointment made by the elected representatives. Victorian municipalities are centrally audited by the Victorian Auditor General's Office (VAGO) and must all operate an audit committee according to section 139 of the Local Government Act (1989) (VAGO, 2015). Central auditing and compulsory audit committees do not currently apply in NSW local government.

Victorian municipalities obtain about 63% of their revenues from taxes and fees. Taxes are calculated on the capital improved value of land and structures and the rate of taxation is currently determined by elected representatives of the municipalities (Drew & Dollery, 2015d). Intergovernmental grants are also an important source of income for Victorian municipalities. FAGs for

Victorian municipalities totalled A$539.8 million in 2015/2016 (Department of Infrastructure and Regional Development, 2015). Initial State FAG allocations are based on population size, hence the lower aggregated quantum for Victorian municipalities.

METHODS

The aim of this chapter is to examine municipal resilience with a particular emphasis on the effect of regulatory constraint. To this end the budgetary position and volatility were assessed for the 231 municipalities making up the jurisdictions of NSW and Victoria. Normalised budget positions were calculated for each municipality by taking the operating result from audited financial statements and dividing same by total revenue for the period. This approach accords with regulatory monitoring practices in Victoria. However, in NSW the regulator excludes contributions for capital purposes in its comparative dataset. To ensure a consistent approach for the two jurisdictions, capital contributions were added onto operating results and total revenue for all NSW municipalities. The mean operating result was then calculated for each of the municipalities over the relevant period (the six financial years from 2009 to 2014: publicly available data does not exist for periods prior to June 30, 2008[1] and as such the analysis in this chapter is limited to the years immediately after the global financial crisis). Near zero mean budgetary position was taken to be between −1 and +1%. To stratify municipalities according to volatility, we conducted Ward's method cluster analysis on the *entire* cohort for the standard deviation of individual normalised budgets calculated over the six financial years (use of the entire cohort in a single cluster analysis is important as it allows for a comparison of *relative* volatility between the two jurisdictions). Cluster analysis is an empirical strategy for arranging municipalities into homogenous groups. Ward's method joins municipalities to groups which result in the minimum increase to the error sum of squares as measured by Euclidian distance (for further information on cluster analysis see Drew & Dollery, 2016). We grouped the analysis into three clusters representing relatively low, medium and high volatilities. A budgetary position and volatility matrix was then constructed over the six financial years (see Table 1).

Notably, the majority of municipalities experiencing a mean negative budgetary position over the six years were located in NSW (27 out of the 28 'negative' municipalities). It is also clear that the level of budget volatility was far higher for NSW municipalities than for their Victorian peers (19 of the 25 high-volatility municipalities were domiciled in NSW).

These results seem to suggest that differences in regulatory approaches might have an important effect on municipal resilience. In order to investigate this matter further we plotted the mean normalised budget position and

Table 1. Budgetary Position and Volatility of New South Wales and
Victorian Municipalities (Number of Municipalities in Each Cell Is Presented
as a Percentage of the Entire 231 Council Cohort in Parenthesis).

Budgetary Position Volatility	Negative	Around Zero	Positive
Low	*17 NSW (7.4%)*	9 NSW (3.9%)	100 NSW (43.3%)
	1 Victoria (0.4%)	3 Victoria (1.3%)	67 Victoria (29%)
Medium	4 NSW (1.7%)	2 NSW (0.9%)	1 NSW (0.4%)
	0 Victoria (0%)	0 Victoria (0%)	2 Victoria (0.9%)
High	6 NSW (2.6%)	0 NSW (0%)	*13 NSW (5.6%)*
	0 Victoria (0%)	0 Victoria (0%)	*6 Victoria (2.6%)*

standard deviation for each *jurisdiction* to examine inter-temporal trends. We
then conducted four case studies drawn from diametrically opposed cells of
the budgetary matrix: two low-volatility, negative budgetary position municipalities (Central Darling (NSW) and Monash (Victoria)) and two positive
high-volatility municipalities (Carrathool (NSW) and Loddon (Victoria)). The
extreme positions of the matrix were selected rather than the most representative clusters under the assumption that regulatory effects were most likely to be
seen first at the margins. This desire to emphasise the effects of regulatory
constraints on resilience was also reflected in the careful choice of exemplar
councils. For instance, Central Darling Shire was selected as it is the sole example of Australian government financial failure and Carrathool was chosen
because it achieved very different budgetary outcomes despite being faced with
quite similar environmental constraints. Moreover, Monash was the sole example of a Victorian council with low-volatility negative budgetary position, whilst
Loddon provided a good example of the need for revenue flexibility in the face
of catastrophic natural disasters. The case studies were based on artefacts taken
from the local media and official documents (such as transcripts of public
inquiries and council submissions to public consultations).

RESULTS

To provide a comprehensive understanding of the effect of regulatory constraint on municipal resilience in the post-GFC period we considered the matter
from two complimentary perspectives. First, we conducted an inter-temporal
comparison in order to establish whether there were in fact clear differences
between the two jurisdictions and therefore provide an empirical basis for suggesting that the disparate regulatory environments might have a bearing on the

budgetary positions of councils. We then conducted a close examination of four councils in order to understand how regulatory settings, in particular, influence municipal resilience.

Inter-Temporal Analysis of Jurisdiction Level Responses Post-GFC

Fig. 1 illustrates inter-temporal trends in budget positions at a state jurisdiction level, as well as a measure of the spread of budget positions for each of the two jurisdictions over the (financial year) period 2009–2014 inclusive. In order to interpret Fig. 1 it is important to be aware of events which occurred over this time. The first major disruption to council budgets occurred as a result of the Commonwealth Government's response to the GFC. To assist municipal cash flows the Commonwealth pre-paid part of the 2010 allocation of FAGs into the 2009 financial year (Parliament of the Commonwealth of Australia, 2009). Later, in February 2009 the federal government partnered with local government to roll out over A$1 billion of the fiscal stimulus programme (Parliament of the Commonwealth of Australia, 2009). At about the same time, Victorian municipalities were faced with infrastructure write-offs and increased demand for welfare assistance resulting from the February 2009 Black Saturday bushfires, which affected 78 communities, covered 400,000 hectares and killed 173 residents (Country Fire Authority, 2015). Municipal natural disaster response explains why Victorian municipalities as a cohort had a steeper downward gradient in

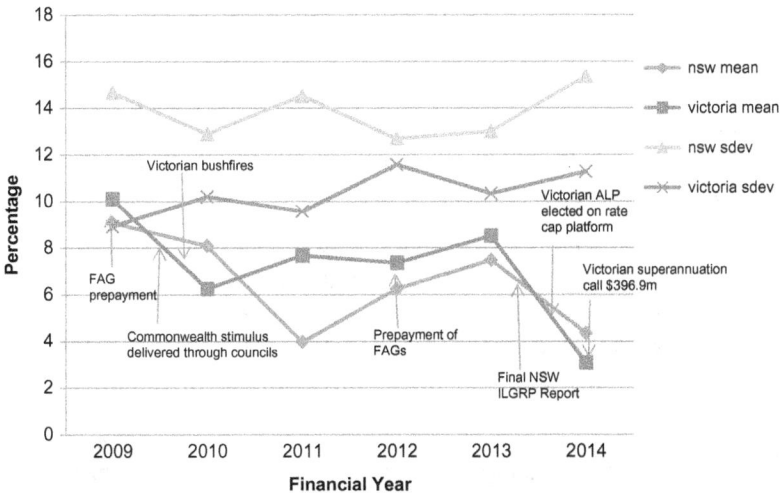

Fig. 1. Budgetary Position and Volatility of New South Wales and Victorian Municipalities since the Global Financial Crisis.

their mean budget position between the 2009 and 2010 financial years (see also, Institute of Public Works Engineering Australasia, 2014).

The strategy of prepaying FAGs was then repeated for the 2012 financial year, wherein half of the FAG allocation for 2012/2013 was paid a year early—this time in order for the federal government to attempt to manufacture a budget surplus for the subsequent financial year (Comrie, 2013). Moreover, NSW municipalities recognised A$384 million in investment losses during 2009–2012, associated with collateralised debt obligations, capital protected and managed fund products (Department of Premier & Cabinet Division of Local Government (DLG), 2015). 'Lehman Brothers, in particular, were active in the WA [Western Australia] and NSW markets' (Parliament of the Commonwealth of Australia, 2009, p. 64). Victorian municipalities had little exposure to high-risk investment products due to more conservative investment regulatory guidelines issued by the state regulator.

Notably, the NSW jurisdiction had higher rates of volatility over the entire domain. This is likely the result of the strict tax limitation regime which made it very difficult for municipalities to mitigate volatile expenditure demands with own-source revenue increases. The NSW jurisdiction also had lower average normalised budget positions for four of the six financial periods. Given that the remaining two periods were characterised by significant shocks to which only Victorian municipalities were exposed, this overall result may be taken to suggest that regulatory settings (in particular tax limitations and investment guidelines) are extremely important to municipal resilience.

The responses of individual municipalities to the various budget disruptions over the (financial) period 2009–2014 inclusive led to two very different regulatory reactions. In the case of Victoria, relatively high increases to taxation rates, executed to arrest declining budgetary positions, led to the state opposition party running on an election platform which *inter alia* included introducing municipal tax limitations (proposing that tax increases would be capped at the rate of inflation as measured by the Consumer Price Index). When the opposition party was elected in May 2014 they quickly introduced preparations to establish tax limitations to commence in the 2015/2016 financial year (however, in response to strident stakeholder objections, the introduction of tax limitations was deferred in early 2015 to the 2016/2017 financial year) (Australian Broadcasting Corporation (ABC), 2015a). In addition, Victorian municipalities were hit with a one-off defined superannuation call in the order of an aggregate A$396 million to meet unfunded defined superannuation liabilities (Municipal Association of Victoria (MAV), 2012). In contrast, NSW municipalities, which had suffered declining budgetary positions principally as a result of the long-standing tax limitation regime, came in for a different type of regulatory intervention. The NSW Government established an 'independent' advisory panel which recommended a programme of radical forced amalgamations (Independent Local Government Review Panel (ILGRP), 2013).

Individual Council Responses to Shocks

Central Darling Shire in NSW (exhibiting a six-year average budgetary position of −2.22%) has had the most spectacular outcome arising from post-GFC budget disruptions, having been placed into financial Administration in December 2013 when it became clear that the municipality was no longer solvent. This period of Administration has since been extended to 2020 following a public inquiry which identified a long history of failed regulatory interventions stretching back to January 2011 (Colley, 2014). It is the first instance of government financial failure in Australia.

Elected representatives (councillors) were quick to cite inadequate levels of intergovernmental grants as the cause behind the liquidity crisis confronting the municipality (Drew & Campbell, 2016). It was argued by councillors that the high infrastructure burden coupled with a small population spread over a vast distance equivalent to one-fifth of the size of the United Kingdom meant that only increased intergovernmental grant transfers could ensure a sustainable municipality. In addition, councillors drew attention to the burden created by an increasing obligation of municipal government to address market failure (such as the purchase and operation of the Wilcannia Post Office after the previous owners fell into receivership) (Drew & Campbell, 2016).

However, the inquiry was scathing of what it perceived to be the 'fatalistic attitude [of elected representatives] about the councils financial viability' (Colley, 2014, p. 9). In particular, the Commissioner of the inquiry condemned 'councillors [who] blamed, and continue to blame the Federal and State governments, including various government agencies for a failure to provide funding to bail the Council out of the financial crises' (Colley, 2014, p. 9). The attitude of the council might indeed have been the result of an extreme sense of fatalism as concluded by the Commissioner. However, it is also a possibility that the events leading up to the Administration period may have been the result of brinkmanship. Rather than reducing services, councillors expanded some services and when it became apparent that the council was approaching insolvency wrote to their Member of Parliament demanding an immediate cash injection of $2 million and a review of the quantum of grant transfers to the Shire (Colley, 2014, pp. 28−31). The state government response seems to have taken the council by surprise: the shire did not get a cash injection and was forced into administration, however, it did receive an increase in its FAG allocations in the order of $800,000 per annum from 2012/2013 levels (Drew & Campbell, 2016). In any event, the conclusion of the public inquiry was that the liquidity crisis could only be addressed through deep and enduring cuts to municipal services. Moreover, the Commissioner determined that the current elected representatives did not have an adequate commitment to the recovery plan and therefore declared that the municipality would need to continue in Administration for a further six years (Colley, 2014).

A number of interesting observations can be made regarding the municipal resilience of Central Darling Shire. In the first instance, it is clear that tax limitations imposed by regulatory authorities exerted a direct influence on the coping capacity of elected representatives, essentially dictating a high level of dependency on intergovernmental grant transfers for revenue side approaches to resolving the liquidity problem. Second, the transcripts from the public inquiry suggest that a combination of municipal tax limitations along with a high level of grant transfers had resulted in a disconnect between resident demand for enhanced services and own-source revenue (Colley, 2014). Finally, it is clear that elected representatives of the municipality suffered from diminished anticipatory capacity: it appears from the transcripts of the inquiry that the councillors really did believe that the state government would bail the municipality out of the liquidity crisis. Moreover, councillors seemed unable to anticipate the outcome of the inquiry: following the release of the Commissioner's recommendations the Mayor was cited as saying that he 'was shocked to hear the suspension will stay' and that the 'councillors were ready to return to work, and even had plans underway for the Administrator to hand back control' (Local Government Career, 2014).

In Victoria there was just one council with a negative budgetary position over the six financial years subsequent to the GFC – *Monash* (six-year average budgetary position of −1.66%). In its submission to the Essential Services Commission (ESC, 2015) regarding the proposed tax limitation framework, the municipality boasted that it 'has consistently kept rates as low as possible and has the lowest rates of all 79 Victorian municipalities' and that it 'has proudly maintained the lowest rating status for several years' (Monash City Council, 2015). In one sense Monash Council appears to have a self-imposed tax limitation regime which has led to similar results to those experienced by some NSW municipalities – deteriorating budgetary positions over an extended period of time. However, unlike Central Darling, Monash Council was able to anticipate a looming crisis and was prepared and able to take actions on the expenditure side to mitigate poor budgetary outcomes. In January 2014, Monash Council voted to sell its two aged-care facilities (housing 165 residents) to Royal Freemasons for A$21.8 million. This sale was expected to save the council approximately A$1 million per annum in subsidies for the facilities as well 'several millions of dollars in capital works in the short term' (Lake, 2015). It is important to note one very big difference between the two municipalities – Central Darling is a rural council situated 950 km west of Sydney, whilst Monash is a metropolitan council located just 25.8 km from Melbourne, the Victorian capital. Consequently, Monash had the advantage of being able to find commercial operators which could make a profit operating council assets, whereas Central Darling had only the option of closing facilities – the shire's remote location makes many commercial operations simply not viable. Therefore, it is clear that Monash had significantly greater coping capacity by virtue of its geographical position, but also greater anticipatory awareness of the need to adapt and mitigate revenue side budgetary constraints.

On the opposite side of the matrix are the two exemplar high-volatility 'positive' municipalities. *Carrathool* (six-year mean normalised budgetary position of 19.77%), like Central Darling, is a rural NSW council located some distance west of Sydney (675 km) and thus faces similar environmental constraints. In the 2012 financial year (prior to the investigations of Central Darling) the two municipalities faced almost identical circumstances. For instance, Carrathool had a population of 2,668 with an average income of A$38,064 and a council operating expenditure of A$17 million, whilst Central Darling had a population of 2,108 with an average per capita income of A$38,248 and an operating expenditure of A$16.3 million (Office of Local Government (OLG), 2015). The big difference between the two NSW municipalities was on the revenue that each was able to extract by virtue of the tax limitation measures. Tax limitations were based on incremental increases on the extant tax rate charged in 1977 – therefore municipalities which had small differences in rate revenue in 1977 could conceivably end up with large differences owing to the compounding effect of almost four decades (Abelson & Joyeux, 2015). Thus, as at 2012 Carrathool was collecting well over four times the municipal taxes as was Central Darling Shire despite roughly comparable capacity of residents to pay (Office of Local Government, 2015). It should be noted that municipalities have the option to apply for special rate variations (SRV) to increase municipal taxes above regulated annual increase levels. However, this process is expensive (owing to the regulatory requirements to demonstrate need and community support) and politically charged, and one to which few municipalities are prepared to commit (in 2012 just 13 municipalities applied for SRVs) (IPART, 2012). In short, Carrathool Council had greater coping capacity (through higher budget redundancies to buffer against shocks) than Central Darling Shire, almost entirely as a result of higher revenue take afforded under the tax limitation regime. This serendipitous situation wherein regulated tax revenues far exceeded need meant that the leadership team at Carrathool could afford to exhibit an attitude of contentment at the same time as their peers were confronted by insolvency.

In Victoria, *Loddon Shire* (six-year average budgetary position of 9.32%) is 215 km NNW of Melbourne. It displayed a highly volatile but positive mean normalised budget outcome over the six financial years, which stands in stark contrast to its Victorian peer of Monash which also had – at least legislatively – the flexibility to adjust taxation revenues to match need. Volatility in the results can be directly attributed to a number of natural disasters which occurred in the rural area: between September 2010 and January 2011, Loddon Shire experience three major flood events which destroyed an estimated A$42 million of road and bridge infrastructure (Institute of Public Works Engineering Australasia (IPWEA), 2014). The municipality was able to access national disaster relief funding and execute the restoration works in the stipulated two-year time frame and A$8 million under budget (IPWEA, 2014). Consistent with other rural municipalities in Australia, Loddon Shire has a number of facilities to meet demand associated with market failure, including five kindergartens and an A$2.5 million home-care service (ABC, 2015b). The council credits its solid budget outcomes to the careful control of costs and the flexibility to set rates at a level commensurate with demand (Loddon was not subject to municipal tax limitations as were the NSW municipalities). For instance, Loddon Shire increased rate revenue by 7% in 2012, 5% in 2013 and 5.9% in 2014. Yet over the same period NSW council tax limitations allowed for increases of only 2.8% in 2012, 3.6% in 2013 and 3.4% in 2014[2] (IPART, 2012). This comparison highlights the importance of municipal tax flexibility in allowing municipalities to respond to shocks and thus produce positive budget outcomes. Indeed, the Mayor of Loddon Shire has recognised that the introduction of similar tax limitations in Victoria would impose severe constraints on the municipal budget, noting that 'we are going to have to start a conversation with our community around what services we might be able to reduce' (ABC, 2015b). Thus, Loddon Shire is exhibiting great anticipatory awareness regarding the effect of regulatory constraints on municipal resilience. However, the Mayor asserts that the plan will ultimately result in unsustainable municipalities because 'our residents do not want a cutback in Council services' (ABC, 2015b). Thus, whilst the past behaviour of Loddon Shire might best be described as adaptive it appears that looming regulatory constraints are creating an atmosphere of fatalism.

CONCLUSION

Australia has been widely lauded as one of the few developed economies to have escaped recession subsequent to the GFC. However, some of the measures taken by the Commonwealth to provide fiscal stimulus in the wake of the economic shock appear to have resulted in significant budget disruption for municipalities. Moreover, local governments have been exposed to a number of other shocks arising from natural disasters, loss of investment principal associated with 'risky' financial products and extraordinary defined benefits superannuation calls.

The financial resilience of individual municipalities seems to have been influenced, at least in part, by jurisdiction level constraints — in particular, investment guidelines and tax limitations. NSW municipalities were exposed to significant risk as a result of inadequate investment guidelines (at the state regulator level) and they produced highly volatile budget outcomes as a consequence of revenue constraints associated with the tax limitations. In contrast, Victorian municipalities had far lower budget volatility and produced higher mean budget positions despite catastrophic natural disasters and almost

A\$400 million of unexpected superannuation calls. In fact, an examination of the financial resilience of all 231 local governments over the period 2009 to 2014 inclusive revealed that just one of the 28 negative budgetary position municipalities was domiciled in Victoria and 19 of the 25 high-volatility municipalities were located in NSW. This is compelling evidence of the critical effect of regulatory policy on municipal financial resilience.

The importance of regulatory settings for financial resilience was further illustrated through a comparison of two municipalities from each jurisdiction drawn from diametrically opposed positions on the budgetary position and volatility matrix. Specifically, we compared the two NSW local governments of Central Darling (a low-volatility 'negative' municipality placed into almost seven years of Administration due to poor liquidity) and Carrathool (a high-volatility 'positive' council). Both municipalities operated in similar contexts and under comparable operating expenditures. However, the resilience of the respective municipalities was entirely disparate as a result of significant difference in revenue take, attributable to the long-standing tax limitation regime. Two illustrative Victorian cases were also examined in order to elucidate post-GFC municipal resilience. In the first case — Monash — significant revenue constraints were also in place (this time as a result of self-imposed tax limitations). However, the evidence suggests that the officials at Monash had a better understanding of their financial predicament than the officials at Central Darling and they have implemented a number of expenditure side measures (such as selling the two aged-care facilities) to mitigate the poor budgetary position. At the opposite end of the spectrum, Loddon Shire in Victoria was able to engineer a mean positive budgetary outcome through careful control of costs and exercising their flexibility to set taxes at a level commensurate with need.

Ironically, the Victorian Government is set to introduce a tax limitation regime which will largely bring to an end the revenue flexibility which allowed Victorian municipalities to produce superior budget outcomes over the post-GFC period. Meanwhile, the NSW Government is in the throes of a forced municipal amalgamation programme, largely designed to arrest the decline of local government budget positions — a decline attributable in large part to the long-standing tax limitation regime (Abelson & Joyeux, 2015).

It might be noted that the absence of some approaches to resilience, evident in our sample, may be due to the sampling approach used in this chapter: We specifically, sought out examples of extreme outcomes to highlight the effect of regulatory constraint which we argued are most likely to be first perceived at the margins. It is entirely possible that local governments in the better represented cells of the budgetary position matrix exhibited other resilience behaviours such as self-regulation. However, our approach has uncovered tentative evidence of a novel resilience behaviour — brinkmanship (Central Darling Shire). In nations such as Australia where an important source of revenue is provided by a system of intergovernmental transfers not determined by robust empirical methodology, there is an incentive for local governments to try to exploit these so-called soft budget constraints (Oates, 2005). As fiscal austerity starts to bight (in combination with exacerbating factors such as taxation limitations) it is entirely possible that we will soon observe new instances of municipalities failing to cut services despite falling revenues in the hope that they might receive a bailout (either directly or through changes to grant transfers) should the finances deteriorate to crisis point.

In summary, this chapter has demonstrated that regulatory policy can exert a large influence on municipal budgetary position and volatility. In particular, tax limitations and lax investment guidelines can seriously diminish resilience. However, it is also true that representatives' understandings of financial vulnerability and the willingness to exercise spending restraint can have important implications for individual municipalities, notwithstanding the aforementioned constraints. In addition, we have demonstrated the importance of geographical context on municipal resilience. Specifically, low population size, low population density and large distance from major conurbations provides both little opportunity to outsource service provision as well as high demand on local government to address market failure. Finally, our analysis suggests bleak futures for municipalities within the two jurisdictions as the first signs of fiscal austerity start to emerge through the three-year freeze to intergovernmental grants. In particular, the imminent introduction of tax limitations to Victoria is a matter of great concern. Moreover, the NSW regulatory authorities seem unwilling to confront the problems caused by the long-standing tax limitation regime and instead have embarked on a disruptive programme of forced amalgamation.

NOTES

1. In Australia the financial year is taken from 1 July to 30 June. Therefore, the data encompasses the period from 1 July, 2008 through to 30 June 2014.
2. Tax limitation levels fluctuate in accordance with IPART's local government cost index.

REFERENCES

Abelson, P., & Joyeux, R. (2015). New development: smoke and mirrors − Fallacies in the New South Wales government's views on local government financial capacity. *Public Money & Management*, *35*(4), 315−320.
Australian Broadcasting Corporation (ABC). (2015a). *Victorian councils praise decision to delay rate capping*. ABC, Melbourne.
Australian Broadcasting Commission (ABC). (2015b). *Loddon shire budget proposes 5.5pc rate rise as mayor airs uncertainty about future council income*. ABC, Melbourne.
Australian Bureau of Statistics (ABS). (2014). Migration, Australia, 2013−14. ABS, Canberra.
Australian Bureau of Statistics (ABS). (2015). *Taxation revenue, Australia, 2013−14*. ABS, Canberra.

Chakrabarti, S., Kodikara, J., & Pardo, L. (2002). Survey results on stabilisation methods and performance of local government roads in Australia. *Road & Transport Research, 11*(3), 3–16.

Colley, R. (2014). Central darling shire council public inquiry report.

Commonwealth of Australia. (2015). *Budget 2015–16: Budget strategy and outlook. budget paper No. 1.* Commonwealth of Australia, Canberra.

Comrie, J. (2013). *Roadmap to financial sustainability for local governments in NSW.* JAC Comrie Pty Ltd, Sydney.

Country Fire Authority (CFA). (2015). *About black Saturday 2009.* Retrieved from http://www.cfa.vic.gov.au/about/black-saturday/. Accessed on September 11.

Day, C. (2011). Chinas' fiscal stimulus and the recession Australia never had. *Agenda, 18*(1), 24–34.

Department of Infrastructure and Regional Development (DI&RD). (2015). *Financial assistance grants to local government.* DI&RD, Canberra.

Department of Premier & Cabinet Division of Local Government (DLG). (2015). Review of NSW *local government investments.* DLG, Sydney.

Dollery, B., Grant, B., & Crase, L. (2011). Love they neighbour: A social capital approach to local government partnerships. *Australian Journal of Public Administration, 70*(2), 156–166.

Drew, J., & Campbell, N. (2016). Autopsy of municipal failure: The case of Central Darling Shire. *Australasian Journal of Regional Science, 22*(1), 81–104.

Drew, J., & Dollery, B. (2015a). Road to ruin? Consistency, transparency and horizontal equalisation of road grant allocations in eastern mainland Australian States. *Public Administration Quarterly, 39*(3), 517–545.

Drew, J., & Dollery, B. (2015b). Inconsistent depreciation practice and public policymaking: Local government reform in New South Wales. *Australian Accounting Review, 25*(1), 28–37.

Drew, J., & Dollery, B. (2015c). Less haste more speed: The fit for future reform program in New South Wales local government. *Australian Journal of Public Administration.* doi:10.1111/1467-8500.12158

Drew, J., & Dollery, B. (2015d). A fair go? A response to the independent local government review panel's assessment of municipal taxation in new south wales. *Australian Tax Forum, 30*, 1–19.

Drew, J., & Dollery, B. (2015e). Breaking up is hard to do: The de-amalgamation of Delatite shire. *Public Finance and Management, 15*(1), 1–23.

Drew, J., & Dollery, B. (2016). What's in a name? Assessing the performance of local government classification systems. *Local Government Studies, 42*(2), 248–266.

Economou, N. (2010). Parties, participation and outcomes: The 2008 Victorian local government elections. *Australian Journal of Political Science, 45*(3), 425–436.

Essential Services Commission (ESC). (2015). *A blueprint for change: Local government rates capping & variation framework review.* ESC, Melbourne.

Fenna, A. (2013). The economic policy Agenda in Australia, 1962-2012. *Australian Journal of Public Administration, 72*(2), 89–102.

Independent Local Government Review Panel (ILGRP). (2013). *Revitalising local government – Final report of the NSW independent local government review panel.* ILGRP, Sydney.

Independent Pricing and Regulatory Tribunal (IPART). (2012). Special rate variations – *Applications* & determinations. IPART, Sydney.

Institute of Public Works Engineering Australasia (IPWEA). (2014). Loddon shire council: Road infrastructure flood program. IPWEA, Perth.

Lake, G. (2015). *Get the facts: Sale of aged care facilities.* Retrieved from http://www.geofflake.com.au/aged-care/. Accessed on September 15.

Local Government Career. (2014). Suspension kept minutes from central darling's return. Local Government Career, North Brighton.

Monash City Council. (2015). *Local government rates capping and variation framework review.* Monash City Council, Monash.

Municipal Association of Victoria (MAV). (2012). Defined benefits superannuation shortfall. MAV, Melbourne.

Oates, W. (2005). Towards a second-generation theory of fiscal federalism. *International Tax and Public Finance*, *12*, 349–373.

Office of Local Government. (2015). Time series comparative data 2012–2014. OLG, Sydney.

Parliament of the Commonwealth of Australia. (2009). *The global financial crisis and regional Australia: House of representatives standing committee on infrastructure, transport, regional development & local government*. Parliament of Australia, Canberra.

Pilcher, R. (2002). Reporting of roads by NSW local councils – Survival of the fittest. *Accounting, Accountability & Performance*, *8*(2), 23–41.

Pilcher, R., & Van Der Zahn, M. (2010). Local governments unexpected depreciation and financial performance adjustment. *Financial Accountability & Management*, *26*(3), 299–323.

PricewaterhouseCoopers. (2006). National financial sustainability study of local government. Sydney: PwC.

Twomey, A. (2012). Always the bridesmaid – Constitutional recognition of local government. *Monash University Law Review*, *38*(2), 142–180.

Victorian Auditor-General's Office (VAGO). (2015). Local government: Results of the 2013–14 audits. VAGO, Melbourne.

Wittenhall, R. (2011). Global financial crisis: The Australian experience in international perspective. *Public Organization Review*, *11*, 77–91.

CHAPTER 4

FINANCIAL RESILIENCE IN BRAZILIAN MUNICIPALITIES

André C. B. de Aquino and
Ricardo Lopes Cardoso

ABSTRACT

This chapter analyses the financial resilience pattern presented by four Brazilian municipalities at the beginning of a serious revenue downturn, which was initiated at the central government as a combination of economic and political crises. The crisis occurred during an on-going public financial management reform and attempts to imbricate IPSAS-oriented accrual-accounting policies in a dominant cash-based budgeting culture. Thus, contrasting those patterns with other democracies depicted in this book, we aim to contribute to the comparative literature on financial resilience under austerity periods. We interviewed secretaries of finance, department directors and accountants of each city hall and businessmen from the four municipalities. Cases were selected among 100,000-350,000 inhabitants' municipalities from one of the three most industrialised brazilian states, varying the cases according to their mean and volatility budgetary surplus over the 10 years before the beginning of the analysed crises. All cases presented no anticipatory capacity or long-term strategic planning. Their usual responses are short-term oriented, such as supplier payments postponement, increasing tax collection or cutting expenditures, rather than based on their weak transformative capacities. Despite the fatalistic and very ineffective reactive behaviours observed in two cases, a proactive mayor, supported by consulting firms, enhanced the responses effectiveness of the two remaining cases.

Governmental Financial Resilience: International Perspectives on how Local Governments Face Austerity
Public Policy and Governance, Volume 27, 53–71
Copyright © 2017 by Emerald Publishing Limited
All rights of reproduction in any form reserved
ISSN: 2053-7697/doi:10.1108/S2053-769720170000027004

Hence, mayor leadership might be a fruitful feature to be investigated by future studies.

Keywords: Brazil; financial resilience; local government; crises responses; mayor leadership; budgetary slack

INTRODUCTION

This chapter investigates the financial resilience of Brazilian municipalities. The global financial crisis affected the Brazilian economy with a significant time lag. In 2014, it hit the country as a combination of different and complimentary aspects: (1) the significant drop in prices of commodities (especially iron and oil & gas); (2) countercyclical initiatives adopted by the central government from 2008 and (3) a political crisis that affected the central government's Executive and Legislature branches.

Due to the drop in commodity prices, many states and municipalities suffered a reduction of royalty revenues. As a result of the central government's countercyclical initiatives (implemented during 2008–2014), municipalities suffered due to (1) reduction of their own tax collection and (2) reduction of intergovernmental fiscal transfers (either in the amount of transfer or in the delay of cash flows). In addition, a political crisis distracted the attention of Legislature members from coping with the economic crisis to deal with the impeachments of Rousseff and the lower chamber's head. The formal argument to support Roussef's impeachment was for breaking the budgetary law and cooking the books and the formal argument to support the impeachment of her main opponent, the head of the lower chamber, was for lying to the chamber when he denied maintaining bank accounts in offshores.[1]

For means of comparison among Brazilian cases and with other cases depicted in this book, we adopted the same constructs and methodological design from Barbera, Jones, Korac, Saliterer, and Steccolini (2017) which is based on a multiple case study analysis from a single country.

Among the results, we highlight that Brazilian municipalities presented responses to the crises that were short-term oriented. We also discuss, following previous literature (Boin, 2003; Kjaer, 2013; Oberfield, 2014; Orazi, Turrini, & Valotti, 2013; Wright & Pandey, 2010), that the responses were broadly and effectively implemented when specific team characteristics were present.

THE CONTEXT

Brazil is a republic federation with a decentralised service delivery responsibility to more than 5,500 municipalities distributed among 26 states, combined with a high fiscal concentration on the central government. The transfer of funds is the main revenue source for the majority of the municipalities (in average 60% of municipalities' total revenues come from transfers, 20% of them are specific-purpose transfers to health and education). For central, state and local governments, the executive official (president, governors and mayors) and the representatives at the Legislature are elected by universal direct suffrage. For the executive, re-election is allowed only once. The mayor and the municipal council elections take place simultaneously every four years.[2]

Fiscal decentralisation allows municipalities to collect property tax and taxes on services.[3] Additionally, municipalities receive intergovernmental fiscal transfers from the central government and their respective states in the form of specific-purpose and general-purpose transfers. The latter are calculated based on tax on industrialised products collected by the central government and taxes on the trading of goods and vehicle ownership collected by states. Hence, these transfers vary in accordance with the economic activity and tax collection by the central and state governments.

Specific-purpose transfers are calculated depending on each programme (input-based conditionality). For example, those related to the education function are a fixed amount per student enroled at schools maintained by the municipality and those related to the health function are a fixed amount per unit of health service delivered by health organisations maintained by the municipality, which vary depending on service complexity. However, whenever the state or central government faces any financial distress, those fixed amounts are not adjusted for inflation and/or the state or central government delay transfer to municipalities. In either case, municipalities are pushed to consume their own resources to complement (or replace) the shortfall in the amount transferred by the state or central government. Notice that the alternative would be municipalities quitting the provision of services and bearing high political costs. The most expensive services delivered by municipalities are health care, garbage collection, social assistance, nursery, kindergarten and primary school. Services can be delivered through city hall departments, agencies, state-owned enterprises, and certain activities can be outsourced to private sector.

The local government in Brazil uses the strong mayor model (Mouritzen & Svara, 2002), where the mayor is the chief of local administration. The mayor depends on municipal council support for critical issues, such as changing tax rates, contract PPP schemes and approving and amending the budgetary framework and budgetary law. Tenured civil servants, that represent the majority of the workforce in city hall and other agencies, are strongly organised in workers' unions, thereby creating barriers to cut payroll expenses or benefits.

The city hall has to comply with the budget voted by the municipal council and also with the public financial management (PFM) framework, which requires that municipalities (1) spend less than 60% of their own revenues on public servants payrolls; (2) spend more than 15% of their own revenues on health care and 25% on education; (3) ensure a balanced budget; (4) comply with the voted budget and amendments; (5) reinvest all capital revenues obtained from sale of assets on capital expenditures and (6) maintain total debt lower than 120% of its annual revenues.

Municipalities cannot contract loans to cover operational expenditures, but they have been known to postpone supplier's payments, which increases their liabilities (unpaid commitments, *restos a pagar*). Unpaid commitments are part of the current carry-over mechanism in Brazil, and its usage by municipalities has grown since 2004, especially intensified in 2013 and 2014 (Aquino & Azevedo, 2016). Although the Supreme Audit Institution (SAI) has criticised the excessive indebtedness by the use of unpaid commitments by the central government, the regional audit bodies (hereafter courts of accounts) take a passive stance towards its increasing use by municipalities.

Regional audit bodies are responsible for enforcing PFM controls. Audit performed by 33 regional audit bodies[4] is only a 'compliance check-list' for the fiscal discipline law 1964, fiscal responsibility law 2000 and the federal constitution 1988. Usually, the audit has little consequences as the board of the audit office is appointed by the state governor; thus political networks play a significant role. Since citizen participation and thus vertical accountability is quasi non-existent, mayors have low incentive to implement innovative management systems, performance measurement mechanisms or programmes to reduce wastes and inefficiencies.

In 2008, Brazil started its convergence process of the previous national cash-commitment accounting standards towards IPSAS. In March 2016 for the first time all levels of governments reported on a new standardised chart of accounts. The current deadlines for the specific IPSAS-oriented accounting policies adoption assume a gradual implementation that stands until 2022.

The sub-prime crisis that shook the US in 2007–2008 and Europe in 2009–2011 was initially mentioned as a 'small wave' by President Lula, despite analysts perceiving it as a 'tsunami' for the Brazilian economy. Notwithstanding, between 2008 and 2014, the Brazilian central government implemented a set of countercyclical policies: increase in wealth distribution programmes called *Bolsa Família* and *Minha Casa Minha Vida*; reduction of VAT on activities that are labour-intensive (e.g. production of motor vehicles and construction building and materials);[5] reduction of tax charged in financial transactions (i.e. an incentive for families and firms to increase their gearing); promoting consumption; subsidising interest rates through state-owned banks for specific firms; subsidising interest rates for states and municipalities through the Treasury. Hence, economic growth experienced from 2010 to 2014 was artificially based and thus not sustainable.

In late 2014, when the prices of oil and iron did not recover as expected, the positive cycle of commodities ended, and the macroeconomic policies adopted did not generate expected results. In spite of the crisis, central government did not cut expenditures in 2014 because it was an electoral year. Later in 2014, President Rousseff's cabinet sent a bill to Congress that retrospectively changed the fiscal surplus target for the year 2014 in order to accommodate a significant deficit. The Congress passed the budgetary target and then acquitted Rousseff of penalties under the fiscal crimes law. In the 2014 elections, President Rousseff was re-elected. In late 2015, her cabinet again sent a bill to the Congress that retrospectively changed the fiscal surplus target in order to accommodate a significant deficit. The latter was caused by reduction on sales taxes, increase in wealth distribution programme expenditures and administrative expenses and the reversal of the previous years' window dressing. The Congress amended the federal government's budgetary target once again. For 2016, the budget suggested a deficit, and not a balanced budget as required by law for all levels of government in Brazil, and it constantly increased during the first months of the year. In parallel, the political crisis achieved a no return point, and Rousseff administration lost significant legislative and popular support. A qualified audit report from the SAI to the Congress identified her administration responsible for accounting information misrepresentations and irregular loan operations. The report supported the acceptance of a call for her impeachment process.

At the time of writing, Brazil is in a macroeconomic and political crises with increasing unemployment, interest and inflation rates, stemming from the worsening economic environment due to the international financial crisis; consequences of police investigations on contracts related to Petrobras and other state-owned enterprises; political crises that affect both the President and the Congress and a reliability-legitimacy crisis.

These crises began in 2014/2015 and immediately affected the most developed states in Brazil (i.e. Minas Gerais, Rio de Janeiro and São Paulo). Following the steps of the central government, state governments did not cut expenditures in 2014, but rather increased expenditure in social programmes, as it was an electoral year in states too.

METHODS

We selected four municipalities from industrialised states in Brazil (Minas Gerais, Rio de Janeiro and São Paulo), as these states were first to be affected by developments at the national level. We focused on medium-sized local governments with a population ranging from 100,000 to 350,000 inhabitants. Following the methodology used throughout this book, we selected cases with different patterns of budgetary performance, which was measured based on the average budgetary position over the last 14 years and the budgetary surplus standard deviation.[6] Fig. 1 presents the average budgetary position (horizontal axis) and volatility (vertical axis) for each case for the period 2000−2013, comparing the four analysed cases with similar municipalities. We used data until 2013 to capture the municipalities' financial position before the current crises

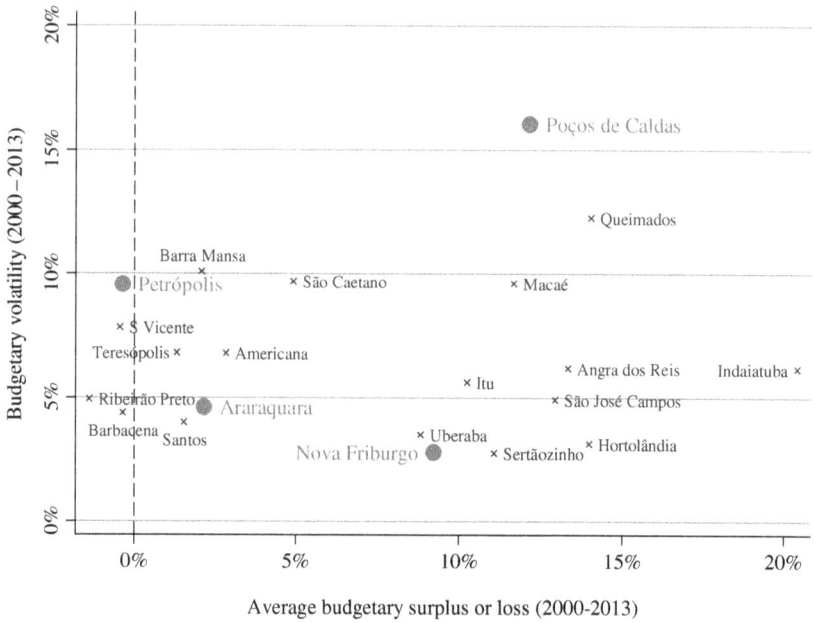

Fig. 1. Mean and Standard Deviation of Budgetary Surplus for Target Sample, Period 2000−2013.

affected them. Selected municipalities represent different combinations of budgetary position and volatility: Nova Friburgo (Rio de Janeiro) showed a high positive average budgetary position (9%) and low volatility (3%). Poços de Caldas (Minas Gerais), despite exhibiting a high budgetary position (12%), showed high volatility (16%). Araraquara (São Paulo) presented low volatility and low average budgetary (4.6% and 2%, respectively). Finally, Petrópolis (Rio de Janeiro) presented medium volatility (9.5%), but an average deficit for the period (−0.03%).

There are some remarkable differences between the cases in terms of geography and economic activity, which are presented in the next section, and summarised in Table 1. Accounting and internal auditing functions are very similar in all analysed cases. All interviewed accountants from each municipality were aware of the accrual-accounting reforms in Brazil. All cases implemented the new chart of accounts in compliance with the accounting reform deadline, but none started the implementation of new IPSAS-oriented accounting policies. Therefore, accounting information is still predominantly cash-based for revenue recognition and commitment-based for expenditures. The decision-making process in accounting is focused on revenue collection and expenditure allocation. Non-financial assets and contingent liabilities receive scarce attention. In

Table 1. Pattern of Municipality Response and the Mayor Leadership.

	Poços de Caldas/MG	Nova Friburgo/RJ	Petrópolis/RJ	Araraquara/SP
Population 2015 (thousands), and its growth (10 years)	164; 10%	185; 5%	298, 5%	226, 10%
Annual budget 2014; % grants	BRL 516 million; 61.5%	BRL 417 million; 74.1%	BRL 907 million; 57.7%	BRL 674 million, 61.1%
Foundation, origins and immigration	1872, sulphur water baths, immigrants from Italy.	1890, Swiss families' occupation planned by the Crown.	1857, Imperial family summerhouse, immigrants from Germany.	1889, earlier corridor to the west exploitation, immigrants from Europe.
HDI[a] (relative position in the state)	0.78, (Minas Gerais Top 6)	0.74, (Rio de Janeiro Top 13)	0.74, (Rio de Janeiro Top 11)	0.81, (São Paulo Top 7)
Distance to the state capital (km, hours by car)	465 km, 6 hours	143 km, 2 hours	66 km, 1 hour	270 km, 3 hours
Geography (area, topography, climate[b] and temperature[c])	547 km², Valley, Warm (Cfb), 14.4°C and 20.7°C	933 km², Mountains, Tropical (Aw) 15.8°C and 21.8°C	796 km², Mountains, Warm (Cfb), 15.2°C and 21.5°C	1,003 km², Flat terrain, Warm (Cfa), 14.4°C and 20.7°C
Budgetary surplus[d]	Positive	Positive	Negative	Low positive
Budgetary volatility[d]	High	Low	Medium	Low
Mayor leadership and executive team	Politically oriented executives and an absent mayor	Technical executives	Mayor as a leader and technical executives	Super CFO
Consulting firms	Not relevant	Relevant presence	Not relevant	Not relevant
Shock/impact	Financial crisis, decrease in grants[e] and taxes	Financial crisis, decrease in grants[e] and taxes	Financial crisis, decrease in grants[e] and taxes	Financial crisis, decrease in grants[e] and taxes

Table 1. (*Continued*)

	Poços de Caldas/MG	Nova Friburgo/RJ	Petrópolis/RJ	Araraquara/SP
Vulnerability	Loss of control over the buffer from the electricity agency	Rigidity of personnel expenditures	Dependence on central government transfers	Personnel expenditures and lack of reserves
Anticipatory capacity	No anticipatory capacity	No anticipatory capacity	No anticipatory capacity	No anticipatory capacity
Coping capacity	Buffering (limited to cuts in personnel expenditures)	Buffering (deferring payments)	Buffering, Adapting (expenditure cuts, adapting tax collection system)	Buffering, Adapting (expenditure cuts, deferring payments, adapting tax collection system)
Pattern	(Powerless) fatalists	(Reactive) adapters	(Reactive) adapters	(Reactive) adapters

[a]Human Development Index.
[b]Climate by Köppen and Geiger classification.
[c]Average temperature in the winter and summer time.
[d]Budgetary surplus is the average budgetary surplus for 2000–2013, and the volatility is the standard deviation for the same period.
[e]Grants include federal and state transferences to municipalities.

compliance with budgetary and fiscal responsibility laws, they periodically prepare financial and budgetary reports to the governmental audit body and to the Treasury. The mayors from Poços de Caldas, Nova Friburgo and Petrópolis appoint the secretary that coordinates the municipality's internal auditing office. In contrast, internal auditing in Araraquara is coordinated by the chief finance officer (CFO), who also runs the accounting function.

A total of 32 interviews were conducted, where the head of the internal control department (Poços de Caldas, Nova Friburgo and Petrópolis) or of the finance department (Araraquara) was the key informant and further interviewees included staff and/or the head of finance, budget and accounting departments. Additional staff or heads of other departments were interviewed on questions that emerged during the initial interviews, including infrastructure and construction in cities affected by the climate catastrophes in 2011. Some relevant political and economic events mentioned by municipalities' interviewees were double-checked with official documents, local newspapers and interviews with local businesspersons. The interviews were conducted on site between August and December 2015, each lasted about 60 minutes, and were audio-recorded.

Each of the following cases is presented with its vulnerability before 2013, and whether its government showed some anticipatory capacity. Following Barbera et al. (2017), we also discuss if the city hall operates tools to 'identify and manage their vulnerabilities and to recognise potential financial shocks before they arise'. We introduce an organisational element to the analysis, verifying whether the team's capability and the mayor's leadership might be relevant to deal with the crisis effects. Additionally, we present the coping capacities observed, or resources and abilities to face the shocks, whether there is a *buffer capacity* (i.e. the ability for absorbing shocks), *adaptive capacity* (i.e. the ability for implementing incremental changes) or a *transformative capacity* (i.e. the ability for taking paths of more radical changes). Finally, we briefly present the resilience pattern.

RESULTS

Poços de Caldas is a former tourist attraction, currently experiencing an industrial expansion. Its diversified economy comprises tourism, agriculture, energy, alumina, clothing and food production. Due to the fact that it is far from the state capital, it developed a self-oriented countryside culture, without significant changes to formal and informal institutions.

Poços de Caldas is a peculiar case of buffering due to electricity production and distribution. Until 2010 it had no debt and a good budgetary position. In late 2010, it re-structured its electricity production,[7] suffering from two consequences: the reduction of the discretionary use of revenues from electricity production[8] and worsening its budgetary performance because the electricity production activities were no longer consolidated.

> [The city] did not have net debt because of the positive financial position of electricity production. However, after restructuring, the picture changed dramatically. Today [December 2015], we have a net debt equivalent to 16% of annual net current revenues. (CFO)

Until 2010, electricity production was a significant source of buffering. The mayor could use the cash generated by the electricity production discretionarily. After the restructuring, the discretion was reduced significantly and consequently the revenues started to be generated in the form of dividends that are capped by a local law. The local government was pushed to find effective solutions to balance its budget due to cash shortage resulting in deferral of payrolls in 2011.

In 2013, despite the municipal council increasing the local tax rate, expenditures (except payroll) and investments had to be cut because it also approved a significant increase in employee benefits. In 2014, revenues decreased by 15%. The multinational aluminium industry interrupted part of its production and the grants from central and regional governments decreased.

Budgeting and planning in Poços de Caldas are centralised. Revenue forecasting is incremental, and adjusted using macroeconomic forecasts, but no scenario planning or risk management tools have been implemented. Thus the disruption of the central government's countercyclical policy was not anticipated. Brazilian budgetary and fiscal responsibility laws allow budgetary amendments during the fiscal year, and thus do not foster anticipatory capacity. In Poços de Caldas, adjustments of up to 30% of the 2014 annual budget were possible,

> By the year end, the executed budget is completely different from the budget approved by the legislature. It is a fluid and untrustworthy provision. Such discretionary power is too dangerous; it is a counter-incentive for planning. (CFO)

Another challenge is administrative leadership. Secretaries (heads of departments) seemed more committed to spending their original budget than coping with the crisis. They did not comply with the CFO's decisions on cutting expenditures, even under the risk of all public servants not receiving their salaries by the year-end. The mayor's attempts to update the local tax code were strongly opposed, partly lobbied by large real estate owners and construction companies. The local government continued to apply short-term actions. In late 2015, the mayor cut some services and tried to access additional revenues; for example reserves from the water agency, additional dividends from the electricity industry. Such attempts were however unsuccessful.

The city's accounting information systems were poorly developed and planning seemed poor. The secretaries presented their budget demands directly to the mayor, thereby creating information asymmetries and fights for budget allocation.

In 2015, a 20% budget cut was enacted, but soon this turned out as insufficient.

> The mayor decided to constrain all current expenditures, including extra hour compensation, motor vehicle maintenance and gas, printing costs, travel, capacity building programs, utilities, etc. (CFO)

However, many exceptions to these budget constrains were agreed.

One could say that the city has been perpetuating the same level of services to a growing population with a small urban area expansion, demanding just modest infrastructure investments. The prior wealthy condition of the local government did not foster long-term planning and efficiency. Poços de Caldas mainly buffered the shock by cutting expenditures, but this practice was identified as deficient.

> We cannot afford an abrupt cost reduction if we have been increasing expenditures year after year, for decades. The drop in revenues neutralises effects of expenditures cutting. (CFO)

Poços de Caldas exerts the characteristics of a powerless-fatalist, not anticipating crisis and relying only on buffering (Table 1), thereby showing a low level of coping capacity. Both spending cuts and intents to increase revenues collection were not coordinated and suffered from implementation errors. Adaptation efforts to reorganise working contracts with the workers' union and to update the tax code were unsuccessful. This seems mainly rooted in the lack of coordination of secretaries, which are not aligned with the agenda established by the leadership (mayor, CFO) to cope with the crisis.

Nova Friburgo is located near Rio de Janeiro city and has an influx of cargo and people to and from there. Its economy is mainly concentrated on tourism, clothing industry (mainly lingerie) and agricultural industry (fruits, vegetables, flowers). The city had however recently developed an innovative urban commerce and service industry.

The city suffered a climate catastrophe shock in January 2011. The city centre was devastated, many buildings and roads were destroyed, and as a consequence, many businesses went bankrupt. Although the city received significant support from the central and regional governments, at the time of writing, it was still under reconstruction. The climate catastrophe was referred to by all interviewees, giving it a central role in the analysis of financial resilience of this case.

During that time (2009–2012), the local government experienced three other minor shocks that led to 'a period of chaos'. A couple of months before the storm, the mayor had an accident and died after several months in hospital. The deputy mayor took office just as the climate catastrophe happened.

The city immediately received financial support from the central and state governments, and a 'wave of solidarity' began, as a variety of companies made donations and participated in rescues and rebuilding the city. Engineering projects were dependent on funds from central and state governments. Reconstruction projects were managed by the local or the state government. At the end of 2011, both local and regional projects were denounced in scandals involving a wide network of bribes. The mayor (former deputy mayor) was involved in misappropriation of public funds and impeached in March 2012. The head of the legislature then became the head of city hall (mayor in post). From 2012, he proved a lack of capacity to coordinate secretaries and staff and the city hall was operating without a central coordination.

Nova Friburgo has a good budgetary position and low volatility. This was true even during the climate catastrophe, which the city did not anticipate, but was able to buffer entirely. There were no disaster plans, so that the city implemented an emergency crisis management system involving firefighters, rescue groups and research institutes as a reaction to that shock. However, poor areas of the city are still at risk as before.

Some weeks after the storm, internal administrative processes that did not depend on political decisions or on additional funds, mostly executed by public servants and mobilised by the 'wave of solidarity', were reintroduced as a normal routine. For example, the finance secretariat started to issue property tax billings; and human resources department was searching for names of civil services among the fatal victims in order to exclude them from payroll.

In 2013, the newly appointed local administration implemented a 'super-secretariat' responsible for a reengineering process to search for opportunities of efficiency gains by cutting operational costs and an economic development plan. Surprisingly, the super-secretariat did not anticipate the reduction in transfers as a result of the 2014 national crisis. However, following consultants' recommendations, local government cut expenditures and was able to buffer crisis' first impacts.

Planning and budgeting are incremental, centralised and dependent on one senior civil servant, 'the budget man'. It caused information asymmetries that have been tackled unsustainably, by increasing the frequency of meetings of the leadership with the 'budget man'. Risk management and strategic planning were non-existent in the local government.

The 'period of chaos' was central to the local government's adaptation attempts. In 2012, some executives who built their careers in multinational firms and lost their jobs after the climate catastrophe, decided to act as 'informal counsellors' to the mayor in post (head of legislature), and were invited to join the new government in 2013. Three professional executives from the private sector were appointed as heads of the finance, budget and tourism secretariats. Three secretariats formed the management super-secretariat (joining budgeting, planning and development functions), which adopted a business-oriented work pattern and had to implement the agenda on economic development and city reconstruction. A consulting firm was hired to promote a management change in the local government in 2013/2014. The consulting was financed through private donations, thus most of the meetings of the administration with the consultants were open to the public. The result were efficiency savings through spending cuts in operating expenditures and health care; improvement in tax collection; negotiations for specific-purpose transfer payments, especially for construction; renegotiation of debt owed to central government. The adaptation was however restricted to specific functions and the accounting and internal control functions were not part of the process. The savings were used to increase employee benefits that were lagging since 2006. Some processes were implemented in daily routine but others were abandoned right after the end of the project. The efficiencies were controversial – some respondents saw it as creating enough buffering to cope with the crisis, but others argued:

> we did everything we could do to enhance efficiency, now we cannot do much more than cutting expenditures. (CFO)

In addition to the consultants' recommendations, the local government implemented a programme to reduce red tape in business permits in order to promote entrepreneurship. In late 2015, with the impact of the crisis amplifying, the local government cut every infrastructure, health and education programme that were funded through their own resources. Confronted with crisis-related delays of central and state government funds that financed construction projects, the municipality decided to not pay suppliers, and many reconstruction works stopped working.

Nova Friburgo shows a reactive adapter pattern of financial resilience. While exerting adaptation efforts before the financial crisis, the local government showed low anticipatory capacity regarding the financial crisis and mainly relied on buffering (Table 1). In contrast to the climate catastrophe and the 'period of chaos', the financial crisis arrived silently and was perceived as a mere administrative problem. The citizen's attention was on reconstruction after the storm, and the local government did not succeed in implementing the adaptation on a long-term basis: planning and forecasting were still done 'using the rear mirror'.

Petrópolis is located in the mountains and is home to the historic imperial family summerhouse. Petrópolis has a diverse economy comprising services (60% of its GDP, ranging from tourism to airplane engine repair) and clothing manufacturing (40%). The same climate catastrophe also hit Petrópolis in 2011. However, it affected primarily rural areas. The local government therefore did not consider it a crisis. Its slow population increase during recent years (5% in 10 years), accommodated small and constant investments in urbanisation and infrastructure and the maintenance of citizens' welfare.

Petrópolis is a case of a low positive budgetary position and low volatility. In contrast to the other cases, the government of Petrópolis was not pressured by its infrastructure demand. The historic city centre is well-preserved and has been continuously improved, and the urban area expanded slowly. Because the historic city centre attracts tourism, it is a critical issue to the city hall. The federal grants received until 2014 were used to expand employee salaries, something that is hard to revoke and the political costs to reduce them are high. In 2015, the central government stopped transfer payments for construction, and the state government stopped transfers for emergency care units – a jointly implemented programme by the state and the local government in 2010. The payroll and operating expenditures of the emergency care units had therefore to be borne by the local government. As a response to revenue decline, the leadership decided to cut many expenditures, including the secretaries' and the mayor's salaries.

The anticipatory capacity of Petrópolis seemed low; revenue forecasting is based on previous figures adjusted by macroeconomic forecasts. Budget execution is monitored on a weekly basis.

The current mayor holds his third mandate and was awarded with the Mayor-Entrepreneur Prize by the federal agency for Micro and Small-sized Businesses (SEBRAE) twice. Six interviewees used the terms 'leader' or 'native leader' to refer him, highlighting his cognitive capacity, organisational insight and accounting and public finance skills; albeit he is a physician. The mayor as a front-row individual seems to be crucial to the local government's resilience, thanks to his confrontation and problem-solving competency, positive and integrative personality and goal-orientation. His role as a leader brings cohesion and self-confidence to the executive team.

Budget monitoring appears goal-oriented and formalised, with the mayor and the CFO having constant information exchange on the development and benchmarking of revenues.

According to the CFO, since 2013 Petrópolis has increased its tax revenues without increasing the tax rate. It did so by reducing red tape in tax collection and on business permits and by amplifying monitoring of tax collection.

> To bounce back from a crisis we might not be afraid of crisis; instead, we need creativity. In addition to creativity, we need planning. Hence, we need accounting information. Public sector managers might use creativity to cope with crises, not increasing tax rates. (CFO)

The coping capacity of Petrópolis builds rather on revenue increase than on expenditure reduction, primarily by reduction of red tape, process innovations and enlarging the base of taxpayers through reduction of non-compliance by large taxpayers (banks, credit card operators and notarial offices). These initiatives led to an increase of taxes by 7% (2014–2015), despite the economic crisis.

The main proposal is to reduce dependence from central and regional government transfers. To increase local revenues without the side-effects (political costs) of tax rate increase, the city hall attempted to enforce the current tax rules and to develop the local economy, stimulating entrepreneurs to start a business.

Later, the mayor decided to enhance the power of fiscal auditors, and the finance secretariat accumulated the coordination of auditing efforts from every secretariat in Petrópolis (environmental, fiscal and traffic surveillance etc.). Databases managed by the finance secretariat to levy property tax were synchronised with databases managed by energy and water suppliers.[9] In addition, the council re-evaluated the taxable value of property located in areas where urbanisation improvements were carried out.

Secondly, the local administration implemented initiatives to reduce the informal economy (non-taxed and weakly monitored activities). Those initiatives can be understood as transformative capacities because it also potentially contributes to a new development path for the city. In order to reduce blue-collar unemployment, the city hall invited unemployed people to register themselves as micro-entrepreneurs or to manage their own stands at market areas managed by the municipality. Additionally, cutting red tape on starting a new business (from 150 days to 48 hours) boosted entrepreneurship. The CFO also started an education programme for citizens (including speeches at schools) and among public servants (especially among those enforcing tax collection), in order to fight tax fraud. These initiatives were started as a response to decreasing revenues in an early phase of the crisis, when it was not yet perceived as a crisis.

Despite the adaptive capacity and signals for transformation, Petrópolis shows a reactive adapter pattern of financial resilience. Anticipatory capacity seemed low and coping with the financial crisis mainly comprised buffering (Table 1).

Araraquara is a logistic hub that has benefited from investments made by the central government and the state of SP in railways and highways from 1950 to 1990. Its economy is diverse, building on services (62% of its GDP), manufacturing – including the largest Brazilian orange juice producer (25%) and agriculture (2%).

Due to an intense population increase (15%), Araraquara invested heavily in urbanisation in the last 10 years. While orange juice producers were affected heavily by the financial crisis starting in 2008, the city was able to create 14,000 new jobs during 2009–2014. However, a significant share of these jobs were public service positions. This led to an expansion of local government workforce of 50% (4,000 public servants in 2006; 6,000 in 2013) and the increase in taxes was counterbalanced by additional expenditures. However, this revenue growth cycle ended in 2013, and in accordance to the CFO:

'In 2014, we received BRL 20 million less transfers from SP state than we expected. Then city hall had to deal with a very thin equilibrium'.

Similar to the other cases, Araraquara shows low anticipatory capacity. Planning is not comprehensive and budget is neither perceived realistic nor as a relevant managerial tool. Decisions are made on an emergency basis in order to balance the budget, mainly deferring payments to suppliers and employee benefits (i.e. increasing unpaid commitments).

The mayor is a political actor who refrains from financial issues. All financial decisions are devolved to a professional CFO, a former financial executive at a multinational private sector firm. The CFO shows high communication and negotiation skills and closely monitors accounting and budgeting. However, he has no authority to direct the other secretaries, thereby coping did not follow a comprehensive development plan but was limited to a few isolated initiatives: enlarging the base of taxpayers, reducing red tape and deferring payments and cutting expenditures.

> Municipalities have no way to cope with crises other than increasing taxes and deferring payments to suppliers. At the end of the day, we say that 'municipalities do not go bankrupt', but we will delay the payment of public servants' wages, and we will be forced to re-structure internally. (CFO)

Public acceptance of tax increase was limited since the city changed the property tax rate in 2009. Thus, the city enhanced tax collection, enlarged the VAT base and took large taxpayers owing taxes to court. The latter was prioritised based on the amount owed, in order to compensate for legal costs. Similar to Petrópolis, Araraquara implemented also an electronic invoice system. As an alternative to increasing tax rates, the city outsourced garbage collection (that was funded from taxation) to a state-owned enterprise, which then charges a garbage collection fee. Expenditures were cut by reducing civil servant working hours from 8 to 6 hours per day, disallowing overtime and re-negotiating employee benefit entitlement with schoolteachers. The city reduced also the maintenance level of roads and reduced the menu of school meals as a response to an unexpected reduction of state transfer payments, both at high political costs.

Araraquara represents a reactive adapter pattern of resilience. The local government was highly vulnerable due to the lack of reserves and showed low anticipatory capacity with regard to the financial crisis (Table 1). Despite the adaptive capacity shown in tax collection initiatives, other secretariats – although affected by spending cuts determined by the mayor – continued to operate as they did before. The mayor concentrates on merely political functions and does not coordinate the secretaries. This impairs the implementation of a comprehensive agenda and accounts for limited coping capacities.

CONCLUSION

As a consequence of the central government countercyclical economic policies the global financial crisis barely affected Brazilian municipalities until 2013/2014, intensifying in 2015/2016. All four cases in this investigation presented virtually no anticipatory capacity or long-term strategic planning. Instead, there is evidence of incrementalism in budgeting and deferring payments to hide and ignore liabilities (unpaid commitments). Budget planning, even though adjusted to macroeconomic expectations, did not anticipate (i) the insufficiency of transfers for specific programmes that were agreed with state and central governments some years ago; (ii) the delay and drop of general transfers from the central and regional governments; (iii) the impact of the economic downturn on VAT and shortage other revenues.

We identified reactive short-term coping rather than transformative capacities in Brazilian local governments. When central and regional government transfers drop, government reacted immediately by increasing tax collection, cutting expenditures or deferring payments (unpaid commitments). The latter is highly problematic since local governments do not include these deferrals in the budget plan for the next fiscal year, as they are not obliged to. This strategy is probably an alternative to borrowing loans, which is not allowed for local governments. However, it is a non-sustainable way of coping. The continuous use of this strategy will inevitably interrupt suppliers' provisions in the near future as the local firms will refuse to contract with the government or may charge a premium.

The four cases stressed the role of the mayor and the CFO (or another relevant secretary – as in the case of Nova Friburgo). When the mayor is a proactive leader and the CFO is technically empowered (Petrópolis), the secretariats show a coordinated response. However, when the mayoral leadership is limited to political functions, the CFO's technical competence is limited to tax collections, and influencing other secretaries on efficiency improvements is impossible (Araraquara). The 'super-secretary' from Nova Friburgo and the consulting firm mitigated the lack of mayor leadership. In the absence of mayoral leadership and with a weak CFO, coping capacities are very low or the responses are uncoordinated and full of potential mistakes and collateral effects (Poços de Caldas). In general, leadership capabilities should be considered when discussing local government financial resilience, at least in countries with strong mayor models as in Brazil. It is more than justified considering the turnover of all high executive staff, including the mayor and his appointed team. New elected mayors and their appointed staffs can suggest another administrative pattern (e.g. routines, rituals, organisational structure, managerial artefacts), which will be weakly embedded in the administration routines, and which will go away at the end of his mandate.

NOTES

1. In August 2016 the Senate found President Dilma Rousseff guilty of responsibility crimes and administrative misconduct and voted (after one year of impeachment process) for removing her from office. Her opponent, the head of lower chamber Eduardo Cunha, in September 2016 lost his position as federal deputy due to breaching of

parliamentary decorum by lying about secret offshore bank accounts, and in October 2016 he was arrested by the Brazilian Federal Police.

2. The elections for president, governors and members of state and central government's Legislature take place simultaneously every four years, but not simultaneous to municipal elections.

3. The mayor has no discretionary power to set or amend the tax code. There are determined taxes and fees the municipalities are allowed to collect (defined by the federal constitution). The local government can implement or not those taxes and fees and can decide the rate and price. But local Legislature must approve such initiatives.

4. We do not use the term 'audit office' because Brazil follows the Napoleonic model. More about SAI models see Stapenhurst and Titsworth (2001).

5. Notice that the VAT collected by the central government is the basis for transfers to states and municipalities. Hence, such countercyclical mechanism negatively affected the finances from states and municipalities.

6. Similarly to Barbera et al. (2017) we measured budgetary surplus as the difference between total revenues and total expenditures from year t, plus financial assets from year $t-1$, less financial liabilities from year $t-1$; normalised by operating expenditures from year t.

7. The electricity business in Brazil is operated by private organisations or state-owned enterprises and regulated by a federal agency. Poços de Caldas is an exceptional case of a municipality that operates a hydropower plant at its waterfalls. The city avoided complying with a regulation from the Brazilian Electricity Regulatory Agency until 2010, when Poços de Caldas's government decided to create a state-owned holding controlling the electricity generation and distribution businesses; as a consequence, the financial statements of the energy business stopped being consolidated in the municipality's financial statements.

8. In 2008, the net income made by the electricity production was equivalent to 81% of Poços de Caldas tax revenues.

9. Energy and water suppliers have more than 140,000 properties units (apartments, houses, commercial and industrial buildings etc.) on their database, but the Finance Secretariat, in order to issue billings, accounts for only 90,000 units in its database. Hence, the CFO expects that such synchronisation might increase property tax collection in 2016, levying taxes from 'phantom real estate units'.

REFERENCES

Aquino, A. C. B., & Azevedo, R. R. (2016). Unpaid commitments and the budgetary credibility lost (*under revision Revista de Administração Pública*).

Barbera, C., Jones, M., Korac, S., Saliterer, I., & Steccolini, I. (2017). Governmental financial resilience under austerity in Austria, England and Italy: How do local governments cope with financial shocks? Public Administration, forthcoming.

Boin, A., & Hart, P. (2003). Public leadership in times of crisis: Mission impossible? *Public Administration Review*, *63*(5), 544–553.

Kjaer, U. (2013). Local political leadership: The art of circulating political capital. *Local Government Studies*, *39*(2).

Mouritzen, P. E., & Svara, J. H. (2002). Institutions, national cultures and political leadership. In *Leadership at the apex: Politicians and administrators in Western local governments* (pp. 47–81). Pittsburgh, PA: University of Pittsburgh Press.

Oberfield, Z. (2014). Public management in time: A longitudinal examination of the full range of leadership theory. *Journal of Public Administration Research and Theory*, *24*(2), 407–429.

Orazi, D., Turrini, A., & Valotti, G. (2013). Public sector leadership: New perspectives for research and practice. *International Review of Administrative Sciences, 9,* 486–504.

Stapenhurst, R., & Titsworth, J. (2001). *Features and functions of supreme audit institutions.* World Bank, Washington, DC. PREM Note 59.

Wright, B., & Pandey, S. (2010). Transformational leadership in the public sector: Does structure matter? *Journal of Public Administration Research and Theory, 20*(1), 75–89.

CHAPTER 5

ENGLISH RESILIENCE IN THE FACE OF AUSTERITY

Martin Jones

ABSTRACT

In the aftermath of the financial crisis, English local government faced a period of significant budget reduction and uncertainty. Austerity measures were effectively rolled out over several budget iterations, resulting in a 37% real-term reduction in core central government funding, equivalent to a 25% reduction in income/spending power (including council tax) between 2010 and 2011 and 2015 and 2016. At the same time, changes in government policy in a range of areas between 2011 and 2012 and 2015 and 2016 created 164 new burdens on local government, with an estimated value of £11.5 billion, many of which were unfunded. All of this during a period when local government was being encouraged to freeze council tax and when natural pressure on locally collected taxation and services was increasing due to the economic recession.

This chapter reviews the responses of four English local governments to the austerity period triggered by the onset of the global financial crisis in 2007. For the English councils the results develop into two main themes. Firstly, there appeared to be a common set of anticipatory and coping capacities employed both in the lead up to the funding cuts from 2010 onwards and in the way councils subsequently dealt with aspects of the crisis. Secondly, despite this commonality, the specific and local contexts experienced by each council, both internally and externally, determined their overall path to

Governmental Financial Resilience: International Perspectives on how Local Governments Face Austerity
Public Policy and Governance, Volume 27, 73–91
Copyright © 2017 by Emerald Publishing Limited
ISSN: 2053-7697/doi:10.1108/S2053-769720170000027005

dealing with austerity. These two paths were self-regulation and constrained adaption.

Keywords: England; austerity; resilience; anticipatory capacity; coping capacity

INTRODUCTION

This chapter reviews the responses of four English local governments to the austerity period triggered by the onset of the global financial crisis in 2007. It starts by considering the context of English local government, before going on to consider the impact of the financial crisis in the United Kingdom and the ensuing period of austerity. In line with other chapters in this edition, the general methodology follows that of Barbera, Jones, Korac, Saliterer, and Steccolini (2015) and develops the typology of resilience given there. The four local governments are then discussed before conclusions are drawn as to possible pathways to resilience.[1]

THE ENGLISH LOCAL GOVERNMENT CONTEXT

The United Kingdom was established in 1921 and is made up of four separate countries (England, Scotland, Wales and Northern Ireland). Despite increasing devolution of some aspects of fiscal and policy making being afforded to Scotland, Wales and Northern Ireland in recent times, the United Kingdom retains a unitary and un-codified constitution, meaning that, on paper at least, the Westminster government holds a high degree of power and control over the constituent countries.

This central control is most acutely felt in England, which has not been granted the same levels of devolution enjoyed by the other three countries. Local government in England is, despite having high levels of local political autonomy, very closely administered from Westminster in both policy and fiscal terms. This sets it apart from many of its European neighbours. A power of general competence was introduced in 2011, affording local government greater freedoms than had previously been the case. However, the un-codified nature of the UK constitution means these powers can be changed relatively easily by the Westminster government through the passing of new legislation, which often include retained powers for the Secretary of State responsible for a given policy area. In this sense, local government in the United Kingdom, and

England in particular, only enjoys 'partial autonomy' (Wilson & Game, 2011, p. 34) and is relatively centralised, even compared to other unitary states.

There are 353 local authorities in England (excluding single purpose authorities) that operate under one of two models: unitary or two-tier. Under the unitary model, a single local government (London borough, metropolitan or unitary council) provides all services and collects all tax receipts within its geographic boundary. Under the two-tier system, a county council provides more strategic and cross-cutting services such as education, social care and highways and transportation, with smaller district councils delivering more locally based services such as refuse collection. District councils collect local taxation and pass on a proportion to the county councils by way of a levy called 'the precept'. Unitary and county councils are collectively known as single tier and county councils (STCCs).

English local government spends in the order of £113 billion annually (Total net current expenditure 2013/2014 – DCLG, 2015, p. 42) which is funded from a variety of national and locally collected sources. Central grants (specific and general) account for around 57% of income, locally collected taxation (domestic and business) around 22%, charges for services 13% and other income (including capital receipts) 8% (DCLG, 2015, p. 14). Local governments have freedom to borrow (within self-managed indicators set out in the Prudential Code[2]), have their own bank accounts and treasury management functions and prepare accounts on an accruals basis, including the annual publishing of an operating statement, statement of financial position and cash flow statement. Accruals accounting is applied to both budgeting and accounting statements and largely follows IFRS[3] with the exception of some statutory provision. Accounts are audited annually and the financial year runs from 1 April.

THE ONSET AND IMPACT OF THE FINANCIAL CRISIS AND AUSTERITY

In the United Kingdom, the global financial crisis first became apparent following the collapse of the Northern Rock Building Society in the autumn of 2007, which was subsequently nationalised in 2008. As the extent of the global financial crisis, and its projected impact on the UK government finances unravelled, so did questions about the sustainability of government spending. This was especially so in local government, which had benefited from increased central funding during the years of the New Labour government (total government grants rose from £60,361 million in 2001–2002 to £103,369 million in 2009–2010 (DCLG, 2008, p. 30 and DCLG, 2011, p. 34)). UK central government debt to GDP stood at 42.7% in 2007 but leapt to 61.1% in 2008 rising to 85.5% by 2010 (OECD, 2016). With an election looming, the New Labour government's response to the crisis was to nationalise a number of failing banks

and introduce a fiscal stimulus package, which included a reduction in the prevailing rate of VAT and an increase in capital spending (Kickert, 2012). There
was also a re-evaluation of spending commitments, with planned reductions in
local government spending if not, at that point, implemented, at least discussed.
The election of 2010 was arguably fought over the Brown/Darling handling
of the UK economy, and, notwithstanding the evident global economic impact
of the crisis, the Coalition government came to power in May 2010 with, as it
thought, a clear mandate for austerity measures and a reduction in the size of
the state (Blythe, 2015).

Austerity measures affecting English local government were effectively rolled
out over several budget iterations; however, in summary the extent of these
measures was that local government would suffer a 37% real-term reduction in
core central government funding, equivalent to a 25% reduction in income/
spending power (including council tax) between 2010/11 and 2015/16 (NAO,
2014). At the same time, changes in government policy in a range of areas
between 2011/12 and 2015/16 created 164 new burdens on local government,
with an estimated financial value of £11.5 billion, many of which were
unfunded (NAO, 2015). All of this during a period when local government was
being encouraged to freeze council tax, or even reduce it, and when natural
pressure on locally collected taxation and some services was increasing due to
the economic recession.

Prior to 2008, financial management in the sector was focussed very much
on budgetary growth and being able to demonstrate efficiency in the use of
resources. After 2008, the financial environment changed dramatically on two
fronts. Firstly, the widely anticipated reduction in resources available due to
significant likely reductions in central government grants and secondly due to
the largely unforeseen regulatory change introduced by the Coalition
Government's business rates and council tax benefits reforms,[4] which gave
greater control and accountability at the local level, but without necessarily the
funding to go with it.

METHODS

The study used in-depth multiple case studies of four Single Tier and County
Councils (STCCs) selected through theoretical sampling with reference to their
financial performance (average contribution to non-allocated reserves) and
financial volatility (the standard deviation of financial performance) over the
10 years 2002–2012, and spanning the onset of the financial crisis in 2008.
STCCs rather than district councils were selected as, given the small scale of
the study, they were thought to offer a wider range of services and therefore
likely to face more significant range of challenges than their district counterparts. Enquiries with accounting practitioners identified the use of the

contribution to unallocated reserves as a key financial measure (see also NAO, 2014) and confirmed this measure as the best possible indicator of the variation in the budgetary position as it essentially represents the only area of flexibility available to decision makers, being, in the absence of a cash budgeting requirement, the 'balancing figure' between the net budget requirement on the one hand and government grants and locally collected taxation on the other. All 152 English STCCs were analysed on the above basis, with the four councils selected for interview coming from the extreme positions across the axes of positive and negative contributions to reserves and their relative volatility (high or low) during the period. They represented a mix of two metropolitan districts, a county council and a unitary authority. Up to three semi-structured interviews (Bryman & Bell, 2003) were undertaken within each of the four local authorities in 2015. To ensure a triangulation of views, the interviews were conducted with the Chief Executive Officer (CEO) or Deputy Chief Executive (Deputy CEO), the Director of Finance and section 151 officer (DoF) and a service department director, which varied across each authority.

The four local authorities selected were Manchester City Council, Warrington Borough Council, Derbyshire County Council and Wigan Council. Information pertaining to the local authorities is given in Table 1.

FINDINGS

Manchester City Council

Manchester City Council is a metropolitan borough council established in 1974. It displayed low negative average performance in terms of the annual contribution to/from unallocated reserves at −0.01% and a low standard deviation of 0.81%. Manchester has an annual net revenue budget (excluding schools) of around £490 million and serves a population of around 510,000. The council saw a reduction in funding of around £250 million between 2010 and 2015 (around 40% of its budget) and at the time of the interviews was planning a reduction of a further £100 million. The council is one of 10-member councils on the Greater Manchester Combined Authority (GMCA), which has regionally based priorities for transportation, economic growth and regeneration across the Greater Manchester region. Interviews were undertaken with the Chief Executive, the City Treasurer and the Director of Health and Wellbeing.

Despite the severity of the cuts, the vulnerability of the council was perceived to be low. This was due to a combination of factors including a healthy reserve balance and low levels of external debt, having halved its debt position following a housing stock transfer. The CEO also described how the council had previously embarked on a programme of economic diversification within the city

Table 1. English Resilience Patterns.

	Manchester (Self-Regulatory – Autonomy)	Warrington (Self-Regulatory – Self-Sufficient)	Derbyshire (Constrained Adapters)	Wigan (Constrained Adapters)
Budgetary position	*Zero*	*Negative*	*Positive*	*Zero*
Volatility	*Low*	*Medium*	*Medium*	*High*
Financial shocks	Grant reduction, reduced business rates income due to appeals (unfunded)	Financial crisis, grant reduction to negligible levels, low business rates retention due to affluence and reduced business rates income due to appeals (unfunded)	Financial crisis, grant reduction, increased demand for services	Grant reduction, equal status scheme, risk transferred from central government due to new council tax benefit scheme and business rates retention appeals (both unfunded)
Perceived vulnerability levels before the shock and their/evolution over time	*Initially low/ stable over time*	*Initially medium/decreasing over time*	*Initially low/ Increasing over time*	*Initially low/Increasing over time*
Level of anticipatory capacity before the shock and their/ evolution over time	*Initially high/ stable over time*	*Initially high/stable over time*	*Initially high/ stable over time*	*Initially high/stable over time*
Levels of coping capacity[a]	*Comprehensive*	*Comprehensive*	*Selective*	*Selective*

[a] Level of coping capacity: selective – several coping actions of buffering and adapting indicate selective coping capacities; comprehensive – the full use of the spectrum of coping actions in buffering, adapting and transforming, indicate comprehensive coping capacities.

in response to shocks that had occurred in the 1990s. '*If the banking crash of 2007 had happened in 1997, you might as well have hung a sign outside the town hall saying "gone for lunch"... because we were too one dimensional in our economic activities .... We're a much stronger diversified economic base [than in 1997], and by having that diversified economic base our dependency on particular sectoral difficulties and crashes is much less [in 2007]*'. This meant that while the impact of the crisis was significant, the scope for recovering from it was improved. In addition, the council had access to external income sources in the form of dividends from stakes in privately owned assets such as airports and a major conference centre. However, while this enabled it to maintain an ambitious capital programme to support economic growth within the city, it did not help solve the significant reductions in the revenue budget. Reserves could only provide temporary respite from the impact of the cuts and what was required were long-term solutions, including a major reduction in staffing across the organisation.

The council had high anticipatory capacity prior to the crisis in the form of medium-term financial planning, risk assessment and other environmental monitoring tools, which informed the budget planning process. As the CEO highlighted, '*what we have done over the last decade is to move much more towards 3 year budget strategies. We started that during the good times and so it became even more important that we had that focus, as you said, in times of austerity.*' This forward looking approach was still evident at the time of the interviews, with the City Treasurer saying '*At the moment, we are looking at about another £100 million, the CEO will tell you that is optimistic, it won't be that much, but if you read the tea leaves that's what the suggested draft settlement says we have got for the next couple of years*'.

In terms of coping capacities, these were a sophisticated mix of buffering, adapting and transforming. The strong financial position of the council going into the crisis gave it buffering capacity to help smooth the impact. Nevertheless, fundamental changes were needed to the scope and scale of services provided by the council, which required systematic reviews of service provision identifying where services could either be reduced or run in different ways. For example, there was streamlining of back office services, some libraries were closed and replaced by community run facilities, leisure trusts were established which allowed for a reduction in funding of leisure services while maintaining quality and increasing patronage and there was a phased withdrawal from children's day care facilities, which were replaced by independent provision. In all there was a staffing reduction of around 3,000 between 2010 and 2015.

There were also changes in the ways budgets were set and managed. The City Treasurer described a process that was much more inclusive. Post-2008, financial and non-financial goals became increasingly interlinked, the view being that the council should not spend on things that do not contribute towards its reform and growth agenda. Understanding how to integrate performance management information with finance was therefore seen as important and the performance management team has been deliberately based within the finance team.

The council also adopted a transformative approach to its future based on developing self-regulatory autonomy not only for the city but also at a regional level. It is now focussed on developing economic growth, employment and skills as well as having a big public health agenda. Gaining control of the public health budget was seen as positive, creating opportunities to join up with NHS Care Commissioning Groups (CCGs).

> Yes we've taken a lot of money out like other public agencies over last three/ four years, but we have done that in a way which has started to address how we as a council need to change, the way in which we view direct public services and what our role is in promoting Manchester as a place where people want to live and invest and visit and all the rest of it. (CEO)

However, caution was expressed about the future potential resilience of the council, meaning that it may be more vulnerable going forward. Even though austerity was said to have been managed fairly successfully, if painfully, looking ahead, the next stage of austerity may be different. Having reduced the head-count and introduced employment changes there was very much a sense of 'where do we go next' without large cuts in services. Looking forward, the ultimate goal is to generate a self-sustaining financial base to balance what is collected in tax with what is spent on services as well as lobbying for enhanced financial autonomy within the Greater Manchester region (something which has now been successful and due to be implemented through greater devolution in 2017).

Warrington Borough Council

Warrington Borough Council was designated new town status in 1968 and became an independent unitary council in 1998. It enjoys a strong local economic climate with high levels of employment and a strong business sector. It has a population of 207,000 and an annual net revenue budget (excluding schools) of around £136,000 million. The council saw reductions in funding of £50 million between 2010 and 2015 (around 30%) and was expecting to have to achieve a further £40 million in the next budget period. Due to its relative affluence it is one of the lowest government-funded councils per head of population and also has a low level of council tax. As a 'new town', Warrington benefits from favourable planning conditions, something that has contributed to its continuing economic and population growth.

Warrington displayed a relatively high negative average performance in terms of the annual contribution to/from unallocated reserves at −1.57% and a high standard deviation of 3.46%. The council maintained a relatively stable unallocated reserve balance of between £4 and £7 million during most of the 10 years 2003/2004 to 2012/2013. Interviews were undertaken with the CEO, the Director of Finance and Information Services (Section 151 officer) and the Director of Economic and Environmental Services.

The council exhibited a medium level of vulnerability prior to the crisis despite its relative wealth and the favourable conditions offered by its new town status. As the town is still growing, income actually increased over the previous 10 years. This was mainly due to an increasing council tax base, but has also been supplemented by inflating fees and charges in line with what the market will bear. Business rates have also grown quite quickly due to the rapidly growing economy in Warrington. However, prior to crisis reserves were at quite a low level and this was seen as a potential threat to their financial condition. As such the council has now followed a managed programme of increasing the level of both its earmarked and unallocated reserves.

In terms of anticipatory capacity, the council used predictive financial modelling to show that in a short space of time the drop off in government funding meant the council would need to be self-sufficient in terms of local income streams (council tax, business rates and income generation). This also contributed to the medium perception of vulnerability referred to above. Despite this, forward planning on the part of the council, meant that it entered the crisis phase in a relatively strong position. As described by the DoF, '*the financial health is reasonably strong if it has changed slightly over the last 4 years. Some of that I would put it down to things that were put in place [in advance of the central budget cuts]. Guessing what was going to happen to Local Authorities at that time, quite a big savings programme had been put into place to try and mitigate what was looking like was coming over the horizon quite quickly, that put us in a good place*'. The front loading of the savings programme before the onset of the funding reduction allowed reserves to start to be built up while external debt levels with the Public Works Loans Board (PWLB) were steadily reduced. This was seen by the DoF as contributing to the relative ease with which the initial austerity period was managed, '*although we have seen it coming, the shock is a lot less [..] and maybe we have over planned and got to a point of where most people haven't really noticed when the shock hit*'.

Coping has seen a combination of buffering, adaptive and transformative capacities. The main financial goals are now focused on increasing levels of income while at the same time reducing costs to become more efficient, especially in terms of statutory services, prompting a change in budget setting approach to one that is more outcome-based. Reserves have been used to both pump-prime savings initiatives within the council as well as providing a means of smoothing shocks across years. There has also been an alignment of financial and non-financial goals, which are increasingly seen as being interlinked and the council is looking seriously at whether non-statutory services are affordable. This adaption has meant some impact on the quality of services delivered, but mainly this was bringing it down to a more acceptable level of quality. There have been adaptations to systems too with the strengthening and embedding of risk management and benchmarking. This has improved the management of risk and elected members now openly discuss risks that have been escalated upwards. Financial risk is automatically considered as part of this and is a standard agenda item on quarterly senior management team meetings. Other initiatives, which could be considered transformative, include co-production with other public partners (including the NHS and parish councils), as well as attempting to gain combined leverage from the economic strength offered by the 'Warrington Pound', of which the council contributes around 1/3 of all agencies in the area. To help maintain services while reducing costs, the CEO stated the council had '*spun out 2 community interest companies, leisure and libraries in the first and in the other we've got our cultural offer, all of our museums. So that's no longer formally part of the council. They have a management agreement with us and we give them a fee every year, they are now delivering in partnership with the council. We're the commissioner of the services, a whole range of leisure and cultural services which the council probably would not have been able to continue to provide directly*'.

The main focus of the council is transformative, based on being able to self-regulate the local context with the aim of financial self-sufficiency in terms of business and local taxes to mitigate the virtual removal of central government funding. This includes facilitating council staff to be more entrepreneurial in approach, engaging in lending to other public bodies and revising processes to enable decisions that benefit the local economy to be taken more quickly, while still lawfully. The DoF stated '*our goals have kind have turned around, that we are trying to make sure we are generating income and that we are self-sufficient and we can do what we want and carry on providing important services without any requirement government funding has on us. In some ways it ought to make it easier planning in the future and not relying on the vagaries of government settlements*'.

However, despite this apparent optimism about what a self-sustaining future might hold, the vulnerability of the council is still at a medium level. In part this is because being successful in growing the tax base will naturally increase demand for services as population increases. However, it is mainly due to the uncertain future financial environment and whether the changes made so far are indeed sustainable. In the words of the CEO, '*We are trying to take it in our stride but particularly in 15/16, I am very anxious about that. I have taken all the low hanging fruit, now I'm having to saw off the tree*'.

Derbyshire County Council

Derbyshire County Council is a non-metropolitan upper-tier authority. Established in 1972, it saw the scale of its services reduce in 1997 when the unitary Derby City Council was created. It serves a population of around 770,000 people and has a net revenue budget (excluding schools) in the region of £470 million. The council faced a budget reduction programme of £250 million between 2010 and 2019 (around 30%). Interviews were held with the Deputy CEO and the DoF.

Derbyshire displayed a position of relatively high positive average performance in terms of the annual contribution to/from unallocated reserves at +2.02% and a relatively high standard deviation of 2.25%. The council recorded an increasing level of unallocated reserves during the 10 years 2003/2004 to 2012/2013, starting with a balance of just £7.1 million and rising to £98 million by 2012/2013.

As a result of having a strong and managed reserves position, Derbyshire was considered to have low vulnerability at the start of the crisis period. Reserve balances are routinely risk assessed to meet items such as uninsured risks, disaster recovery and any underestimation of budget reductions. They are also used to soften the impact of cuts by phasing them in over time.

Anticipatory capacity was also high, due to the presence of already embedded medium-term financial planning processes and early risk management systems. The council identified early on the need to prepare for the budget cuts expected post-2008, even though these were ultimately worse than expected. This translated into early action with the DoF describing that '*about 2008 time, [the council was] preparing for fairly significant budget reductions which we expected to come on stream. Admittedly we didn't expect them to be as bad as they [were], but we started taking quite severe measures even then, particularly in slowing down capital to produce longer term budget reductions that we could benefit from*'.

Historically, the council had actively used the slack resources within its reserve balances to avoid making changes to service delivery. However, in the early 2000s it was identified this had become a risky policy, exposing the council to financial risk. Over time, reserves were built back up to meet specific provisions for known risks and to provide a more substantial general reserve balance. During the early 2000s the council increased its level of council tax and also received favourable government settlements in some years, giving surpluses that were put into reserves.

Despite anticipating significant potential savings of £127 million, the council may have pursued an approach more based on buffering than adapting had it not been for an increase in the cuts in the final settlement to £157 million. It was this that provided the lever for change in approach from the elected officials, forcing them to deal with the issues and ultimately having a positive impact. They were comfortable with £127 million but the additional £30 million changed their approach and concentrated their minds on required change.

In coping with the effects of the crisis, the council predominantly used buffering approaches with some adaptations taking place. Initially, reductions were made on a 'salami slicing' basis, with each department shouldering the same proportion of pain, encouraging directors to work collegiately and act corporately. A change of political control in 2013 saw the adoption of a more prioritised basis of budget reduction, although initially this resulted in a hiatus with too many priorities and a resulting lack of focus immediately after the local elections. The council still operates a prioritised approach, but paradoxically this produced similar results to those had salami slicing been adopted, the only difference being that central support departments have had to make proportionately greater savings than service departments.

Around 40% of the required savings were a result of grant going down and 60% because of increasing service pressures (e.g. demographics and inflation). In the first round of cuts, roughly one third each of savings came from either becoming more efficient, additional sources of income (e.g. charging for adult social care) or managing demand for services. Going forward, it will be less about efficiencies, as most of this has been done, and more about the other two approaches. The DoF identified that charges have been particularly effective in the management of some budgets. '*You look at charging for what you don't charge for, or you charge less than other people charge ... so yes we have made big "cuts" in adult care but a lot of it is because we now charge for that which we hadn't done previously*'. Similarly he pointed out that service levels had been maintained through being more efficient rather than cutting them back. '*The vast majority of reductions made are not made by reducing [services]. Over the years the majority have been made because we do things better. We cut out the waste. You don't see a reduction in services, it's just cheaper to produce*'.

Austerity savings from 2010 onwards have been managed through base budget reductions as part of a five-year planning process, and not by using reserve balances as was the case in the 1990s. This has been a deliberate policy and one that has transcended changes in political control during the period. Reserves have still been used to help deal with austerity but not in the same way as in the past. Instead they are used to help facilitate change and to soften the impact of slippage in the savings programme. The current five-year plan provides for the running down of unallocated reserves to £29 million by 2018/2019, considered to be a prudent level of reserves at that time.

Although there have been some necessary moves towards multi-agency collaboration (e.g. in health care), adaptation has so far mainly come in the form of changes in approach within the organisation to financial management and strategic capability. The Deputy CEO identified a more cross cutting and collegiate approach to dealing with the cuts than had previously been the case. '*I think we have a financial plan that is honest, in terms of the reserves, the long term cuts programme, how we tackle the challenges we face. I think we have a strong corporate management team where there is a huge amount of honesty and challenge and for me that's probably the biggest differences from 10 years ago. I think we are being more honest with each other across departments and honest with Members [elected officials] and staff in terms of what some of these things mean*'. There was also a strengthening of the approach to risk management within the council. Departments and projects now produce their own risk registers that are consolidated into a corporate risk register reported to the strategic level and audit committee. Embedding the positive management of risk has been the hard part of this, moving it on from just producing a risk register. In facing the cuts the Deputy CEO described a position where now '*we have basically one massive piece of paper which has our cuts on of £157 million, and then behind each line there is a business case. So that business case, has the more detailed financial risks, equalities, HR kind of issues identified and then it is looked at collaboratively. Again the thing for me is getting people from all the services around the table*'.

Looking forward, in dealing with the period of austerity, Derbyshire has moved from an approach primarily focussed on buffering, with some internal adaptation, to one that is more transformative in outlook, although it had not reached this stage. The Deputy CEO talked a lot about plans for the future, which were much more transformative in nature than the responses in the early years of austerity. Fundamentally, she identified a shift in mind-set within the organisation that may not have arisen had not the severity of austerity taken place. '*We talk about one direction, one approach, and we talk about Derbyshire as a place now, not Derbyshire as an organisation, which again is a shift, a big shift. This is new responsibility that we have completely, overall, turned over the way that we write. We now write for people not the organisation, [by which is meant] our 5 year financial plan and all the intermediate work*'.

Derbyshire's approach would be identified as being a constrained adapter. They entered the crisis period in a favourable financial position, typified by strong reserves and an apparent level of either redundancies or the capacity to introduce charges that has meant the funding reductions were absorbed with little direct impact on service delivery. However, despite this the organisation is constrained by a high reliance on external funding streams and has now begun to adapt its internal process and capabilities to be better able to face similar challenges going forward. Ultimately this has started to evolve into transformative approaches that look to set the scene going forward. Interestingly, and perhaps because of this path through austerity, of the three English councils in this study, Derbyshire was the most optimistic about the future after 2016.

Wigan Council

Wigan Council is a large metropolitan borough, serving a population in excess of 300,000 and with an annual net revenue budget (excluding schools) in the order of £232 million. The council saw a reduction of funding of £66 million between 2010 and 2015 (around 30%) and was facing the prospects of a further £40 million by 2017. Wigan is also a member of the GMCA.

Wigan displayed a low average performance in terms of the annual contribution to or from unallocated reserves at +0.01%, but was of interest as it had a relatively high standard deviation of 4.47%, one of the highest in the STCC group. This was mainly due to a large contribution being made to unallocated reserves in 2008/2009 that was subsequently drawn down in 2010/2011 and 2011/2012. At the interviews it was found that this movement was related to the financial impact of 'equal status', a financial shock faced by all local authorities around this time. Interviews were undertaken with the Deputy Chief Executive (and senior financial officer) as well as the Director of Adult Social Care and Health.

Wigan is not the most affluent of towns and suffers from a low council tax yield, lacks a defined industry base and struggles in terms of attracting inward investment. It also has an aging population and high levels of disabilities. Despite this, the financial vulnerability of the council was considered to be low before the onset of the crisis. Mainly this was due to the council having a strong reserve base (on average around 10% of net expenditure) and having relatively low levels of debt, which had been reducing leading up to the crisis.

Anticipatory capacity was high within the council and measures had been put in place to start to mitigate the potential effects of the cuts before they occurred. The Deputy CEO stated, *'before the general election [of 2010], we knew whoever came in was going to cut. We didn't know the size of the cuts, but we took a paper and agreed it with the Leader (of the council) about taking the money out as quickly as possible, and not waiting for the grant to fall out'*.

In terms of coping capacities, Wigan tended to use a mix of buffering and adaptation. Buffering through the use of reserves was not used to stave off the crisis. It was recognised early on that the scale of the cuts would require a response based on more substantial changes to the way the council operated. Alongside these spending reductions, reserves (allocated and unallocated) were used to not only both help smooth the under/over achievement of spending plans at the corporate level, but also to help incentivise departments to over-deliver on savings by allowing these savings to be used within departments in the following year in the form of invest to save schemes. Reserves were also used to absorb unforeseen challenges at the corporate level (such as an increase in National Insurance contributions), without necessarily impacting on departmental budgets. A key element of dealing with the crisis was said to have been addressing the required cuts in expenditure early. This was a strategic approach, driven by the finance directorate and resulted in achieving the four-year spending reductions within a three-year period. Alongside this, over-programming of savings was used in order to give year-on-year flexibility. This approach effectively forced cash out of the base budget at an early stage, combined with a programme of service change that resulted in a reconfiguring of services. The Deputy CEO explained *'because we took action quickly, we got some flexibility in terms of how we deal with the problem. We are about a year ahead of where the money is falling out .... So I always feel like there's wriggle room in terms of what we are going to do'*. Its success was attributed to strong support from the senior politicians within the council as well as from the CEO.

Prior to 2010, balancing the budget was undertaken by salami slicing and expecting departments to come back with proposals for reducing their controllable budget. However, service directors are now required to meet their budgets in year and demonstrate delivery of savings through the council's performance monitoring system. After 2010, things changed significantly in terms of the way budget decisions were taken and implemented. Departmental savings targets were not now undertaken using salami slicing, but rather directors were required to identify real and significant savings based on fundamental changes to the ways services were delivered. As part of this the CEO required directors to be '*humble and honest*' about service priorities and required a greater level of corporate understanding across the management team. This was aligned with a strengthened approach to risk management, with a more open dialogue of risks and their impact between and across service directors and the DoF, giving a better understanding of the wider implications. This was something recognised by the Director of Adult Social Care, '*What goes on under the current regime is more "Get on and deliver it and we'll back you .... Let us know what you need and we will help you" rather than "That looks really hard and you're a problem and if you don't get every aspect of it right you've got the lifespan of a world war one fighter pilot" .... I think the organization is trying to point the resources at the things it needs to*'.

In terms of financial management, there was a change here too. The Deputy CEO described a situation where '*when I started you concentrated more on expenditure, and in those days you'd even look at growth, you'd have growth bids and things like that. And now I take just as much interest in income. So business rates, what is happening in the local economy, in terms of business ... and a number of them are things outside of our control .... So I think in 2005 – 2008 we were looking at growth. Now it just seems like you are looking at the local economy, council tax yield, business rates ... we are probably spending as much time there as on expenditure*'.

Similar to Derbyshire, the approach adopted by the council is one of constrained adaptation. While this includes working collaboratively with other agencies, for example the Police and Care Commissioning Groups, unlike Manchester, Wigan is less able to directly influence its local environment and is more susceptible to the impact of changes to and within the local government financing system. Its membership of the GMCA gives some scope for sharing spatial impacts, but unlike its neighbour, it is faced with reshaping services within the resources available to it.

Looking forward, there was concern that after 2016/2017 any further savings reductions may be unsustainable given the level of change that has already occurred within the council. So, according to the Deputy CEO, vulnerability was increasing. '*If it goes on, what can we deliver in 2016? ... but no one knows how the financial outlook is going to be after that. Some people are talking about the same level again, but that's just not sustainable with the current breadth of services that local authorities have to deal with... I don't think we can do what we have done again*'.

CONCLUSIONS

For the English councils interviewed, the results develop into two main themes. Firstly, there seems to have been a common set of anticipatory and coping capacities employed by each council both in the lead up to the funding cuts from 2010 onwards and the way they subsequently dealt with aspects of the crisis. The second theme shows that despite this commonality of systems and processes deployed, the specific and local contexts experienced by each council, both internally and externally, determined their overall path to dealing with austerity. These two paths were self-regulation and constrained adaption which, along with the more common capacities, are discussed below. What seems key in understanding the English response to both the central cuts and the economic and social demands the financial crisis placed locally, is how they were able to understand and manage their vulnerabilities during the crisis using a common set of capacities that helped them respond accordingly to their situation. As such it seems that financial resilience is a useful framework for considering how local governments respond to shocks in their financial environments (Steccolini, Barbera, & Jones, 2015).

The English councils interviewed all displayed a high level of anticipatory capacity before the direct funding reductions hit in 2010. Once the global crisis started to bite in the United Kingdom in 2008, the councils recognised that there was going to be a significant impact on their central funding allocations and started to map out the effects, planning how to respond and recover. This was mainly driven by the officers, and especially DoFs, but they were relatively easily able to marshal the elected officials and other service directors behind plans to make significant budget reductions fairly early on. Derbyshire was perhaps initially behind the curve on this and ultimately it was the additional scale of the cuts that galvanised the elected officials into action. The build up to the general election in 2010, while leaving outcomes uncertain, probably helped councils to understand that significant change was coming, no matter which political party came to power (something that was repeated in 2015). This capacity to recognise that change was coming was uniformly displayed across all four councils, with medium-term financial planning, risk management systems and 'reading the tea leaves' at the national and local level all cited as part of this foresight. In 2008, such systems were already in place within the councils, even if at a more rudimentary level than they subsequently developed into, becoming more sophisticated at the time of the interviews with plans in some councils to develop them still further. This left the councils with stronger anticipatory capacity as the longer term impacts of further funding reductions started to unravel. This high initial level of anticipatory capacity going into the crisis, in part reduced the level of vulnerability each council experienced. Despite the severity of the cuts so far, all councils claimed to be in a strong financial position at the time of the interviews, with most citing taking action early, as part of a planned coping strategy, being responsible for this.

So, in part vulnerability can be moderated by having good anticipatory systems in place, allowing scenarios to be mapped and actions taken. However, vulnerability can also be understood in terms of the control a local authority has over its own funding streams. Those with greater ability to manage the local economic environment, and importantly the tax base, could go some way to redressing the cuts in central funding and were probably less vulnerable going forward, at least in terms of dependency on central funding. Those less able to manage such factors, due to unfavourable social and economic contexts, were more vulnerable to changes coming from the centre. This seems to have resulted in two generic approaches to resilience within the English councils. To take control of their own destiny through the active management (self-regulation) of their local contexts, with the aim of stretching opportunities for income generation. Or to take a more constrained view, necessitating the need to better monitor and understand the overall financial envelope in order that services can be adapted within the available resources. In the former view, autonomy for Manchester and financial self-sufficiency for Warrington, there was a sense that services could still be grown and developed even in times of financial cut back. In the latter view, the focus appears to be more on squeezing out efficiencies and managing demand, once opportunities for increasing income through price and tax adjustments have been achieved.

Financial reserves also play a part in understanding both vulnerability and the way in which responses to the crisis played out. Some already had 'healthy' reserve balances in place in 2008 and saw this as a source of strength. Warrington was the odd one out, but quickly embarked on a period of reserve replenishment, something that Manchester and Derbyshire had done fortuitously in the years before 2008. The way in which reserves were used to respond to the crisis was relatively uniform. All councils recognised that reserves could not be used to directly buffer the impact of the funding reductions, as had previously been the case. They could not just sit it out, but rather reserves were used more sophisticatedly to help fund change management initiatives and invest in saving schemes, as well as providing a degree of financial flexibility should saving initiatives not come on stream when planned. This was linked with making an early start, commencing the reductions in advance of the cuts to spread the impact over a longer period of time and provide budget savings in the early years to add to reserves. This approach was cited by three out of the four councils, with Wigan also utilising over-programming to add additional flexibility.

Notwithstanding the above discussion, fundamental changes were made by all councils to accommodate the cuts in funding, mainly through staffing reductions. Nevertheless, each council was also keen to point out that this had not necessarily diminished the quality or take up of services and in some cases this had improved. Some councils saw an opportunity to bring about necessary changes, the crisis merely became the trigger that allowed them to drive the changes through. Each council suggested the crisis provided a galvanising event, on the back of which decision making became much more collegiate across senior management teams. The impact of the crisis was so bad that it forced new ways of working at the strategic level with greater tolerance and less silo management. This was reflected in budget management systems, where salami slicing was replaced with cuts linked to outcomes, and financial and non-financial performance management systems became more closely intertwined.

Finally, the English councils showed a high propensity to work collaboratively with other public agencies when responding to the crisis both within statutory requirements, but also voluntarily. The GMCA to which Manchester and Wigan belong, is the most formal of such arrangements discussed in the interviews (and one which at the time of writing other regions are exploring), but the 'Warrington Pound' initiative and other examples given by the councils show a future where increasingly budgets will be pooled and services shared across agencies, particularly for public health and wellbeing. This desire to collaborate, while helping to instil further efficiencies at the spatial level, also offers the option of safety in numbers, whereby the pain of further cutbacks can be shared across a network, rather than being suffered alone.

Looking ahead, all councils considered that they had so far been successful in meeting the initial round of spending reductions through a combination of efficiency, prudent use of reserves, reforms to service delivery and income generation. However, they were less optimistic about their ability to respond to the next wave of cuts and 2016/2017 was seen as a particularly difficult year. Each council recognised that it would need to rethink its approach to financial management yet again in the coming years, further demonstrating the presence of anticipatory capacity as a component of financial resilience. Nevertheless, at senior levels confidence going forward was lower than it had been in terms of responding to future financial pressures. This view was explicitly or implicitly evident in all the councils and was irrespective of the outcome of the general election in 2015, with resignation that though a change of political control nationally may bring with it a different relationship between local and central government, financially it was likely to have little impact.

NOTES

1. The author would like to thank CIMA's General Charitable Trust for helping to fund the primary research used to inform this chapter.
2. Since 1 April 2004 local authorities have been under the Local Government Act 2003 and the CIPFA Prudential Code, and are free to finance capital spending from self-financed borrowing without the need to have government approval as long as it is affordable and prudent to do so. This new system replaced central dictated credit approvals and reduced the direct impact central government had on local government capital spending.

3. Local authority accounts are produced following The Code of Practice on Local Authority Accounting in the United Kingdom: a statement of recommended practice and the Service Reporting Code of Practice. Both documents are published by the Chartered Institute of Public Finance and Accountancy (CIPFA).

4. From April 2013, local authorities that are collection authorities were allowed to retain up to 50% of business rate growth as an incentive to grow their local economies. The changes increased the level of financial uncertainty for local authorities by transferring the risk of business rate appeals and business rate avoidance to local authorities (Local Government Association, 2013a). From April 2013, the national Council Tax Benefit system was replaced by local Council Tax Support schemes in tandem with a 10% reduction in central government funding. This increased financial risk for local authorities that are billing authorities in terms of both the additional financial burden of a demand led benefit and the uncertain impact on collection rates (Local Government Association, 2013b).

REFERENCES

Barbera, C., Jones, M., Korac, S., Saliterer, I., & Steccolini, I. (2015). Bouncing back and bouncing forward – Applying an alternative perspective on European municipalities' responses to financial shocks. EGPA Annual Conference, Toulouse, France, PSG VI: Governance of Public Sector Organizations, August 26–28.

Blythe, M. (2015). *Austerity: The history of a dangerous idea*. Oxford: Oxford University Press.

Bryman, A., & Bell, E. (2003). *Business research method*. Oxford: Oxford University Press.

DCLG. (2008). Local government financial statistics England, No.18. Department for Communities and Local Government, London.

DCLG. (2011). Local government financial statistics England, No.21. Department for Communities and Local Government, London.

DCLG. (2015). Local government financial statistics England, No.25. Department for Communities and Local Government, London.

Kickert, W. (2012). How the UK government responded to the fiscal crisis: An outsider's view. *Public Money & Management, 32*(3), 169–176.

Local Government Association (LGA). (2013a). Rewiring public services. Business Rates Retention, the story so far. LGA, London.

Local Government Association (LGA). (2013b). Rewiring public services. Council tax Support, the story so far. LGA, London.

National Audit Office (NAO). (2014). *Financial sustainability of local authorities 2014*. Report by the Comptroller and Auditor General Norwich: TSO and London Houses of Parliament Shop, London.

National Audit Office (NAO). (2015). *Local government new burdens*. Report by the Comptroller and Auditor General Norwich: TSO and London Houses of Parliament Shop, London.

OECD. (2016). *OECD stat. Central government debt*. Retrieved from https://stats.oecd.org/index. aspx?queryid=8089. Accessed on September 1.

Steccolini, I., Barbera, C., & Jones, M. (2015). *Governmental financial resilience under austerity: The case of English local authorities*. CIMA Executive Summary Report (Vol. 11, 3).

Wilson, D., & Game, C. (2011). *Local government in the United Kingdom* (5th ed.). Hampshire: Palgrave Macmillan.

CHAPTER 6

RESILIENCE PATTERNS OF FRENCH MUNICIPALITIES: A CASE STUDY

Céline du Boys

ABSTRACT

French municipalities are in charge of a large number of local public services and benefit from a good, even if decreasing, financial autonomy. They have been until recently and despite the 2008 crisis, in a good financial situation supported by stable tax revenues and protective national policies. But they are now weakened by strong cuts in their main operating grant operated from 2015.

Through a case study, this chapter attempts to better understand French municipalities' patterns of financial resilience in times of austerity. Interviews have been driven in four middle size municipalities in various financial situation, to understand the effects of the crisis on their vulnerability and the influence of their financial and organisational capacities on their resilience patterns.

The study shows that all four municipalities enhanced their responsiveness following the 2015 cut in grants. The latter appeared as a major shock that prompts them to change their behaviours and strengthen their resilience. But municipalities took up different paths of resilience, building up or investing in different anticipatory and coping capacities. Buffering capacities, such as cost cuts, were present in all cases to cope with shocks. Conversely, adapting and transforming capacities were not as prevalent. The pro-active resilient

Governmental Financial Resilience: International Perspectives on how Local Governments Face Austerity
Public Policy and Governance, Volume 27, 93–113
Copyright © 2017 by Emerald Publishing Limited
All rights of reproduction in any form reserved
ISSN: 2053-7697/doi:10.1108/S2053-769720170000027006

municipality relies on a mix of capacities. But three out of four cases show
patterns of financial resilience that leave them insufficiently prepared for
future shocks. This research shows the necessity to develop and constantly
maintain anticipatory and coping capacities that are suitable for tackling the
municipalities' specific vulnerability sources.

Keywords: Local governments; crisis; financial resilience; organisational
capacities; financial situation; France

INTRODUCTION

The French Republic is a unitary state whose organisation is decentralised, as
regard to article one of the Constitution. The three levels of local governments
(LGs) (Region, Department and Municipality) have a very similar legal system
and are placed on an equal footing regarding the State. They are freely adminis-
trated by elected councils and do not exert control on each other.

From 1982, they have received a growing number of responsibilities. Their
autonomy is limited to local administrative responsibilities, as the State keeps
all sovereign responsibilities such as enacting laws, justice, army or diplomacy.
Local public finances are quite healthy thanks to measures such as mandatory
requirement to produce a balanced budget, debt restrictions and that the State
pre-pays and guarantees the amount of taxes voted locally.[1]

After the 2008 crisis, LGs' financial health has been preserved thanks to successive national economic recovery plans (26 billion euros in 2009 and 35 billion euros in 2010) that limited the economic recession.[2] Even despite the freeze
of their main grant, the 'DGF' (a general operating grant),[3] from 2011 to 2013,
a majority of LGs managed to preserve their financial situation.

However, the deterioration of the State deficit and debt[4] led to important
budgetary cuts. A 1.5 billion euro decrease in DGF was announced for 2014
and an 11 billion euro decrease between 2015 and 2017 has been felt as strong
and unexpected shock for most LGs.[5] In 2017, the DGF will have decreased by
28% from 2011.[6]

This provides an interesting environment to study municipalities' reactions
to shocks and their patterns of financial resilience. This chapter aims at analysing, through the examples of four French municipalities, the influence of the
crisis on LGs vulnerability and the effects of their financial and organisational
capacities on their resilience patterns. The methodology used to investigate the
financial resilience of French LGs follows the general approach used in the
book (Barbera, Jones, Korac, Saliterer, & Steccolini, 2017). Similar to other
countries, the results show various patterns of resilience.

The municipalities mainly cope with crisis using buffering capacities such as
cost cuts. In three out of four cases, they have insufficient anticipatory, adaptive

and transforming capacities and show patterns of financial resilience that leave them insufficiently prepared for future shocks. The crisis appears as a major shock that prompts them to change their behaviours and to strengthen their resilience. Our study suggests that so far, some municipalities felt they were protected by the State and so haven't developed sufficient resilience capacities. In Case D, it is the mistrust of the State that have led to better anticipatory and coping capacities.

This chapter is divided into four parts. After introducing the French LGs' context and the methodology of the study, we will present the main results and discuss the resilience patterns of the four cases.

LOCAL GOVERNMENTS' CONTEXT IN FRANCE[7]

Local Institutional Framework

The decentralisation process took place gradually since 1982. In the early 2000s, decentralisation and LGs' financial autonomy were registered in the Constitution.

In 2015, there were 36,658 municipalities (but only 958 over 10,000 inhabitants), 101 departments and 27 regions. From 1999, the large number of municipalities pushed to the development of intercommunalities (public organisations for the cooperation of municipalities:[8] 2133 in 2015), that make up a kind of fourth level of LG. In 2016, this territorial organisation evolved:[9] merger of some regions (18 regions left) and creation of some big intercommunalities around major municipalities, the 'métropoles'. This has generated a strong uncertainty for LGs concerned.

Each LG has specific competences. The municipality and the intercommunality are in charge of organising the services and facilities related to everyday life such as water, sanitation, garbage or town planning. The department's responsibilities are oriented towards social assistance (towards children, disabled, older or unemployed persons) and rural equipment. The region is involved in territorial planning, and sustainable and economic development. LGs also share some transversal competencies related to culture, sport or tourism. Transportation and childhood responsibilities are divided between LGs.[10]

LGs are freely administered by elected councils, who decide the general policy. The president of the council (the Mayor for municipalities) prepares and implements the decisions. To ensure the daily management and the actions which he is responsible for, the council establishes the administrative and technical services organisation. Depending on services, it can be done through internal services composed of civil servants, autonomous administrations and/or externalisation to public or private organisations.

Since 2010, LGs' autonomy is challenged by successive reforms that have devolved new tasks to LGs and cancelled some local taxes. In 2010, the removal of an important business tax called '*Taxe professionnelle*'[11] resulted in a great loss of flexibility in revenues and has been a challenge for LGs. But the decrease of the '*DGF*' in 2015, mentioned in introduction, constitutes the first major shock for LGs.

Local Public Finances Framework

The budget is the central element of local public finances. It plans and authorises resources and expenditure, provided it is balanced. It is split in two sections: operating (or current) activities and investment ones. Borrowing is only allowed for investments, not for operating activities. Debt repayment is mandatory and must be done from own-resources. The budget is voted by the local council and must be validated a posteriori by the Prefect.[12] Its implementation may still give rise to a deficit. In that case, measures to restore equilibrium must be implemented in the following budget. The Prefect and the Court of Auditors monitor or impose measures to return to the balance. Bankruptcy procedure does not apply to LGs and their assets are exempted from seizure.

Full accrual accounting is applied both to general accounting and budget. The local public representative (such as the mayor for municipalities) establishes an administrative account which traces the budgetary flows of the past year. The accounting officer (who is a member of the State accounting department) establishes the balance sheet and the cash-flow statement. LGs must also produce a statement of their off-balance sheet commitments and the list of funded organisations where they took on liabilities, such as associations. However, no consolidation of accounts is required.

Overview of Local Public Resources and Expenses[13]
Expenses keep increasing each year up to now.[14] Personnel costs represent a large part of operating expenses (52% of the 67 billion euros operating expenses of all municipalities in 2013). Investment spending, excluding debt repayment, have been of 27 billion euros in 2013 (equivalent to 40% of operating expenses).

Operating resources represented 80% of 2013 municipalities' total resources (79.1 billion euros). They come from taxes (60%), State grants (23%) and to a lesser extent from service fees:[15]

– Local taxes are collected directly and indirectly from citizens and companies. LGs vote the rate of main direct taxes, and the State ensure the tax collection and bears the risk of non-payment.
– State grants and subsidies represent 23% of municipalities' operating resources. The main one is the DGF '*Dotation globale de fonctionnement*', a

general operating grant (16.4 billion euros in 2013, 86% of operating grants). The 2015 finance act stood a decrease in the DGF paid to all LGs of 11 billion euros by 2017 (municipalities and intercommunalities bearing 56%, department 31% and Regions 13%).

Investment resources represented 20% (19.2 billion euros) of municipalities' total resources in 2013. They come from grants (11.9 billion euros in 2013 for municipalities, 12% of total revenues) and debt (7.3 billion euros of new debt in 2013, 7.4% of total revenues).

Local debt is low, but is increasing since 2003 and reached 115.4 billion in 2013 (5.9% of the national public debt − 62.9 billion for municipalities). From 2008 to 2011, LGs were limited by the bad market liquidity and attempted to limit their debt growth. The 2012 debt market's dynamism pushed LGs to increase debt again and to build cash reserves in order to face uncertainty over access to bank financing in the future.[16] As a consequence and for the first time in 2013 and 2014, LGs used their cash reserves to finance some investment expenditure. Moreover, many LGs suffer from a risky debt structure due to an important proportion of toxic loans.[17] There is no systemic risk (Observatoire des finances locales, 2014), but many LGs are affected and some suffer from a high increase in their financial expenses.

2008 Crisis in France: A Delayed Impact on LGs

The 2008 crisis has had a delayed impact on LGs financial situation. LGs were first preserved by State policies such as the economic recovery plans pursued in 2009 and 2010. But from 2011, the deterioration of national public finances pushed the State to several austerity measures, and from 2014 to the decrease in grants to LGs. Thus, it is only in 2014 that LGs have harshly felt the crisis, with the announcement of an 11 billion decrease in '*DGF*' combined with a still depressed economic climate.

This delayed impact of the 2008 crisis at the local level gives an interesting environment to study French LGs' resilience.

METHODS

In order to study the financial resilience of LGs and in line with the other case studies of the book, we focused our research on municipalities. It is a level of LGs that exists in most countries and so that is more easily comparable. Our focus is on middle size municipalities, between 40,000 and 200,000 inhabitants. Beyond the fact that they host a large part of the population (almost 10 million inhabitants, 15% of population), they offer a diversity of managerial practices, at the border of small and big cities, that is interesting to study.

In accordance with the other case studies of the book, two variables have been used for case selection: budgetary position and volatility. Budgetary position is measured by the average surplus or deficit generated by all operations divided by the average annual current revenues, on the period 2003–2012. Volatility has been computed as the standard deviation of the budgetary position over the period.[18]

Out of 125 municipalities in this population range, four have been selected for further investigation within the lowest or highest 20% budgetary positions and standard deviations (Table 1). Over the period, no municipality showed a negative or null average budgetary position.

Municipality A (south-east of France) is in a difficult financial situation, with a high debt and some risky toxic loans. A significant part of the population is considered as poor. The city hosts a few historical important industrial companies, but lacks from attractiveness. A new Mayor has been elected in 2014, in a right wing tradition.

Municipality B (Brittany) is in a difficult financial situation with a high level of personnel expenditures, but a quite low debt. The population is quite poor. The economic activity is low, with only small businesses and public administrations. The present Mayor, at the centre right, has been elected in 2001.

Municipality C (Parisian suburbs) was, in 2014, in a good financial situation with a relatively low and healthy debt. A large part of its population is poor, with a high level of social housing, but the city hosts some big industries and its territory benefits from a great attractiveness. There is a strong political stability at the head of the city, at the very left wing. The present Mayor, who was the former deputy mayor, was elected in 2015.

Table 1. Cases Selection and Main Financial Data.

	Case A	Case B	Case C	Case D
Volatility	Low[a]	High[b]	Low[a]	High[b]
Budgetary position	Low[a]	Low[a]	High[b]	High[b]
Population (and trend)	50 000 (=)	46 000 (↘)	88 000 (↗)	49 000 (↗)
Global annual revenues 2013 in ME[d] (in euro Per capita)	90 (1,800)	85 (1,847)	215 (2,443)	110 (2,244)
DGF[c] 2013 → DGF 2015 in ME[d]	10.2 → 8.3 (−18.6%)	16.5 → 14.9 (−9%)	20.1 → 15,5 (−22.9%)	16.8 → 14.3 (−14.9%)
Projected DGF evolution up to 2017 (According to our interviewees) in ME[d]	−4	−3	−7	−3

[a]Within the 20% lowest.
[b]Within the 20% highest.
[c]DGF: 'Dotation global de fonctionnement' (general operating grant).
[d]ME: Million euros.

Municipality D (Parisian suburbs) is in a good financial situation, with a low debt. The population is mainly well off and the city hosts some major services companies and benefits from a great attractiveness. There is a strong political stability at the head of the city, at the centre right. The mayor was first elected in 1994.

All four municipalities suffered from a decrease in DGF, but not in the same proportion due to equalisation arrangements, but also because of a very complex DGF calculation.[19]

Within each municipality, three or four semi-structured interviews were undertaken. They were conducted with the Chief Executive Officer (CEO) and the director of Finance, and depending on cases, with some department directors or Deputy CEOs in charge of services to the population. Each interview lasted between 60 and 120 minutes, and focused on the municipality's financial health during a 10-year period, its main financial and non-financial goals, the main risks and shocks that the municipality had faced and how it had identified and responded to these. Interviews were recorded, transcribed and used for qualitative content analysis. Within-case analyses were used to identify general themes and categories.

As mentioned above, the decrease in 2015 of the 'DGF' was a major shock to all municipalities. Our interviews took place in March 2015, while the municipalities were achieving their 2015 budget. Therefore, they reflect the first decisions taken to address this shock.

RESILIENCE OF FRENCH MUNICIPALITIES: CASE STUDY RESULTS AND DISCUSSION

The analysis of the four municipalities shows that they all suffered from major events in their external environment that have been perceived as affecting finances. But while they all underwent a large decrease in their resources, the capacities deployed, especially anticipatory and adaptive ones, and the evolution of their vulnerability have been different. Since there are differences in the existence and build-up of capacities, the concept of resilience provides an interesting framework to analyse those cases.

In the four cases, the economic crisis resulted, from 2010, in lower revenues and increased demand for social care from the population.[20] Several national reforms also resulted in significant increases in the cities mandatory expenditures,[21] in the abolition of some taxes and in decreases in grants. But, it is the DGF decrease in 2015 that has been perceived as the major shock that challenged their situation. Moreover, in City A, the increase in the Swiss Franc exchange rate has been perceived as another important shock, because of the city's toxic loans indexed on it. At last, for Municipalities C and D, the creation in January 2016 of the Paris Metropolis, a huge intercommunality in the Paris area, was also a major shock. Indeed, the sharing out of tasks between municipalities and the metropolis, the organisational or governance framework were still a matter of debate in March 2015, and the impact on municipalities' financial situation was still very vague.

We will first describe, for each case and in line with the resilience model, the evolution of their vulnerability facing those shocks and the anticipatory and coping capacities deployed. Those elements will be sum-up in Table 2. We will then discuss the different dimensions of the resilience framework and related issues.

Case Study Results

Municipality A

The city shows a *high vulnerability*, before and after shocks. Its financial health is bad and has alerted the national office for public finances.[22] It is expressed as follows: high debt, toxic loans (but the new Mayor succeeded in securing one), a low level of DGF with regard to its size,[23] numerous properties but poorly maintained resulting in a small market value and in some needs for maintenance spending. At last, A is the central city of its urban area. As such, it assumes important expenses in services and infrastructure that benefit a much wider population than its own (cultural, sport, social and health facilities…).

From a socio-economic point of view, the city is also perceived as vulnerable. It suffers from a poor population, with great needs for public services but no tax potential. It lacks attractiveness for the benefit of nearby cities. Moreover the municipal geography makes it very difficult to manage and organise the territory and its public services (old city with narrow streets, past chaotic urbanisation, big differences in height that make the city centre difficult to access…).

Anticipatory capacities are weak. The financial crisis and its consequences on the city's resources have been downplayed by executives and politicians. At the date of the interviews, there were neither a chief financial officer, nor an elected representative in charge of finance, and there were no will to replace them. Except the financial department employees, no one seems to have financial competencies and recently elected representatives have a low awareness concerning financial issues. All this prevented the development of anticipatory capacities. As a consequence, planning and budgetary processes are very succinct and have not evolved with the crisis: incremental budgeting method, no management control or use of key indicators. Financial services provide some long-term planning, but its use for strategic reflexions seems limited.

This situation can be explained by serious issues with the organisational structure (very compartmentalised and characterised by a lack of communication between departments) and with the human resources management. There is at the same time a rapid turnover in top executives and no staff turnover. Coupled with an apparent lack of training and development for employees, it results in a lack of internal competencies.

Few coping capacities to be deployed. To face shocks on the budget balance and address financial vulnerability, the city mainly focused on buffering capacities: new ways of funding like developing private sponsorships for some small municipal events, increasing fees for organisations that use municipal assets, cost cuts through reduction of some secondary public services and cancellation of some cultural events and sell of assets even if a large part of them are in a bad condition. There is not much possibility to incur new debt as the repayment is limited by the small operating margin. And there is not much leeway on tax leverage as it would make the tax pressure unbearable for inhabitants and so there is no political will to activate it.

On the investment side, few buffering capacities were deployed as the city is committed on continuing projects because of some financing it has obtained. The mayor has so far refused to postpone the city-centre renewal project, as he believes it is key for the future of the city. This project could be characterised as an adaptive capacity launched to answer the problem of attractiveness, with the limit that its expected results are very uncertain. Moreover, it turns the city more vulnerable due to its financial scale (even if some important subsidies have been obtained).

Facing the crisis, the Mayor wants to strongly downsize, with not replacing 60% of staff retiring, and with reorganising the structure and the working methods, but so far, no reorganisation project was materialised to do so. To answer issues relative to the organisational structure and the lack of competencies, executives expressed the will to hire a management controller. At last, a restructuration of service pricing is also envisaged to increase resources. These elements could be seen as attempts to develop adaptive capacities, but in 2015 nothing had been implemented.

To conclude, City A was and is now even more vulnerable, and is perceived as such by managers. The city has already used most of its buffering capacities, and is trying to develop a few new ones to face the present crisis. But, this seems insufficient to face the next decrease in DGF. The development of adaptive capacities seems unsure and no transforming capacities have been identified. Moreover, anticipatory capacities are weak and has not been developed yet. These elements lead us to characterise the pattern of resilience of the city as a *powerless fatalist.* The crisis has not yet pushed to an evolution of the resilience pattern (see Fig. 1).

Municipality B
The city shows a high vulnerability. It has a fragile financial health with a very low operating balance. Despite a careful and strict management, expenses are high. As the central city of its urban area, it assumes important expenses in services and infrastructure (culture, sport but also social actions). Moreover, the city's political vision has led to high and rigid personnel costs (high level of public service with lots of employees, no externalisation at all, vision of the city as a job provider, strong influence of trade unions). At last, the aging and degraded properties require significant maintenance expenses.

From a socio-economic point of view, the city is perceived as vulnerable because of its poor population with high needs and a low tax potential (half of the population is tax-exempted). The city has low attractiveness because of the high tax pressure and an unattractive city centre. Economic competition by nearby cities is strong, and several shops, firms and administrations have moved to nearby cities that are more convenient and accessible. The relationship with those cities are strained, in particular inside the intercommunality.

City B has low anticipatory capacities, but is developing them thanks to the crisis. Executives and politicians have not well anticipated the present deterioration of public finances and the difficulties to come. Elected representatives lack of managerial competencies. They have great difficulty defining a strategy that takes into account the present threats and difficulties. They are not sufficiently aware of financial constraints and lack of leadership in defining and implementing a coherent political project. The awareness and the responsiveness is coming from managers recently hired that push others managers, but above all politicians, to change. Under their pressure, politicians' mindset is slowly changing. This pushes to the development of anticipatory capacities. By the past, incremental budgeting was the only method. But, in 2015, the executive team chose to elaborate the budget via the development of prospective scenarios, in order to better engage and raise elected representatives' awareness of the current situation. Long-term financial planning that only covered investment has changed to integrate operating activities. Some services are implementing dashboards and indicators, but there is no overall monitoring tool at the municipal level.

The city deployed few coping capacities, mainly buffering ones. For years, to balance budgets, taxes and operating charges (heat, commodities, supplies...) have been the only levers, but the city is now bound to find other solutions. Thus, in 2015, they decided to reduce personnel expenses and to lower subsidies to non-profit associations.[24] However, decisions were taken in a hurry and without a strategic vision, and savings are likely to be much lower than expected. The debt leverage will also be used, even if managers know it will quickly become unsustainable due to the weakness of the city self-financing. In addition, there are reflexions on properties sale or on postponing some investments.

Interviewed managers were conscious that those buffering capacities may permit to balance the 2015 budget, but will let the city more vulnerable in the close future. So, they are thinking about implementing some deeper changes that address the city's factors of vulnerability, reflecting the attempt to build-up adaptive capacities. Thus in 2015, a reflection, not supported by any management control process, has begun on the reorganisation and restructuring as a key prerequisite to lower personnel costs. Managers wish to question management methods, the organisational structure and the managerial culture. They plan to build an administrative development plan with employees, top managers and elected representatives. It should permit to mobilise employees, to clarify with elected representatives the strategic objectives and to raise their awareness of financial constraints. It should also help to change the culture towards greater efficiency and performance. Still, this plan is only at its first stage and it can only be hoped that it will strengthen the municipality coping capacity in the future. These actions are perceived as a challenge to managers and elected representatives.

An important structuring project, the rehabilitation of the city centre, is also emerging in order to stop departures of businesses and residents. However, this project appears to be beyond its means, to come late and to be an incomplete answer to the complex lack of attractiveness of the city. At last, managers interviewed have not mentioned a strategy to increase business tax revenues. From their point of view, it is the responsibility of the intercommunality and they are not aware of an existing strategy on this point.

To conclude, City B was and is still very vulnerable and its situation is likely to deteriorate in the close future. It has insufficient anticipatory, buffering and adaptive capacities and no transformative capacities. The development of more elaborated planning and budgeting methods should enhance the city's resilience. The large reorganisation plan wanted by the administration seems essential to cope with future crisis, but has not been put in action yet. These elements that remind the situation of Municipality A, lead us to characterise the pattern of resilience of the Municipality B as a *powerless fatalist, but with a growing level of responsiveness* (see Fig. 1).

Municipality C
City C had a low level of vulnerability before the crisis. Thanks to a political will to develop an industrial area, tax revenues are high and the city's financial health is good: low debt, contained personnel costs. There is a tradition of cautious management, with no eccentric or wasteful expenses. The staff is competent. However, the crisis has damaged the financial health and reduced the city's leeway.

The municipality's strategy, social-oriented due to the left wing tradition of the city, is at the same time ambitious and costly with lots of social housing built and a high level of public services. It is, on the one hand, a factor explaining the attractiveness of the city. On the other hand, it is a factor of financial vulnerability through the high level of expenses it generates and the low taxes generated by the population attracted by social housing.

With the crisis, City C has developed some anticipatory capacities. Before the DGF decrease, they were at a medium level: incremental budgeting, long-term planning of investment operations and to a lesser extent of operating flows, use of some monitoring tools but a lack of rigorous management control and of a cost analysis process. Most executives had not anticipated the DGF decrease and a majority of elected representatives do not comprehend well the financial challenges and are reluctant to alter the city's political project for financial reasons. However, with the crisis, executives try to raise elected representatives' awareness of the financial situation. And for the 2015 budget, cost analysis has been developed to assist decision making and to question each budget item. But there were still no will to hire a management controller.

Coping capacities also evolved thanks to the crisis. Before 2015, the city coped with previous crisis using its buffering capacities, mainly cutting departments operating costs. But in 2015, remaining buffering capacities appeared insufficient: few reserves, low tax leverage and limited assets (most of municipal properties had yet been used to build social housing). Leeway were in increasing debt, in cutting back personnel cost (mainly with not replacing retired staff), in postponing some investments and in questioning the extent of public services and their pricing, even though elected representatives were reluctant to do so.

The weakness of buffering capacities from 2015 and the scale of the DGF shock pushed executives and the Mayor to question and develop their adaptive capacities. Top managers are urging to change working methods towards more efficiency. In collaboration with employees, they attempt to create new leeway in operating costs and payroll. Even if the municipal culture is very reticent towards externalisation, managers mentioned the possibility to externalise some small services. The performant organisational structure (good cooperation between managers, good communication between civil servants and with elected representatives, well-established decision processes) and the culture of cautious management should enable an efficient restructuring.

Moreover, for 10 years, the city has built an ambitious urban development strategy that provides it with a healthy development in the long time. They have been preserving and developing an industrial area that have provided the city with important business tax resources (now it's the intercommunality that collects them, and then repays a static part to the city). In the residential development projects, managers in charge showed very good capacities to find co-funding. This strategy can be seen, on the one hand, as a strong adaptive capacity permitting to face financial shocks as it ensures the town future revenues and dynamism and on the other hand, as a vulnerability factor as it increases investment and operating costs and brings rigidity (investment cannot be postponed because of commitment to co-financiers).

To conclude, City C's vulnerability is perceived as increasing with the crisis. In response, the city has developed new anticipatory capacities and deployed buffering and adaptive ones. However, no transforming capacity has been identified. At the time of our interviews, managers perceived that coping with the DGF would be easier than with the new territorial organisation of the Metropole. Facing this latter situation, they felt lost and didn't know how to cope or what capacities they should deploy. These elements lead us to characterise the pattern of resilience of the municipality as a *reactive adapter* (see Fig. 1).

Municipality D
City D has a low vulnerability. Its financial situation has been healthy for a long time, with strong and diversified resources and important financial reserves. The organisational structure and the political stability of the municipality are

also factors that lower vulnerability. The city benefits from a great attractiveness to businesses and inhabitants, which is partly the result of the strategic vision of the Mayor and the CEO.

Over time, the city deployed high anticipatory and coping capacities. The city has well-developed management control and planning tools and systems. However, they limit long-term planning due to institutional and financial instability and favour flexibility and a careful management of reserves. Politicians and executives have a good understanding and awareness of financial risks and are risk averse. Interviewees claimed that this latter characteristic is essential, as it often spare them being in difficult situations.[25] Unlike the three other cities, they anticipated from 2008, the effects of the economic crisis on local finances.

To cope with shocks, the municipality has important buffering capacities. The CEO is permanently managing to create and maintain some leeway, with a will to preserve low operational costs, tax and debt level. The city also have important financial reserves that can be used as buffers to absorb possible decrease in resources. When debt market conditions are good, managers incur new debt to constitute reserves and anticipate shocks. To absorb the 2015 decrease in DGF, the city plans to slightly increase taxes and to decrease some operating costs, such as grants to associations.

The city also shows good adaptive capacities. Managers are permanently working on adapting the organisational structure and the internal communication to enable low costs and to adapt public services to population needs. They look for efficiency gains in operating and investments activities (e.g. assets that are not used are systematically sold). To do so, management control processes have been implemented for six years. The CEO insisted on hiring a management controller to assist him on successive reforms and restructuration. The management controller has a support role to chief departments in designing and implementing new policies. Moreover, managers have a good awareness of financial constraints and integrate them in their day to day management. They often compare themselves to nearby cities through informal knowledge exchange with neighbours' managers.

There is also a will to preserve flexibility that is much more marked than in the three others municipalities, as illustrated by the following elements. A special attention is paid to the people hired to ensure their open-mindedness. Binding internal procedures are limited and staff autonomy is favoured. The CEO is reluctant to invest in projects only to benefit from a grant: he doesn't trust the central government and fears that the grant stops while rigid operating costs would continue. The city managed to keep its business taxes and have not transferred them to the intercommunality.[26] The CEO and the mayor are reluctant to communicate some precise long-term objectives to the population, and prefer large missions that are easier to adapt or adjust in a changing environment.

Last adaptive capacity, the city implemented a consistent attractiveness strategy towards inhabitants and especially businesses.

Table 2. Comparison of Resilience Dimensions.

	A	B	C	D
Budgetary position	*Low positive*	*Low positive*	*High positive*	*High positive*
Volatility	*Low*	*High*	*Low*	*High*
Financial shocks	Exchange rate – Successive State decisions towards LGs[a] – DGF decrease	Successive State decisions towards LGs[a] – DGF decrease	Territorial reforms – Successive State decisions towards LGs[a] – DGF decrease	Territorial reforms – DGF decrease
Level of vulnerability and evolution after shocks	*High/increasing* Bad financial health, High debt, toxic loans, many assets but poorly maintained, high centrality expenses Socio-economic factors: Poor population, low attractiveness	*High/increasing* Bad financial health, high & rigid personnel costs, high centrality expenses, degraded assets Socio-economic factors: poor population, low attractiveness and competition by nearby cities	*Low/increasing to medium* Good financial health (but in deterioration), high level of business taxes Socio-economic factors: poor population, strong attractiveness	*Low/increasing* Good financial health, high level of business taxes (even if volatile), important but decreasing reserves Socio-economic factors: strong attractiveness
Anticipatory capacity and evolution after shocks	*Low* (Before) Low financial awareness and competencies – Incremental budgeting – weak financial planning – No management control or monitoring tools (After) growing financial awareness, will to implement management control processes	*Low* (Before) Low financial awareness, Incremental budgeting, weak financial planning, no management control (After) Long-term operating and investment planning, growing financial awareness, scenario analysis for budgeting	*Medium* (Before) Low financial awareness, Long-term planning, Monitoring tools, but incremental budgeting, lack rigorous management control and cost analysis process (After) Development of cost analysis for budgeting process, growing financial awareness	*High* (Before) Great financial awareness – Good anticipation of shocks – Management control processes – Tax and LT planning (After) Switch from long term to medium term planning because of increased instability

Coping capacity	Low	Low	Medium	High
	Buffering: low — Cost cuts, selling of assets, reduction of secondary public services, deferring investments, new way of funding services	*Buffering: low* — Decrease in subsidies to associations, in personnel costs, reduction of public services quality and number, deferring investments, selling of assets	*Buffering: medium* — Cost cuts, debt increase, tax leverage, reduction of secondary public services, deferring investments	*Buffering: high* — Important reserves, cost cuts, prioritisation of investments, high tax leverage
	Adapting? — Urban renewal plan (but with uncertain effects)	*Adapting?* — Reorganisation plans (but nothing implemented yet). Urban renewal plan (but with very uncertain effects)	*Adapting: high* — Strong and coherent urban renewal and development plan, pro-active in attracting businesses, organisational restructuration	*Adapting: high* — Pro-active in attracting businesses, assets selling policy, control management and search for efficiency, search for flexibility
	Transforming: No	*Transforming:* No	*Transforming:* No	*Transforming:* Re-positioning capacity
Pattern of resilience	*Powerless fatalist*	*Powerless fatalist*	*Reactive adapter*	*Pro-active adapter*

[a] Decreases in grants, reform of local taxes, increase in LGs mandatory expenditures.

The city also shows a strong transforming capacity. A few years ago, to face the loss and ageing of its inhabitants, the city has operated a new strategy to attract younger population. Some big long-term investments in housing and transportation have been done. This was thanks to a great political ability of the Mayor to negotiate with central and other local governments.

These elements lead us to characterise the pattern of resilience of the Municipality D as a *pro-active adapter* (see Fig. 1).

Discussion

Our study shows that all four municipalities enhanced their responsiveness with the 2015 crisis, but the deployment of their anticipatory and coping capacities have been different, showing different resilience patterns. Municipalities A and B appeared very vulnerable before and after the crisis, with few capacities to cope with the crisis. Municipality C was less vulnerable, with a solid financial situation before the crisis. But after having used most of its buffering capacities and because of a lack of anticipatory capacities, the municipality turned more vulnerable after the crisis. Municipality D has a low vulnerability that it could preserve, thanks to its anticipatory and coping capacities (Fig. 1).

This case study first permits to better describe resilience dimensions and to catch their evolution to the crisis. Vulnerability of the four cities have increased with the crisis. It is determined by a large set of internal factors, changeable across cities: financial health (cash-flow, debt, toxic loans, level and condition of assets), performance of the organisational structure, management team skills, political stability…

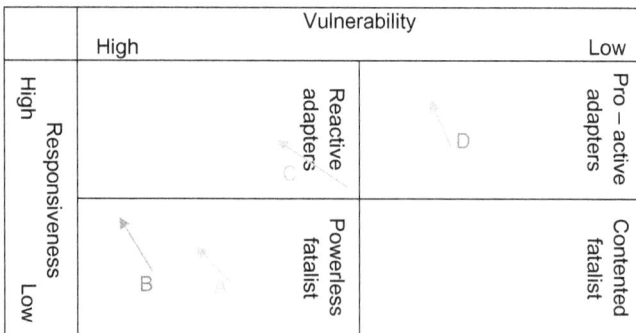

Fig. 1. Patterns of Financial Resilience of the Four Municipalities Studied.

Important centrality expenses are also a cause of vulnerability, as shown in Municipalities A and B. In Case B, this is also the consequence of a bad relation with the intercommunality that should share out those costs.

Socio-economic factors can cause vulnerability to be perceived as higher: population level of poverty, municipalities that are in areas out of the way, lack attractiveness or face an exodus from their city centre and territory as in cities A and B. In those cases, developing the necessary capacities to attract population and businesses and boost the territory is perceived as a great challenge.

The 2015 shock that have been perceived as a major one, pushed to the development of anticipatory capacities. Municipalities A, B and C attempted to improve their budgeting methods and short-term planning to face the crisis and its resulting uncertainty. At times, the uncertain present conjuncture also results in the general drop of long-term planning as the figures are not perceived as reliable, as shown in Case D.

General awareness and awareness of financial vulnerability sources from managers, but above all from politicians, also increased. This variable appears as a key anticipatory capacity, as shown in Municipalities A and B where newly elected politicians focused on implementing their election pledges and haven't integrated the financial consequences of the crisis, leading to an increased vulnerability.

All municipalities relied on buffering capacities to cope with crisis (increasing taxes, fees and debt, downsizing and cutting operating costs, postponing investments, selling assets, and for Municipality D a careful management of reserves…) but Cities A, B and in a lesser extent C, relied almost exclusively on them. In those cities, buffering capacities had been already deployed to face previous minor shocks and were perceived as insufficient to cope with the 2015 crisis.

Some adapting capacities appears key to cope with shocks. Municipality D focuses on flexibility as an important adapting capacity. In all four cases, managers and politicians believe that the capacity to develop and preserve the city's attractiveness is a key factor, for example via long-term development projects. But the pertinence and the implementation quality of these projects is crucial to the development of an adapting capacity. Cities A and B mayors focus on projects of redevelopment of their city centre and perceive those projects as a relevant solution to answer attractiveness issues, but managers, in particular in City B, think it is insufficient to cope.

At last, our case study suggests that municipalities have not developed much transforming capacities, as only Case D showed some. The few shocks that affected the local environment may explain this situation and future shocks may enable their development.

Second, the study underlines the fact that the various resilience dimensions influence each other without a clear causes and consequences framework. It well illustrates the dynamic of the concept and the interdependence of factors.

The prior sources of vulnerability and the perceived level of vulnerability affect the municipality vulnerability after a financial shock has hit. A lack of anticipatory or coping capacities drives to an increase in vulnerability, but perceived vulnerability can push to develop adapting capacities. Relations between coping capacities are also stressed as adapting capacities appear as solutions to develop buffering ones.

The two-way relations between vulnerability and capacities and between capacities is well illustrated by Case C. There, the low perceived vulnerability prevented the development of sufficient anticipatory capacities. Before 2015, existing buffering and adapting capacities had permitted to cope with minor shocks and to maintain a low vulnerability. But when facing a major shock like the DGF decrease, managers perceived an increasing vulnerability that pushed them to develop different adapting capacities (restructuration, new working methods) in order to develop new buffering capacities (leeway in personnel costs).

Moreover, *the level of anticipative capacities explains the development of coping capacities.* The low awareness of politicians in Cases A, B and C has inhibited the development of adapting or transforming capacities and has pushed to rely mainly on buffering capacities. On the contrary, in Case D, the mistrust of the State and the awareness of risks linked to the economic conjuncture has led to the development of various type of coping capacities.

Adapting capacities appear as key elements to re-create buffering capacities, but their development must be anticipated, meaning a need for anticipatory capacities. In the four municipalities, managers believe it is necessary to implement restructuration plans or management control process (that can be characterised as adapting capacities) to re-create buffering capacities (such as leeway in labour costs or in operating costs of departments), but only City D really set them up. In this case of pro-active resilience, adapting capacities offer a long-term perspective that enables to maintain its buffering capacities. On the contrary, in Cases A, B or C, it is the use and destruction of buffering capacities that acted as a signal of the necessity to restructure the organisation and work processes. As a consequence, it came too late to prevent a deterioration in their vulnerability.

Third, the study illustrates how the political strategy interacts with the municipality pattern of resilience, sometimes in an antagonist way. A high social orientation not coupled with a dynamic strategy to attract businesses leads to a high vulnerability, such as in Case B. There is a need for a mix, as attempted in Case C where the social missions are very ambitious thanks to high revenues from industries. But this situation is difficult to reach for some municipalities that do not have the power to attract businesses (e.g. because this task is assumed by the intercommunality) or that are in depressed areas. In Case B, the municipal strategy orientated towards social issues is disconnected from the intercommunality strategy that is in charge of the economic development. The situation is worsened by the managers' perception that nothing can be done to attract businesses and do not wish to cooperate with the intercommunality.

In the absence of a mix, social policies can be analysed as a factor of financial vulnerability. They often lead to higher expenditure (investment in social housing, higher demand for services...) and lower resources (low price of services, attraction of poorer population with lower tax leverage...). This result illustrates the complex role of municipalities nowadays, aiming to strengthen their resilience, but also to achieve their public goals. This questions the role of the central government in designing LGs' financial environment, to enable the social missions. For example, the compensation the French State pays for social housing appears insufficient to favour resilience of socially oriented cities.

Moreover, resilience concept is also questioned by some policies that can at the same time be factors of vulnerability and interesting coping capacity. For example, urban renewing policies can be considered as a strong adaptive capacity that prepares the city to future challenges, in a long-term perspective. The capacity to find co-funding is also key. But those policies are also a vulnerability factor as they bind to high investment expenses that can hardly be modified, even in time of crisis and even more when co-funding exists. It is the case of Cities A and C that received State subsidies that bind them to continue their projects and to complete the funding. These elements question the concept of resilience in its short and long-term perspectives and illustrate the dynamic and dependent nature of resilience. A pro-active behaviour would try to anticipate effect of those policies on vulnerability, and would develop capacities to cope with their potential negative effects

CONCLUSION

This chapter presents a case study on the resilience of four French middle size municipalities, following the 2008 crisis. In France, the crisis has had a delayed impact on French LGs. Municipalities, even if they were aware of the bad economic conjuncture, have felt the 2015 decrease in the DGF as the major shock that affected their situation.

Our study shows that all four municipalities enhanced their responsiveness with the 2015 crisis. Depending on how the shock has been perceived, municipalities took up different paths of resilience, building up or investing in different anticipatory and coping capacities. Buffering capacities were present in all cases to cope with shocks. Conversely, adapting and transforming capacities were not as prevalent, but most executives consider them as key elements to develop.

Pro-active resilient municipalities are likely to rely on a mix of capacities. This research shows the necessity to develop and constantly maintain anticipatory and coping capacities that are suitable for tackling the municipalities' specific vulnerability sources. If the vulnerability sources and their scope is not understood well by key actors such as politicians, it is the task of executives to warn in time or to implement tools and instruments that enable politicians to recognise and tackle vulnerabilities. The central State has also a role to play in urging LGs to develop anticipatory capacities such as management control or more sophisticated budgeting processes. For the moment, their development is dependent on each municipality's choice.

The case study confirms the importance of the resilience concept in professionals' thought. In four cases, even if they were mostly not aware of the theoretical concept, interviewees were concerned by resilience issues: they wondered how to cope with the crisis, they have discussed the limits of what we characterised as buffering capacities and the necessity to develop what we analysed as adapting capacity. They questioned their capacity to resist, to become less vulnerable and to keep offering the same level of services. They wondered how they should adapt to this morose economic conjuncture.

This study also has implications for research. It supports the interest of the financial resilience concept to understand and explain divergent impact of crisis on financial situations. It offers a more dynamic and broader framework than classic performance models, as it includes an analysis on capacities that goes beyond 'classic' efficiency instruments. However, it is a complex model of relations between capacities and perceived vulnerability, each elements being a determinant as well as an antecedent of the others. Research needs to go further into these relationships and needs to better categorise each variable.

NOTES

1. Article 34 of Law n° 77-574, 7 June 1977.
2. GDP decline in 2009: −2.9% in France, −5.6% in Germany, −4.3% in the United Kingdom or −4.4% in average for UE (INSEE).
3. DGF = Dotation globale de fonctionnement. It represented 24% of LGs current revenues in 2008 (Observatoire des finances locales, 2014).
4. French public deficit rose from 3.2% in 2008 to 6.8% in 2010, while LGs' deficit reduced from 0.5% in 2008 to 0.1% in 2010 (*source*: National Accounting − INSEE).
5. 'LGs in shocks' run as a headline 'La gazette des communes', the local public sector newspaper.
6. DGF evolution in billion euros: 2008: 40/2009: 40.8/2010: 41.2/2011 to 2013: 41.4/2014: 40.1/2015: 36.6/2016: 33.9 (Observatoire des finances locales, 2015).
7. Information in this section is from www.vie-publique.fr (Legal and Administrative Information Branch, under the authority of the Secretary General of the Government) and from www.collectivites-locales.gouv.fr (official website of the national offices for local governments and for public finances ('Direction générale des Collectivités locales' and the 'Direction générale des Finances Publiques'). Statistics and numbers are from INSEE (National institute of statistics and Economic Studies), from (Observatoire des finances locales, 2014) and from (Direction générale des collectivités locales, 2015).

8. Intercommunalities are public organisations that enable municipalities to cooperate on actions going from a shared management of public services to the development of collective local development projects.

9. Law n° 2015-991/7 August 2015.

10. For example, primary school is the responsibility of municipalities, middle school: departments, and high school: regions.

11. Tax paid by businesses, based on the value of their fixed assets. The rate was set by LGs. It represented 44% of LGs' tax revenues. It has been replaced by several taxes which are smaller in amount. Moreover, some of them are very volatile and their rate is not set by the LG.

12. State representative at the local level.

13. Numbers in this paragraph concern the municipal level for 2013.

14. In line with inflation, but also due to decentralisation, to increase in personal costs, social expenditure and debt interest.

15. Numbers on service fees are very difficult to obtain, but it can be evaluated at less than 10% of operating incomes.

16. If the budget must be balanced, its implementation can lead to surplus and so to cash reserves: debt is issued to cover an investment, but the investment is postponed.

17. Structured debt combining traditional bank loans and derivatives. Often linked to non-traditional indexes as the Swiss exchange rate.

18. Source for accounting data: www.collectivites-locales.gouv.fr

19. The DGF calculation, based on population, surface area and other criteria, is opaque. It often creates inequalities between what is received by comparable municipalities. The need for a reform is certain, but it has not been implemented so far.

20. Even if departments have the lead for social missions, municipalities also animate a social action at their territorial level, through a dedicated municipal social centre.

21. In particular, the 2012 primary school timetables reform bound municipalities to organise and finance extra activities in schools.

22. The national office for public finances (Direction générale des Finances Publiques) monitors LGs, on the basis of financial ratios related to taxes, debt, operating expenses and profit.

23. See footnote n°16 for precision on the DGF calculation.

24. In France, LGs are active financiers of non-profit associations working at the local level in fields such as culture, education or social. Lately, these associations are suffering a lot from a decrease in their subsidies.

25. For example, just as many municipalities were incurring structured (and often toxic) loans that seemed very profitable at that time, City D executives kept refusing pressure from banks to sign up such contracts, as they judge it was too uncertain and risky.

26. This situation changed in 2016 with the Paris metropole.

REFERENCES

Barbera, C., Jones, M., Korac, S., Saliterer, I., & Steccolini, I. (2017). Governmental financial resilience under austerity in Austria, England and Italy: How do local governments cope with financial shocks? Public Administration, forthcoming.

Direction générale des collectivités locales. (2015). *Les collectivités locales en chiffres 2015*.

Observatoire des finances locales. (2014). *Les finances des collectivités locales en 2014 État des lieux*.

Observatoire des finances locales. (2015). *Les finances des Collectivités locales en 2015*.

CHAPTER 7

A CUSHIONED IMPACT OF THE FINANCIAL CRISIS – LOCAL GOVERNMENT FINANCIAL RESILIENCE IN GERMANY

Ulf Papenfuß, Iris Saliterer and Nora Albrecht

ABSTRACT

This chapter investigates financial resilience of German local governments. The local governments included in this analysis challenged the applicability of the financial resilience concept by reporting no significant direct impact of the financial crisis during the last 10 years. This is also in line with more general observations suggesting that Germany weathered the financial crisis successfully and without the dramatic effects on its local governments that are observable in other countries. During semi-structured interviews with key administrative decision-makers, it turned out that the financial crisis impacted the local governments' commercial tax revenues only in its aftermath, and respondents rather highlighted the refugee crisis in 2015 and sudden changes in the tax base caused by relocation, bankruptcy or economic turmoil as financial shocks. More general trends, for example, upper governmental levels devolving more service and administrative responsibility without sufficient compensation, and in particular long-term issues, that is, high debt levels magnifying effects of financial shocks, seem to challenge German local governments. Some cases included in this investigation seem reluctant to make conflict-laden, but necessary changes, and feel exposed to policies and regulations by upper governmental levels. This creates uncertainty and at

Governmental Financial Resilience: International Perspectives on how Local Governments Face Austerity
Public Policy and Governance, Volume 27, 115–134
Copyright © 2017 by Emerald Publishing Limited
ISSN: 2053-7697/doi:10.1108/S2053-769720170000027007

times leaves them in a sense of helplessness and infeasibility of proper planning. However, the need for investing resources to build up internal capacities has already been pointed out. From a financial resilience perspective, this seems even more important in a context where relying on buffering was feasible, but might prove insufficient once other internal capacities are required to tackle local governments' financial vulnerabilities.

Keywords: Germany; local governments; debt; refugee crisis; task devolvement; resilience

INTRODUCTION

Germany is the largest economy in the Euro area and the fourth largest economy in the world; it holds a top position in international trade – its share of world exports of merchandise and commercial services accounts for 6.6%, succeeded only by China (10%) and the United States (12%) (figures based on World Trade Organization, 2016). The country can be described as a wealthy society (annual GDP per capita of 47,221 US dollars, OECD, 2016a) with low-income inequality in comparison to other countries (Gini coefficient of 0.283 in 2013, World Bank, 2013). Germany has 82.2 million inhabitants, of which a considerable number are foreign citizens (8.7 million or 10.5%). An even higher number of citizens have a migration background (17.1 million or 20.8%) (Statistisches Bundesamt, 2016a, estimated figures for 2015). The country's population has undergone considerable changes during the last decades, not least due to the German reunification process of 1990, where the former German Democratic Republic (DDR) has been dismantled and the transition from socialism brought economic turmoil for the population of the new eastern states of the Federal Republic of Germany. Unemployment rose almost immediately from an official zero to over 15%, and people massively migrated to the western states (6% of the eastern population during 1989–1991) (Burda & Hunt, 2001).

While the number of foreign citizens immigrating to Germany – after a high in 1992 (about 600,000) – stayed under 200,000 for over two decades, Germany saw a large influx of non-EU citizen immigrants and refugees in 2015 (about 1.1 mio., see Statistisches Bundesamt, 2016b). Germany's working age population has been constantly decreasing over the last decades (OECD, 2016a), however, the recent inflow of refugees and migrants bears the opportunity to add to the labour force after effective integration into society (OECD, 2016b). During the financial crisis in 2008 and 2009 and the subsequent economic recession, Germany's strong economic position did not protect it from a severe impact on the nation's GDP (decrease in GDP by 6.8% during 2008 and 2009).

Public finances deteriorated as a result of stabilising the banking sector and issuing stimulus packages for the economy: after three years of constantly reducing national debt in the mid-2000s, it rose markedly during and immediately after the crisis from 64.1% in 2007 to 84.5% in 2010 and 86.6% in 2012. A similar picture is also shown for the government deficit, where after a slight surplus in 2007 (0.19%) the deficit peaked at −4.22% in 2010 (OECD, 2016a). However, following the definition applied in this book (Barbera, Jones, Korac, Saliterer, & Steccolini, 2017), financial resilience goes beyond merely resisting a disturbance and encompasses both the anticipatory capacity to set early counter-measures, as well as the rapidity of returning to a stable or even a more favourable point. On the one hand, four years after the crisis, the country was recovering well with a solid annual growth of 2.1%. In fact, it was among the few Western European countries that had surpassed its pre-crisis peak in real GDP (OECD, 2014). Both the budget deficit as well as the debt level began to decrease again in 2011 (OECD, 2016a).

On the other hand, Germany was able to constrain the national unemployment rate, which saw only a marginal rise during the crisis years (from 7.53% in 2008 to 7.74% in 2009, and still below the OECD average) (OECD, 2011, 2016a) and continued its long-term decrease (4.98% in 2014) soon after accounting for the lowest unemployment rate in both the Euro zone (11.6% in 2014) as well as the European Union (10.21% in 2014) area (Eurostat, 2016, OECD, 2016a). Adopting fiscal consolidation measures like tight limits to the federal government deficit and balanced budget requirements for its states (*Länder*) early in 2009, the country seems to have positioned itself well to cope with the crisis impact and to facilitate early recovery of its economy and public finances. In addition, by creating a Stability Council of the Minister of Economy, Minister of Finance and the Finance Ministers of all states, Germany developed its capacity to avoid future budgetary crises by monitoring the federal as well as states' budgets and building an early warning system of fiscal distress (OECD, 2010).

However, what might sound like a success story in fact reveals a different picture when focusing on the sub-national level. First, it has been pointed out that the institutional setting of division of responsibilities in the federal republic might have complicated the required rapid decisions on all governmental levels. Second, the federal government issued several investment packages to stimulate the economy also at the state and government level. The funds were dedicated mainly to additional investments in municipalities, focusing on the areas of education and infrastructure, explicitly excluding waste water systems and public transport. The argument was that the additional federal funds not be used to replace municipal funds for regular maintenance (OECD, 2011). Considering the increased expenditures in unemployment benefits, cuts in taxes and social contributions as a result of the economic distress after the financial crisis, as well as the long-term development of increasing social security expenditures put a squeeze on local government budgets, leaving them in a seemingly worse off

situation for the years to come. This chapter therefore aims to explore the
financial resilience of German cities. Situated in a wealthy country context and
one of the strongest local government systems in Europe (Wollmann, 2004),
they represent a highly interesting setting for the research on financial resilience. The chapter is structured as follows. First, we describe the main features
of local governments in Germany and thus introduce the context of research.
The methods section provides the case selection and investigation process
before the results of the analysis are presented from a within-case perspective.
Findings from an across-case analysis and conclusions are provided in the last
section.

LOCAL GOVERNMENT IN GERMANY

Germany is a federal state in which the principles of subsidiarity and local
autonomy play an important role. Each of the 16 states (Länder) has its own
rules regarding the organisation of local government. The German local government is the nearest to the citizen level within the administrative layers (federal, state, local level). It is subdivided into counties (*Kreise*), municipalities and
municipalities associations (Reichard, 2003). Although according to the constitution, municipalities are an integral part of the country's states, the principle
of self-administration offers certain autonomy. From a formal view, Germany
therefore is characterised by a two-layer administration (federal and states
level), but the functions and competencies devolved to the local governments in
fact accounts for them to be the third administrative level (Kuhlmann &
Wollmann, 2013, p. 77). The country has 11,084 municipalities with an average
population of 1,711. The number of municipalities varies highly across the 16
states, from 52 (Saarland) to 2,305 (Rheinland-Palatinate), and so does the
average population per municipality — excluding the three cities with special
statute as city states,[1] the population per municipality ranges from 559
(Rheinland-Pfalz) to 20,824 (Nordrhein-Westfalen). The latter is also the state
with the most large cities — 15 out of 39 cities with a population over 200,000
are located in Nordrhein-Westfalen. The vast majority, 86% of the municipalities, have less than 10,000 inhabitants.

   Local governments consist of the local council and a directly elected 'strong
mayor' who, besides exercising political leadership as the chair of the council,
also serves as the chief executive officer and thus the administrative leader of
the local government (Wollmann, 2004). Municipalities serve a dual purpose:
their own responsibility comprises social and cultural services, water and sewer,
and public transport as well as urban planning and development, and tasks
delegated to them by the respective state, for example, construction supervision,
local policing (see Kuhlmann & Wollmann, 2013, Wehling & Kost, 2010). With
regards to their total expenditure, German municipalities' main functions

however are social protection (33.2%), 15.9% on education and 12.9% on economic affairs. About 18% is spent for general public services (Eurostat, 2016)

This wide variety of competencies accounts for a high autonomy of German local governments in political and functional terms. However, allocation of resources is centralised and local governments rely strongly on revenue shares distributed by the federal level and on state grants, which significantly constrains their fiscal autonomy (Wollmann, 2004). Grants account for 35% of total revenues (non-earmarked grants 21.7%, earmarked grants 13.2%) and revenue shares for 17.6% of local governments' total revenues (income tax shares 15.6%, value added tax shares 2%). Their main own revenue sources are own taxes: business tax (17.9% of total revenues), land tax (6% of total revenues) and other municipal taxes like dog tax, amusement tax, or hunting and fishing licence tax (together 0.4%), as well as service fees (9.7%) (Federal Ministry of Finance, 2014). Local governments can set business tax and land tax rates individually. However, on the one hand, businesses are geographically mobile, which in fact sets limits to raising tax rates. Moreover, this tax source is highly cyclical, which has been shown not least during the financial crisis, where business tax revenues plummeted by 21% in 2009 (Federal Ministry of Finance, 2014). On the other hand, the land tax is based on outdated valuations of the land value, thus this revenue source is stagnating (OECD, 2016b).

It has to be pointed out that the respective share of sources differs across the states, largely due to the special status of eastern states after the German reunification. Roughly 10 years after the reunification, GDP per capita in the eastern states accounted for about 60% of that in the western states, and overall, the figure did not change much in the last years (67% of GDP per capita in the western states) (Bundesministerium für Wirtschaft und Energie, 2016). This relative economic weakness in the eastern states required western states to provide special financial support to their eastern counterparts. However, the significantly lower GDP per capita in the eastern states puts considerable pressure on the financial situation of local governments in the east. In 2013, land tax revenues per capita in eastern states accounted for only 70.3% of those in western states, and business tax revenues in eastern states equalled 57.7% the amount in western states (Federal Ministry of Finance, 2014).

The financial situation of local governments during the decade before the financial crisis was marked by an up and down – the local government budget balance in 2001 was –4.09 billion Euro and the deficit peaked in 2003 with –8.4 billion, only to recover significantly in 2006 to a plus of 2.76 billion, followed by two extraordinary strong years in 2006 (+8.18 billion) and 2007 (+8.35 billion). The crisis hit the local level in 2009 with a slump in budget balance of –7.47 billion. Recent years brought a budgetary ease with a slight plus (+2.59 billion in 2012, +0.24 billion in 2014), but short-term borrowing at the local level more than doubled between 2004 and 2013. Local governments have claimed that urgent investments in transport infrastructure and educational facilities in municipalities would require additional resources of 3–5% of GDP in 2015 (Arnold, Boettcher, Freier, Geißler, & Holler, 2015; Federal Ministry of Finance, 2014). This investment gap results partly from high spending on social cash transfers (e.g. basic social benefits and housing benefits for the long-term unemployed). Federal transfers equalise tax revenues per capita across the states, but do not take social cash transfers into account. Since local governments that exert high social cash transfers invest significantly less, in 2015 the federal government introduced a special fund to support financially weak local governments. This will provide grants for investment in hospitals and educational facilities, urban development, telecommunication infrastructure, energy efficiency, clean air and noise protection between 2015 and 2018 (OECD, 2016b).

Earmarked grants by the federal government are an important source of local government revenues also in two other topical areas: child care and refugee and migrant settlement services. Between 2015 and 2017, the federal government will support municipalities in the expansion of child care with three billion Euro. This is a result of a law enacted in 2013 (KiföG, 2008) entitling all children older than 12 months to a place in a kindergarten or similar child care facility. However, the constitution limits federal government funding for child care to capital spending and prevents co-funding for compulsory education services. Municipalities provide consultation services and housing for newly arriving asylum seekers (refugees) and migrants and are obliged to take in a certain number of this group according to a formula that takes into account states' population and income levels. The federal government supports these services with additional funds and provides grants for projects of conflict prevention and social cohesion at the local level (Bundesamt für Migration und Flüchtlinge, 2016; OECD, 2016b).

Governmental accounting in Germany can take a cash-based approach (*kamerale Haushaltswirtschaft/Kameralistik*) or an accrual-based approach (*Doppelte Buchführung/Doppik*). While accounting reforms towards accrual accounting are implemented at the state and local level, the central government maintains a cash-based accounting model. Each state regulates the accounting system for local governments located in its territory, which is why accounting practices differ from one state to another (Ridder, Bruns, & Spier, 2005). Most states have started implementing accrual accounting from the mid-2000s with transition periods until 2016 latest, however three states allow their local governments to choose between (modified) cash accounting and accrual accounting (Bayern, Schleswig-Holstein, Thüringen) (see Ernst & Young, 2012, Holtkamp, 2012). It has been criticised that the German states apply very heterogeneous standards that are not based on IPSAS, which leads to a complexity in the accounting arrangements in place and hinders comparability across states and with other countries (Ernst & Young, 2012).

METHODS

The methods of data collection and analysis followed a similar approach as in the other country examples presented in this book. The first step of the purposive sampling of cases was the selection of local governments that would be comparable across the different regions and states (*Länder*). In light of their functional and administrative responsibility as well as institutional pressures, comparability of local governments is ensured among the country's 'single-tier' cities (*kreisfreie Städte*), that are not part of a county and thus are responsible for all local government services. These local governments generally are the ones with the most population within a state. On average, single-tier cities have about 250,000 inhabitants, ranging from around 34,000 to 3.5 mio. (represented by the capital Berlin). However, the selection of this type of local government means that local governments of one state (Saarland) were excluded from further analysis, as this state has no single-tier cities. In a second step, we used the combination of (1) the average cash balance *(Finanzmittelsaldo)* and (2) its volatility over eight years (2006–2013)[2] to select cases that are polar, but at the same time also well represented, that is, occur frequently. Due to missing financial data we included 84 of the 103 single-tier cities in the analysis. G1 was selected as it shows an average cash balance around zero (−0.01%) and medium volatility (6.3%). G2 was selected as it shows a positive cash balance (−3.48%) and low levels of volatility (3.0%). G4 was selected as it shows a positive cash balance (10.12%) and high levels of volatility (14.2%) while G3 and G5 show opposite signs, a high negative cash balance and high levels of volatility. The following table shows the development of the cash balance for the selected cases between 2008 and 2013 (Fig. 1).

COLLECTION OF DATA AND ANALYSIS

The data collection comprised semi-structured interviews with administrative leaders in the selected local governments, collection of statistical data, reports and financial statements. The interviews were conducted in March 2016. In three of the five cases, we carried out two interviews each — with the Chief Executive Officer (CEO — *Leiter Hauptamt/Allgemeines Amt*) and the Chief Financial Officer (CFO — *Kämmerer*). In the other two cases, recurring requests for interviews with both respondents were non-successful and we were able to carry out only one interview per case: in G5 with the CEO, in G2 with the CFO. This resulted in a total of eight interviews, which on average lasted between 30 and 75 minutes and included open-ended questions on the financial health of the local government, its main financial and non-financial goals, main risks, shocks that the local government had experienced during the last 10 years, how it had identified them and how it responded to the impact. The

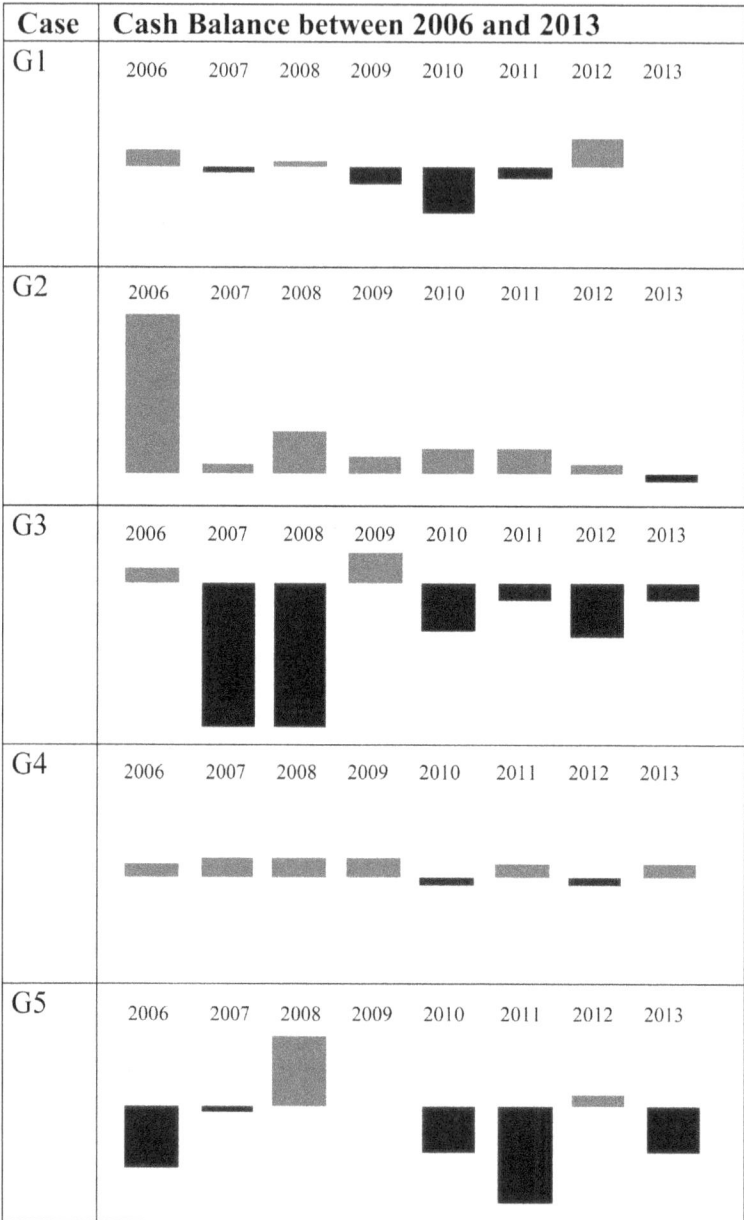

Fig. 1. Cash Balance of the Selected German Cases.

interviews were recorded, transcribed in full and a qualitative content analysis was performed to provide information on the different dimensions of the local governments' financial resilience. However, perceptions about the financial condition, main risks and actions of coping with shocks as a surface expression for coping capacities were verified using triangulation of data from the secondary sources mentioned above. First, within-case analyses allowed the identification of distinct resilience patterns of the five local governments. In the following, the respective results are presented for each case separately. In a next step, an across-case analysis was performed to trace out the recurring themes with relevance to local government financial resilience in the German context.

RESULTS

Before discussing the results and findings for each case, it is important to point out that across all cases, the respondents did not seem used to discussing financial shocks or events that impacted the local governments' finances over time. This issue accounted for a varying quantity and quality of the collected data and limitations in the content analysis. Performing the interviews at times proved difficult, as most of them did not identify unforeseen events that had a negative impact on their financial condition during the past years and, even more surprisingly, did not mention the global financial crisis at all. As the respondents did not identify significant major events, information on the different dimensions of financial resilience were harder to grasp. As no reference point is provided for the analysis of deployed anticipatory and coping capacities, financial resilience needs to be analysed in a different way. In the following, we present the general information on the socio-economic context and the financial situation of the cities included in this analysis, as well as the main within-case findings on the perceived shock(s) and the respective impact on the local government, the financial vulnerability, anticipatory and coping capacity. The combination or dynamic interplay of these dimensions gives an understanding of which resilience pattern is represented by the different cases.

G1

G1 is located in an economically favourable context with several large industrial employers. Nevertheless, the unemployment rate is considerably higher than the German average. The city showed a relatively high level of debt over the last years and succeeded in reducing it only in one budgetary year. Considering also the debt of municipally owned enterprises, respondents doubt that the city will be able to decrease its debt over the next years. The debt level also seems to be perceived as the largest vulnerability of the local government.

The service level and citizen satisfaction however are considered as high and are expected to increase further in the future. While large businesses offer the potential to raise a significant amount of commercial tax, the respective revenues have been decreasing constantly over the last years. In this regard, the city seems somewhat reluctant to raising commercial taxes out of fear of business relocation and sees its financial wiggle room rather in charges and fees. When the financial crisis hit the German economy, it enhanced the negative effect of the sudden decrease in commercial tax.

The financial crisis ... a very bad thing. (CFO, G1)

As several investment projects had already been planned, respondents reported that the city could not back out and thus had to pull through a phase of massive increase in debt. Accordingly, respondents perceived the city's financial condition as continually worsening over the last 10 years. Reaching its trough in 2014, the subsequent year brought a short recovery, just to prove even worse with a significant deficit in 2016 again, and to present a negative prognosis for the year to come. During the last 10 years, G1 also experienced the corporate tax reform at the federal level with its effect on local government finances as a massive slump and thus as a financial shock. Since respondents did not see this shock coming, it seems that the city's anticipatory capacity was rather low. However, also professional associations were unaware of these changes. This specific event seems to present itself as a shock rather due to the relatively low financial autonomy of the German local level, leaving local governments with a low voice anticipating the respective developments and almost no choice in coping but buffering. The latter was also the main way to cope with the difficult financial situation the city found itself in during the last years. While breaks on expenditures, hiring freezes and virement were used to stabilise the local government, there is a sense of helplessness when it comes to the possibilities to raise own revenues and personnel cuts which cannot be implemented rapidly. While local political decision-makers instructed the administration to consolidate, the priority seems to be cutting expenditures rather than opening up the discussion for possible tax increases. These conflict-prone decisions are either avoided at all or shifted to upper governmental levels, where, for example, the state had to mandate an increase in property tax.

Having experienced a phase of a quite challenging financial condition, and the effects of two financial shocks over the last years, G1 still did not invest in building its anticipatory capacity. While the local government drafted a long-term investment plan and a risk report is presented to decision-makers twice a year, there exist no scenario analyses or contingency plans, and financial shocks are regarded as 'too exceptional' to be anticipated. In addition, there is no formalised monitoring system and decision-makers rather build on experience and intuition in foreseeing significant events. The sense of helplessness prevails in G1, as risks to its financial situation are detected in more general, upper governmental level policies that the local level cannot control or influence, for example monetary policy or immigration policy. Some responsibility for the difficult situation is also shifted to political decision-makers that are described as hampering effective risk control. Unable to build up buffering capacities again, and left with pressing investments in the field of education, G1's debt level is even expected to increase in the near future. Exerting weak anticipatory capacities, a strong focus on buffering, and low-conflict strategies in order to cope with shocks in the past, over the long term, a further increase in vulnerability is expected.

G2

G2 is a city that has experienced economic turmoil in the early 1990s when the German Democratic Republic collapsed. Its population is growing, but compared to other cities of similar size, G2 has a relatively high unemployment rate. Selling the local government's assets in the 2000s, it showed the lowest debt level in its state and also the most recent figures point to almost no debt in the municipal core budget. The municipally owned enterprises show a level debt that is still low compared to other local governments. However, the audit office has criticised it as partly disguising the local government's debt.

With its diverse picture of medium-sized businesses, the city exerts a stable commercial tax base and operates with a balanced budget. Within the last years, G2 has carried out several big infrastructure projects and has invested in child care due to the respective requirements by the federal level. In this context however, respondents highlight the steady devolvement of responsibilities to the local level without adequate compensation and thus the low local autonomy in functional terms. The overall service level of the local government is perceived as good, and the city sees itself as proactive with respect to citizen demand and in the use of new communication technologies. When the financial crisis hit local governments in Germany, G2 did not experience it as a shock. At this time, the city had repaid all its debt, making it financially robust. However, respondents identify an expenditure issue in the city's financial situation due to a significant increase in social expenditures, particularly in youth services.

There is no formalised long-term planning in G2, and the city's vision and mission are mainly drawn from political goals inherent in the election and government programme. Having experienced several natural disasters in recent years, the city has implemented contingency plans for these risks. Scenario planning is used in specific areas such as grants, but in terms of other financial risks, decision-makers rely solely on a prudent adherence to bookkeeping rules. With regard to its financial goals, the G2's anticipatory capacity seems to build mainly on cautious planning. When preparing the budget and the financial statement, the CFO carries out an informal risk analysis based on proactive monitoring of the economy and a best-estimate of future revenues and expenditures. The city seems to have become more cautious in budgeting and planning of infrastructure investments after but not due to the financial crisis. While G2 is in a favourable situation with almost no debt, from a long-term perspective, this is perceived as contingent on the respective political decision-makers in power. The respondents expect a rise in local government expenditures as a consequence of the refugee and migrant influx. Despite the special federal grants designed to cover the additional expenditures in first response services, local governments are left with a significant increase in expenditures in the long term, for example, for child care and housing, where they will have to bear approximately 30% of the costs themselves. G2 is a case where according to the respondents, decision-makers used a window of opportunity to sell assets in order to achieve a good financial condition. The city thus had high buffering capacity and was not vulnerable to decreases in revenues indirectly caused by the financial crisis. Its anticipatory capacity however – especially from an instrumental perspective – did not increase over the last years. The interview did not allow conclusions about the city's adapting and transforming capacities, which is however not surprising as these types of capacities are hard to grasp and – in most cases – only become visible in times of crisis. In particular, adapting and transforming capacities need to be deployed once buffering capacities (e.g. in form of financial reserves) are exhausted.

G3

G3 is the biggest city included in this study – however, respondents viewed the service infrastructure of the local government critically, arguing that it stands in no relation to the city's size in population terms. Probably also stemming from the strong identity as a hub for particular services, the service level is regarded as high, in particular in the areas of public transport, cultural facilities and child care. Although G3's financial situation is perceived as insufficient to sustain this level, citizens seem to view even slight decreases in the accustomed service level as extraordinarily negative. The city's debt level is described as 'exorbitant' and it is expected to rise over the medium term. This perception of the financial situation is supported by objective data: G3 shows a higher debt level than the average of single-tier cities (Burth, 2016). Since the mid-1990s, the debt level has doubled, partly also due to the loss of special grants by upper governmental levels. This accounts for high debt service and issues in short-term liquidity. An even worrying situation is shown with regard to cash credits and therefore short-term borrowing, as their level is classified as extremely high (Burth, 2016). Moreover, this figure is also expected to rise until 2020. The case also shows that cash credits seem to be a rather new way of ensuring liquidity for the local government – 10 years ago, G3 had no cash credits at all. According to the respondents, however, there is a window of opportunity for cash credits due to the favourable interest rates. Acknowledging that, were the interest rates to increase again, the impact on the city's financial situation would be 'fatal', it is unlikely that in such a case G3 would be able to repay its short-term debt to mitigate the threat.

G3 has an undiversified tax base which is considered a vulnerability and has been struggling with budget deficits for years, achieving the last balanced budget in 2009. This prevents the city from pooling funds for necessary investments. The long-term deficit is also the reason for G3 having to comply with consolidation rules by the state since 2015 – a measure the local government attempted to avoid in order to ensure autonomy in financial decisions. The local government did not experience a financial shock during the last 10 years – it was rather long-term developments and a lack of counteractions that have aggravated the financial situation of the city. Asked about the financial crisis of 2008/2009 specifically, respondents described it as a 'problematic situation' in the financial sector that affected local governments only indirectly, by a decrease in commercial tax. The city's anticipatory capacity in general can be described as low, political decision-makers are described as losing perspective for the big questions in the local government. The cash-based accounting system (in place until 2008) additionally contributed to the low awareness of, for example, maintenance need by decision-makers. However, respondents acknowledge that administrational leaders did not succeed in pointing decision-makers to pressing issues, resulting in neglecting emerging vulnerabilities and refraining from taking existential decisions. The city uses only a standard set of financial indicators, which is perceived as providing insufficient information. Although G3 received an overwhelming number of suggestions for consolidation by the state, the case reveals shortcomings in its coping capacities. In order to cope with its worsening financial situation after 2009, the local government took actions like raising fees, deferring maintenance, small structural adaptations and prioritisation of expenditure items. However, apart from difficulties to deconstruct the (oversized) administrative infrastructure, the political will to adapt it is described as low. After the first significant increase in service fees (about 30%), resistance by citizens was very high. In combination with the citizens' negative reactions to possible decreases in the service level, the city's leeway in stabilising its financial situation is limited. In order to reduce resistance, G3 holds budget presentations for citizens, the success of this measure however is questionable. In the near future, the local government plans investments in child care, education, and youth and elderly services. The city's anticipatory capacities seem to be increasing – according to the interviewees G3 develops a coherent set of key performance indicators, monitors expenditure uses a traffic light system to report to political decision-makers and plans with financial cushions (e.g. 20% of budget is blocked by the CFO). This facilitates mitigating

certain risks and buffering smaller financial shocks, but main financial vulnerabilities, that is, cash credits and overall debt level, remain. Much uncertainty
prevails also about the (financial) consequences of the refugee crisis/migrant
influx, since the current federal grants dedicated for the respective services and
distributed to local governments do not cover the actual expenses they are faced
with. Although anticipatory capacities seem to be increasing, they prove insufficient to fuel also decisions to build up coping capacities beyond buffering.
From a resilience perspective, the local government thus can be described as a
city that once benefited from favourable conditions but struggles to make substantial structural changes needed to deal with its vulnerabilities, or to develop
a new vision in order to be able to cope with future challenges.

G4

G4 is a fast growing city which, nevertheless, shows a relatively high unemployment rate. From its size, general geographical and economic context, G4 is
somewhat comparable to G2. The most evident difference, however, is shown
in the local government's financial situation. G4 has an undiversified tax base
and a low percentage of own tax revenues compared to other local governments. Over the last few years, its debt level in the core budget has decreased
slightly, and the debt of municipally owned enterprises also decreased considerably. The city's dependency on state grants and earmarked federal grants
accounts for low financial autonomy, but G4 is able to cover operating expenditures with operating revenues, and hence does not depend on cash credits.
However, the city has a relatively high level of liabilities which creates financial
risks. Respondents describe the city's service level as good and as having
increased over the last years. Training and development of the local government's employees accounted for an enhanced citizen orientation. In contrast to
G2 that seems to have embraced new communication technologies, G4 identi-
fies an urgent need to improve the use of information and communication tech-
nology in its service delivery. During the last 10 years, the city had experienced
several shocks that impacted its services as well as its financial condition. Some
of which however can be described rather as 'slow-burning incidents'
(Crichton, Ramsay, & Kelly, 2009), for example, the long-term effects of a federal reform on the commercial and property tax, changes in the energy policy
and the impact on revenues from industry, as well as the increase in unemployment and the subsequent effect on social expenditures. While respondents identified the impact of the financial crisis on the city's possibilities to borrow and
on its financial condition due to its high debt level, they did not perceive it as a
huge shock. Rather, G4 perceives the refugee crisis as a (minor) shock, especially considering the political movements that have formed in the former eastern part of Germany in general, and in the city's vicinity in particular.

However, it also experienced an internal shock with financial impact with a corrupt act in one of its municipal enterprises.

The local government's anticipatory capacity seems rather limited; and similar to almost all other cases described in this book, decision-makers in G4 did not see the financial crisis coming. However, G4 was also unaware of developments like the increased demand in the area of education as a result of the increase in the city's population, and respondents described the relocation or bankruptcy of large businesses, that is, tax payers, as non-foreseeable.

This is always a surprise which one has to cope with as good as possible. (CFO, G4)

This approach may be insofar problematic as, considering its undiversified tax base, the relocation or bankruptcy of large businesses is described as one of the main vulnerability sources for the city. With regards to financial vulnerability in general, G4's financial situation was described as very critical from the 1990s up until the mid-2000s. During the last 10 years, it was described as stable, which is why the city was able to pull through the financial crisis without any substantial damages. Respondents however doubt that the debt level can be decreased, in face of the mandatory services the local government has to provide. This somewhat passive approach is mirrored in the way the local government copes with financial shocks. The search for efficiencies is an ongoing process in G4, but the city mainly builds on buffering; first by virements and cross-departmental funding, followed by deferring expenditures, applying for specific federal and states grants or increases in taxes to cover additional expenditures.

Quarterly budget monitoring and topic-related meetings and reports are the main instruments used for anticipating vulnerabilities and possible harmful events. However, the focus on financial indicators is perceived as being too narrow to enable comprehensive monitoring and control, and respondents acknowledged the need to be aware of weak signals in order to take early actions. While some effects of the socio-demographic changes have been recognised rather late, G4 has developed a vision for the city that focuses on further increasing its population figures and expanding its service level. However, when it comes to the effects of this positioning, anticipatory capacity again proves rather low: on the one hand, the current financial condition and its trend over the next years allow only a limited increase in the service level, and on the other hand, the local government's infrastructure is not sufficient for accommodating a significantly higher number of inhabitants. G4 thereby further reinforces its 'plan as you go' approach, where ways of funding investments or covering expenditures are discussed when the full extent of events has unfolded. The city seems to operate on a shoestring, where operating revenues in fact cover the operating expenditure, but where the debt level is still perceived as too high and several investment projects inhibit debt repayment. The lack of comprehensive plans and necessary measures to equip the city to cope with future challenges

mirrors a rather low anticipatory capacity. Coping with financial shocks
seems to be understood mainly as buffering, where the local government often
relies on upper governmental levels to provide enough resources for buffering
(e.g. through grants), rather than implementing measures that would allow
building up financial reserves or decreasing vulnerabilities.

G5

G5 is located near two metropolitan areas and is a growing, and from a
socio-demographic perspective, young city. Its population increased by
10% during the last years and it exerts a relatively strong workforce basis
(36% of its inhabitants are between 18 and 40) compared to the state's (ca.
24% between 20 and 40 years) as well as the national average (ca. 22%
between 18 and 40 years) (own calculations based on Statistisches
Bundesamt, 2016a, the state's demographic report, and the city's key socio-
demographic figures report). The city has positioned itself as a research and
business hub, focusing strongly on IT services. This accounts for a relatively high number of businesses and hence a broad revenue base. However,
despite being located in a favourable context, G5 shows the highest unemployment rate of the cases included in this analysis, being almost 10 percentage points above the German average. In a comparison by the national
statistical office in 2012, the local government showed one of the highest
debt levels of all single-tier cities in Germany. For over 10 years, the city
has been struggling with deficits, leading to a high share of cash credits
which – until 2016 – were also used as a debt restructuring instrument and
for amortisation payments. Although the financial crisis was not perceived
as a shock, G5 experienced a phase of a dramatic financial situation as a
result of growing budget deficits five years ago. As a consequence, G5
enacted a plan for budget consolidation, and some years ago also fell under
the state's regulation for financially stressed local governments, which
ensures special grants in exchange for the implementation of measures to
reduce the budget deficit. These measures are expected to come into full
effect only recently. Respondents perceive the city's service level as offering
'room for improvement'; G5 is still perceived as financially highly vulnerable and shocks are seen as prevalent. Currently, the perceived main risk for
the local government's finances is the refugee crisis. The city tackles this
issue by creating special organisational forms to provide first response services, by expanding affordable housing possibilities in the short-run, and by
working on enhanced citizen participation in the long-run. However,
respondents feel that responsibility for these services is devolved to the local
level with only insufficient compensation.

In financial terms, the main goal for the future is to ensure a balanced budget. The respondents report that the city uses a performance measurement and management control system to identify risks, and that accrual accounting is used to prevent (financial) risks. However, there is no formal risk management system in place and there exist no specific plans of how to deal with external shocks. Although the financial situation has improved and respondents are positive about the financial trend in the future, the city will be confronted with several investment needs in roads and education over the next years. In order to align planning in this context, G5 launched the development of a new vision for the city. Considering its debt level however, the respective anticipatory capacity in G5 seems rather low. Despite the opportunities that come along with a young and growing population, the local government seem to struggle with building the capacities needed to embrace this development and provide the conditions needed in order to become a financially resilient city. G5 appears rather as a case where the local government recognised branches of industry that will become more important in the future, but struggles in translating these opportunities to the workforce within its local government territory.

CONCLUSIONS

Taking an overall view on the themes that emerged across the cases, it seems that local governments struggle with the uncertainty of upper governmental levels devolving more and more service and administrative responsibility to the local level, while at the same time not providing adequate financial compensation and even reducing grants. Local governments thus perceive themselves as restricted in their self-administration by a set of (primarily) state rules, regulations and standards. As this development has been observed already more than a decade ago (see Reichard, 2003), it cannot be classified as a financial shock. However, it puts pressure on local governments and thus restrains them in building up certain (coping) capacities.

In general, respondents in the local governments in this investigation were unfamiliar with the term or the concept of financial resilience. Although in all cases, at least after a follow-up question on financial shocks, respondents identified the global financial crisis as a financial shock, they unanimously reported that the latter had no direct effects on their cities' finances. It was rather the effect of its aftermath, when turmoil spilled over to the real economy and large businesses had to lay off staff or implement short-time work, both of which impacted local governments' commercial tax revenues. When respondents identified other shocks (than internal business crises), the events that dominated the discussion were the refugee crisis or the refugee and migrant influx, and sudden changes in the own tax base caused by relocation, bankruptcy, or economic turmoil affecting large businesses. In general, there are three overarching vulnerability sources that are at play in German local governments. First, the sometimes relatively high debt level that magnifies the effects of any external financial shock, second, the long-term trend of increasing social expenditures and third, the low autonomy of local governments.

As to the first point, the overall debt of local governments accounts for approximately 130 billion Euro and has been growing constantly. However, there is a caveat in this aggregated view. Local government debt in the western states is remarkably higher than in the eastern states, the former part of the German Democratic Republic. In the latter, local governments have repaid much of their debt in recent years, accounting for half a billion Euro decrease in debt in these states in just one year (Arnold et al., 2015, p. 56). A significant part of local government debt is found in municipally owned enterprises and thus non-consolidated budgets (33–72% of total local government debt is secluded in separate budgets) (Arnold et al., 2015, p. 25 f), which points at the importance of including these organisation in the international debates and research activities on resilience and related questions. Cash credits amount to one third of overall debt; in some states reaching up to 50%. In general, local governments that exert a high level of debt in absolute figures are also the ones making heavy use of cash credits (see Arnold et al., 2015). The currently favourable interest rates provide a window of opportunity to restructure and repay the debt. However, in financially stable local governments, this goal is equally important as investments in infrastructure which, over the last decades, have been deferred in favour of paying for operating expenditures – especially in the area of social services (see Anton & Holler, 2016). The vulnerability caused by increasing social expenditures is a long-term trend that has been prevalent for almost decades, and also professional associations acknowledge the common perception of local government budgets changing from a dominance of 'investment funds to social funds' (Anton & Holler, 2016). As an integral part of their respective state (*Land*), German local governments' self-administration is limited both in functional, but even more in financial terms. Although being situated in a federal administrative context, the cases analysed in this contribution also feel exposed to policies and regulations by the federal government. This creates uncertainty and at times leaves local governments in a sense of helplessness and infeasibility of proper planning.

In hindsight, these findings are surprising, as the German association of cities (*Deutscher Städtetag*) addresses the mentioned aspects in its latest report on local government finances (Anton & Holler, 2016). With regards to the refugee crisis, it is suggested that rapid and collaborative actions across hierarchical levels require replacing lengthy negotiation and legal processes by political agreements over the short-term. Here, trust between the actors is a prerequisite. As a response to the uncertainty arising from changing upper governmental level policies, the association points to negotiating contingent compensation payments that come into effect automatically, and to the availability and quality of data that can facilitate these mechanisms. The authors acknowledge local governments being bound to upper governmental levels' decisions, but point to uncertainties being an integral part of the daily business at the local level. They state that local governments have to accept that unforeseeable changes of the external environment are likely and that they cannot be stopped. What local governments however need to do is create frameworks for action that allow rapid response in democratic processes and implement mechanisms that automatically take into account changing service demands. These aspects tap into building anticipatory capacity in order to deal with uncertainty. More interestingly, the authors highlight that local governments need to improve their robustness through financial reserves, and their *resilience* – not to reduce risks, but rather to enhance the capacity to cope with negative effects. Apart from building up financial reserves and thus robustness, this requires building organisational competences and capacities. It is this resilience that enables local governments also to deal with risks that arise from decreasing commercial tax revenues. These are described as a double-edged sword: in a wealthy local government with volatile commercial tax revenues, it is regarded as the local government's own responsibility to build up enough reserves to survive two years of a slump in these revenues. In the case of industry-dependent, crisis-ridden local governments, the perception prevails that this is not possible. Attempts to detach tax revenues from the local economy in order to make local government finances less elastic are however regarded as counter-productive. Rather, it is suggested that local governments need to invest resources to build up their resilience going beyond buffering capacities.

NOTES

1. The cities of Berlin, Bremen and Hamburg hold special statutes as cities and at the same time function also as states.
2. See Bertelsmann Stiftung: Wegweiser für Kommunen (http://www.wegweiser-kommune.de).

REFERENCES

Anton, S., & Holler, B. (2016). *Gemeindefinanzbericht 2016* [Local government finance report 2016]. Integration fair finanzieren – gute Ansätze weiterverfolgen. Köln: DeutscherStädtetag. Retrieved from http://www.staedtetag.de/publikationen/gfb/079279/index.html. Accessed on October 26, 2016.
Arnold, F., Boettcher, F., Freier, R., Geißler, R., & Holler, B. (2015). Kommunaler Finanzreport 2015 [Municipal Financial Report 2015]. Bertelsmann Stiftung, Gütersloh.
Barbera, C., Jones, M., Korac, S., Saliterer, I., & Steccolini, I. (2017). Governmental financial resilience under austerity in Austria, England and Italy: How do local governments cope with financial shocks? Public Administration, forthcoming.
Bundesamt für Migration und Flüchtlinge. (2016). Leitfaden für die Beantragung, Durchführung und Abrechnung eines gemeinwesenorientierten Integrationsprojektes [Guidelines for the application, administration and accounting for a community oriented integration project]. Juli 2016, Berlin.

Bundesministerium für Wirtschaft und Energie. (2016, August). Wirtschaftsdaten neue Länder. Berlin.

Burda, M. C., & Hunt, J. (2001). *From reunification to economic integration: Productivity and the labor market in eastern Germany*. Brookings Papers on Economic Activity No. 2. Brookings Institution, Washington, DC.

Burth, A. (2016). *Pro-Kopf-Verschuldung der kreisfreien Städte Deutschlands* [Per-capitadebt in German single-tier cities]. Retrieved from http://www.haushaltssteuerung.de/weblog-pro-kopf-verschuldung-der-kreisfreien-staedte-deutschlands.html. Accessed on November 4, 2016.

Crichton, M. T., Ramsay, C. G., & Kelly, T. (2009). Enhancing organizational resilience through emergency planning: Learnings from cross-sectoral lessons. *Journal of Contingencies and Crisis Management, 17*(1), 24–37.

Ernst & Young. (2012). Overview and comparison of public accounting and auditing practices in the 27 EU Member States. Prepared for Eurostat.

Eurostat. (2016). *Government finance statistics*. http://ec.europa.eu/eurostat/web/government-finance-statistics/data/database.

Federal Ministry of Finance. (2014). Finanzbericht 2015. Stand und voraussichtliche Entwicklung der Finanzwirtschaft im gesamtwirtschaftlichen Zusammenhang [Financial Report 2015. Status quo and projected developments of the macroeconomic financial situation]. Bundesministerium der Finanzen, Berlin.

Holtkamp, L. (2012). *Verwaltungsreformen. Problemorientierte Einführung in die Verwaltungswissenschaft*. Wiesbaden: Springer VS.

KiföG. (2008, Dezember). Gesetz zur Förderung von Kindern unter drei Jahren in Tageseinrichtungen und in der Kindertagespflege [Law on the promotion of children under three years in day care facilities]. Bundesgesetzblatt Jahrgang 2008 Teil I Nr. 57, ausgegeben zu G3 am 15 (pp. 2403 – 2409).

Kuhlmann, S., & Wollmann, H. (2013). *Verwaltung und Verwaltungsreformen in Europa. Einführung in die vergleichende Verwaltungswissenschaft* [Public dministration and administrative reforms in Europe. An introduction to comparative public administration]. Wiesbaden: Springer VS.

OECD. (2010). *OECD economic surveys: Germany 2010*. Paris: OECD.

OECD. (2011). *Making the most of public investment in a tight fiscal environment*. Paris: OECD Publishing.

OECD. (2016a). OECD data. Retrieved from https://data.oecd.org

OECD. (2016b, April). *OECD economic surveys Germany*. Paris: OECD Publishing.

Reichard, C. (2003). Local public management reforms in Germany. *Public Administration, 81*(2), 345–363.

Ridder, H.-G., Bruns, H.-J., & Spier, F. (2005). Analysis of public management change processes: The case of local government accounting reforms in Germany. *Public Administration, 83*(2), 443–471.

Statistisches Bundesamt. (2016a). Bevölkerung [Population]. Retrieved from https://www.destatis.de/DE/ZahlenFakten/GesellschaftStaat/Bevoelkerung/Bevoelkerung.html

Statistisches Bundesamt. (2016b). Pressemitteilung Nr. 105 vom 21.03.2016. Retrieved from https://www.destatis.de/DE/PresseService/Presse/Pressemitteilungen/2016/03/PD16_105_12421pdf.pdf?__blob=publicationFile

Wehling, H.-G., & Kost, A. (2010). Kommunalpolitik in der Bundesrepublik Deutschland – eine Einführung [Local government policy in the federal republic of Germany – An introduction]. In A. Kost & H.-G. Wehling (Hrsg.), Kommunalpolitik in den deutschen Ländern. Eine Einführung. 2. aktualisierte und überarbeitete Auflage. Wiesbaden: VS Verlag.

Wollmann, H. (2004). Local government reforms in great Britain, Sweden, Germany and France: Between multi-function and single-purpose organisations. *Local Government Studies, 30*(4), 639–665.

World Bank. (2013). *World development indicators 2013*. World Bank, Washington, DC. Retrieved from http://data.worldbank.org

World Trade Organization. (2016). *World trade statistical review*. World Trade Organization. Retrieved from https://www.wto.org/english/res_e/statis_e/wts2016_e/wts2016_e.pdf

CHAPTER 8

FINANCIAL RESILIENCE OF GREEK LOCAL GOVERNMENTS

Sandra Cohen and Nikolaos Hlepas

ABSTRACT

The crisis exposed Greek municipalities to bilateral financial pressures from cutbacks and increased needs for social assistance. They were directly affected by cheese-slice austerity measures that were implemented in the whole public sector (hiring freeze, cutbacks of salaries, dismissal of employees on contract basis) and successive cutbacks of state grants. In this chapter we discuss the case of four Greek municipalities. The sample was selected by taking into account the average financial performance of municipalities in terms of accrual accounting surplus/deficit over operating revenues and the volatility of this measure of financial performance over the period 2002–2012. In all four municipalities, interviews with an elected politician and municipal officials were conducted on the basis of a structured questionnaire that has been given to the interviewees before the meeting. The analysis revealed that all cities did not show significant anticipatory capabilities. This might be due to several shocks related to central government policies that were difficult to predict and to the ambiguity of the financial condition in the country. Municipalities proved to be particularly flexible and open towards social innovation and responded to the crisis through adaptation but they exhibited limited internal transformation. Nevertheless, the shock due to the crisis and the unprecedented decrease in municipal budgets has triggered a cultural shift towards more prudent management and parsimony. These

Governmental Financial Resilience: International Perspectives on how Local Governments Face Austerity
Public Policy and Governance, Volume 27, 135–152
ISSN: 2053-7697/doi:10.1108/S2053-769720170000027008

findings show that Greek municipalities are still rather vulnerable to future shocks and especially to a further deepening of the on-going financial crisis.

Keywords: Greek local governments; austerity; accrual accounting; financial shocks; resilience

INTRODUCTION

Broader contextual, institutional and policy-related conditions in Greece were not offering incentives for prudent financial management and building of anticipatory capacities in Greek local governments (LGs). On the one hand, both financial and human resources of LGs kept growing for decades, as local government was a rising institution, taking advantage both of domestic decentralisation policies and growing European funding (Hlepas, 2011). On the other hand, long-standing centralism characterises the socio-administrative system, whereas the LGs are highly dependent on state subsidies and regulations (in 2011 63% of LGs revenues were subsidies). While financial resilience was a matter of concern for national governments who were politically accountable for the well-being of the economy, they have acted quite often in an unpredictable and case-by-case way following political priorities. Therefore, long-term financial strategies made no sense for LGs which would rather concentrate on traditional roles as providers of elementary services, as local agents of vertical party-political mechanisms and as integral parts of various patronage networks. Local leaders often acted as political brokers of localities, promoting their demands at higher levels of governance, while in their own communities they were prone to spending instead of saving money mostly stemming from state subsidies. Surprisingly enough, Greek LGs proved able to face the crisis and in some cases their reflexes revealed significant capacities that shaped their resilience. While they might have shown limited anticipatory capacities, they definitely exhibited strong buffering ones.

The crisis exposed Greek LGs to bilateral financial pressures from cutbacks and increased needs for social assistance. They were directly affected by cheese-slice austerity measures that were implemented in the whole public sector (hiring freeze, cutbacks of salaries, dismissal of employees on contract basis) and successive cutbacks of state subsidies. At the same time, the unprecedented rise of unemployment and poverty rates that reached record levels since World War II, considerably increased needs for social services and assistance at the local level. However, their buffering capacity proved to be quite strong, probably also because over-spending in the past, which had built up a lot of slack in the budget, had left enough space for rationalisation in spending. Undoubtedly, they managed to adapt to this multidimensional shock. However, it is still a question whether this shock was an opportunity for the LGs to further develop or build up new capacities that would contribute to their resilience when faced with new shocks. Another question is whether, in spite of unitary, top-down implemented austerity policies, centralist patterns and path dependencies, heterogeneous responses could be detected among the different LGs.

In the following parts of this chapter, the general context (economic situation, local government and accounting systems and reforms) is presented before methods of case selection and findings of empirical research in four selected LGs is explained. The chapter concludes with implications for Greek local governments from a resilience perspective.

THE ECONOMIC SITUATION IN GREECE: A CRISIS THAT LASTS

Since the mid-1990s, the Greek economy experienced remarkable growth rates, even though exports remained low, reflecting weak competitiveness combined with overregulated closed markets. At the same time the Greek public sector is characterised by a deeply cultivated bureaucracy (Sotirakou & Zeppou, 2005). Initially, the 2008 crisis did not seem to shake Greece as hard as it shook other economies at least as it was depicted in the official reported numbers of that time. Government spending kept rising and 2009 marked a tremendous increase in state deficit which had firstly been officially budgeted as 2% of GDP, but it was revised to 3.7% in April and to 12.7% in October 2009 before, finally, reaching 15.4%. While deficit was actually out of control (deficit was −5.9% of GDP in 2006, −6.7% of GDP in 2007 and −10.2% in 2008 as reported now in the official Eurostat portal), no one seemed to have a comprehensive view of the problem, since hiding deficits through various methods was a common practice in many public entities (hospitals, LGs, etc.) in order to deceive public opinion and various decision-makers and supervisors both at home and abroad. Finally, in May 2010, following the Memorandum of Understanding (L. 3845/2010) between the Greek government and the Troika (i.e. European Commission, International Monetary Fund and European Central Bank), a rescue package was offered to Greece. This bailout plan was updated in 2012 with the new medium-term framework for financial strategy (MTFS − L 4093/2012). These two bailout agreements were implemented according to the conditionality principle, meaning that each tranche of the bailout money would be provided under the precondition that concrete measures would be implemented and quantified targets would be reached. Despite the furious resistance against reforms by the opposition, protests from citizens and extensive strikes, a series of reforms were attempted but their implementation was rather weak (with the exception of severe cuts in salaries for governmental employees across the board, cuts in pensions and multiple increases in taxes). By the end of 2014, early elections were held, and the new government initiated a new circle of

Table 1.   Main Indicators of Greek Economy.

	2009	2010	2011	2012	2013	2014
Change in % GDP	−1.0%	−3.9%	−6.5%	−6.5%	−6.1%	−1.8%
Deficit % of GDP	−15.4%	−10.9%	−10.2%	−8.7%	−12.3%	−3.5%
Unemployment rates	9.60%	12.70%	17.90%	24.50%	27.50%	26.50%
Government debt % GDP	129.40%	148.33%	171.35%	156.9%	174.95%	177.07%

Source: Eurostat (http://ec.europa.eu/eurostat)

negotiations with debtors that drastically worsened the situation of the economy (e.g. lack of liquidity at the central government level, increase in the level of arrears to the private sector, capital controls). In August 2015, Greece was officially the only one out of the former 'crisis-countries' of the Eurozone that returned to recession and had to implement a third bailout programme. In Table 1 there is an overview of basic indicators of the Greek economy from 2009 to 2014.

It has to be underlined that while by 2016 other European countries apparently improved, the crisis in Greece is still in progress. Therefore, the year 2010 signals the beginning of the crisis but the financial distress is still on. It is obvious that reform failure in Greece has multiple systemic aspects that offer space for case studies and theoretical discussions (Hlepas, 2015).

MAIN CHARACTERISTICS OF GREEK LGs

LGs in Greece provide, apart from the traditional functions (e.g. the local registry, refuse collection, development and maintenance of local infrastructure, cultural activities and events etc.), several other services to their constituents due to the decentralisation policy followed by the central government (e.g. kindergartens). LGs revenues include own revenues (i.e. taxes, fees and charges) and subsidies covering operating and investment needs. More specifically, in 2011 the breakdown of LGs' revenue was 63% subsidies − 37% own revenues while in 2015 it would read 53% subsidies − 47% own revenues. This shift in the balance between the two was mainly due to a subsidy reduction from central government rather than an increase in own revenues. As for taxes, even though LGs have a relative flexibility in levying them, they are forbidden to institute their own taxes. As for fees and charges, they can only be varied between certain levels and they can only be used for specific purposes (e.g. garbage collection, street lighting etc.). LGs are subject to the restrictive expenditure control mechanisms[1] that govern the public sector finances. Local government expenditure totalled only 3.3% of GDP in 2012, while in 2009 it reached its highest score of 4.1% over GDP. These rates are very low compared to other EU countries (DEXIA, 2008, 2011). The average budget of a Greek LG is not higher than 20 million Euros and the mean number of employees is not bigger than 250 people[2] although their mean population since 2011 is one of the biggest in Europe (33.800 inhabitants on average). The mayor, the economic committee and the municipal council perform the management of LGs. The citizens of the LG directly elect the mayor and the members of the municipal council for a five-year term.

The outbreak of the crisis coincided with the 'Kallikratis reform' (L. 3852/2010) that was launched in 2010 narrowing the number of LGs from 1,034 to 325. This move was separate from the crisis and it was not a response to it. This amalgamation left only 86 LGs (mostly in islands and metropolitan regions) unaffected.

The crisis triggered a series of additional measures as public financial management and budgeting reforms were a priority with the declared aim to address both the short-term financial challenges and longer term performance, accountability and transparency issues.

The most important were the following:

- The void of the renewal of the contracts of LG employees that had as a result a sharp decrease in the number of employees in LGs and a significant decrease in the contribution of salaries cost to the operating expenses. Within this realm the municipal policemen and the school guards were fired. As a result police services stopped being provided at the local government level until the end of 2015 when the municipal policemen were hired again.
- The sharp across the board cuts in public sector salaries.
- The decrease in subsidies given to LGs.
- The introduction of rigid procedures for procurement and assuming expenses purposes.
- LGs could only submit a balanced budget for approval to central government (prohibition of deficit).

Main effects of these measures on the financial condition of LGs were the following: Between 2011 and 2015 subsidies reduced by 24% while own revenues increased by 12%. This combined produced a net drop in income of 11% that was met by reductions in personnel costs of 31% and operating costs (not including personnel costs) of 8%. Moreover the contribution of salary costs to the total operating expenses fell from 45.6% to 38.5%.[3]

Apart from the development described above, a new institution, called the Observatory of Financial Autonomy of LG's (OFALG) was set up. Its responsibility was to coordinate oversight roles, to agree on targets and secure budget execution according to the MTFS projections. Finally, a central data base where LGs were obliged to present the execution of their budget on a monthly based was created. Due to the rather successful performance of LGs, compared to the central level, the new bailout plan signed in August 2015 did not introduce any additional requirements regarding the oversight of local governments.

ACCOUNTING SYSTEMS IN GREEK LGs

Greek LGs operate a dual accounting system in which cash accounting and accrual accounting co-exist and operate simultaneously and independently (Cohen, 2015; Cohen, Kaimenaki, & Zorgios, 2007). The cash-based accounting system tracks the execution of the (cash) budget by monitoring expenditures and revenues throughout all phases and procedures via double-entry journal entries. Apart from the cash budget, all public sector entities are obliged to register on an on-going basis their expense commitments in registers applying, in a sense, commitment accounting. In this way, central government can have an updated and accurate view of arrears and liabilities necessary for reporting purposes.

On the other hand, the accrual accounting system registers transactions in a similar way to Greek private sector accounting standards pertaining (until 2014) to non-listed companies (P.D. 315/1999). While the accounting standards for the private sector changed in 2015, the municipal ones remained unaffected. In general, these new standards are in conformity with the directions of the 4th EC Directive for company accounts.

METHODOLOGY

In this chapter we aim to shed light on the way Greek LGs have coped with the financial crisis and the underlying capacities that enabled them to do so. We try to portray their resilience patterns by following the typology developed by Barbera, Jones, Korac, Saliterer, and Steccolini (2015). As a longitudinal analysis on the financial resilience of LGs newly formed through amalgamations could offer blurring results, our sample was extracted out of the territorially unchanged LGs. This decision was made on the basis of focusing on authorities subject to similar institutional pressures.

The sample was selected by taking into account the average financial performance of LGs in terms of accrual accounting surplus/deficit over operating revenues[4] and the volatility of the above mentioned measure of financial performance over the period 2002–2012. The selection of the accrual accounting information for the purposes of the sample selection is justified on the fact that it provides an accurate view on the revenues and the expenditures. Accrual accounting numbers apart from presenting revenues earned and resources consumed for service provision during a period are also audited. Moreover, while the financial statements of LGs are published, the execution of the budget is not. Therefore, cash basis information was not available for the entire analysis period as the data basis containing budget execution information is operational since 2011. However, none of the cases is an extreme one.

The characteristics of the four selected LGs are presented in Table 2 and discussed within each case study. In all four LGs, three interviews were conducted

Table 2. Resilience Dimensions of the Selected Cases.

LG	City A	City B	City C	City D
Budgetary position	Positive	Around zero	Negative	Around zero
Volatility	Medium	Medium	High	Low
Size (citizens) census 2011	664.612	68.623	137.129	71.950
Shock-impact	Grant reduction, higher demand for services, tightening of fiscal targets, centralisation of financial controls, increase in bureaucracy, personnel decline	Grant reduction, higher demand for services, tightening of fiscal targets, increase in bureaucracy, personnel decline, litigation against the LG	Grant reduction, higher demand for services, tightening of fiscal targets, bureaucracy, personnel decline, litigation against the LG	Grant reduction, higher demand for services, tightening of fiscal targets, centralisation of financial controls, increase in bureaucracy
Perception of the crisis	Threat/focus on self-sufficiency	Threat/dealing with the threat	Threat/dealing with the threat	Threat/dealing with the threat
Vulnerability (before)	Medium	High	Medium	Medium
Anticipatory capacity (before)	Low	Low	Low/medium	Low
Copying capacity	High	Medium	Medium/high	Medium
Anticipatory capacity (after)	Medium/high	Medium/low	Medium/high	Medium
Vulnerability (after)	Low	High	High	Medium
Pattern of resilience	Reactive adapter	Contented fatalism	Reactive adapter	Contented fatalism

(in total 12 interviews) on the basis of a structured questionnaire that has been given to the interviewees before the meeting. The interviews were conducted during the period November–December 2015. The interviewees were the Deputy Mayor responsible for Financial Management, the Chief Financial Officer and the Manager of the Accounting Department (or respondents with similar positions). Therefore in each case both an elected politician (Deputy Mayor) and municipal officials were interviewed. The interviews were recorded and lasted 30–40 minutes each.

RESULTS

City A

City A is the biggest Greek LG (665,000 inhabitants) and has had a positive financial position during the last 10 years. This condition is characterised by stability that is achieved though revenue generating capacities and rationalisation of expenditures and liabilities. The sovereign debt crisis sharply decreased the level of state subsidies (from 54% of total operating revenues in 2011 to 44% of total operating revenues in 2014). However the city had managed to buffer this shock. Actions aiming at broadening the tax base (e.g. putting more taxes on business activities) to counterbalance the 15% decrease in city population between the census of 2001 and 2011, had borne fruit. Nevertheless, the crisis had affected the capability of citizens to pay their taxes, which resulted in an increase in receivables. Moreover, in order to cover the gap in revenues and reduce its vulnerability, the city managed to considerably increase European funding (mainly funding from the European Social Fund for vulnerable groups such as elderly, children, homeless, immigrants etc.), showing therefore significant adapting capacities. Also it attracted voluntary and private donations to provide the resources needed to support specific initiatives. The city maintained the quality and quantity of its services, while it is very active in providing food and taking care of the homeless and has developed a social pharmacy and a social supermarket providing support to the poor. There last initiatives were brought on board during the crisis period.

From the expenditure's angle, the city was able to decrease its operating cost albeit the increased needs for rendering the aforementioned services. This was mainly thanks to the sharp decrease in the number of employees with short-term contracts and improvements in financial management that encapsulated among other the modernisation of the procurement systems and the development of modern and transparent materials management systems. The city was able to meet its term loan obligations on time and decrease the level of its indebtedness.

The financial management of the city includes the monitoring on a constant basis of the execution of the budget as well as the calculation of a set of financial ratios. These ratios provide an overview of the financial condition and performance as well as the efficiency in the flow of collecting revenues and incurring expenses. The city has a rather short and medium-term view on revenues and expenditures. While accrual accounting information is available, financial management seems to rely mainly on cash flows. Professional accountants with private sector experience constitute the accrual accounting team. The use of private sector expertise signals anticipatory capacity. The city has recently developed an interactive web based application where the execution of the budget is available online. This move signalled the intention of the city to become more transparent and accountable. However, the disclosure is related solely to financial information and it does not provide any non-financial performance indicators. Long-term financial planning seems to be difficult, as several central government decisions directly influence the financial condition of the city. Therefore, while the crisis did actually drive City A towards building anticipatory capacity, the coping capacities were developed to a greater extent.

Interestingly, the most important shocks are related to state interventions on the way the LG operates. The most striking ones are (a) the law that voided the renewal of the contracts of city employees and the motives given to city officials for early retirement which resulted in a sharp decrease of municipal personnel and (b) the introduction of cumbersome and bureaucratic procurement procedures that crucially influence operational efficiency and smooth service provision. The abolition of the municipal police and school guards fall in the same realm; decisions that the city had to abide by were made at the national level. These measures are not specific to City A but affected all Greek LGs with a comparable size in terms of monetary units and employees. Of course, other shocks faced by the city refer to the increase in the level of poverty that inflates the demand for services provided to the homeless and destitute, as well as the large number of immigrants and refugees overwhelming City A which caused increased hospitality needs. The city showed significant buffer capacity as it managed to deal with these important shocks. The fact that services were extended while staff decreased provides insights into adaptive capacity that became apparent after the crisis took effect. Municipal staff improved working efficiency, acting as an important facilitator to buffer the shock of sharp personnel decline and contributing to the city's resilience.

City A officials argue that several shocks are difficult to predict and demand close monitoring of the central government policy making and of the reforms agreed with the Troika. Apart from monitoring, close cooperation with state authorities would facilitate municipal revenue collection. In order to increase its revenues, City A needs access to information about income and property of citizens and enterprises but faces unwillingness of tax services to share these data. City A has set the strategic goal to become less dependent on state subsidies. Therefore, the city treats the crisis as window of opportunity to act proactively and reduce, at least, this source of vulnerability, by substantially increasing and diversifying its own resources.

Furthermore, financial resilience is seen as highly related to efficiency; the more efficient the LG is, the easier it is regarded to adapt and to be agile; the inadequacy of financial resources makes it easier to properly handle financial difficulties as it keeps the LG in an alert condition. Also, resilience is highly linked to high quality and motivated personnel that is willing to support the city during periods in which it is understaffed.

According to the interviewees in City A, resilience is related to the qualities of being durable, well prepared, well informed and careful while trying to find ways to be flexible within the boundaries imposed by the central government. In this realm, resilience is related to taking advantage of European funding or/ and to cooperating with private sector and social actors.

City B

City B is a medium-sized LG of approximately 70,000 inhabitants showing a financial position around zero and a medium level volatility. It is a typical case of a working class district at the western side of the Athenian basin. After several decades of rising industrialisation and rapid population growth, City B was affected by the decline of industrial activities but has soon attracted several important retail enterprises and shopping malls who took advantage of newly built transport networks crossing the city. These new businesses increased own municipal revenue, while state subsidies were also growing until 2009. This 'growth-euphoria' that culminated at the time of the Athens Olympics in 2004 was not providing incentives for prudent financial management in the city. On the contrary, the prevailing socio-political atmosphere favoured the careless reproduction of traditional political patronage and its wasteful practices that have been characterising the Greek political system for many years.

At the outset of the crisis, City B was not one of the LGs that were categorised as 'over-indebted' LGs according to the corresponding criteria introduced by the Kallikratis law in June 2010 (the debt ratio had to be under 60% of total revenue and the debt service ratio had to be lower than 20% of operating revenue). But the city experienced the shock of a sudden drop in subsidies provided by the state, especially since 2012 (second bailout agreement). This shock was partly counterbalanced by financial consolidation means imposed by the central government like cutbacks in salaries and the implementation of the overdue liabilities programme, which provided earmarked grants in order to acquit suppliers. The financial condition of the city was further stabilised through other top-down austerity measures, such as the abolition of unoccupied employment posts, the merging or dissolution of municipal enterprises and the dismissal of employees working on limited contract basis. Dealing with unprecedented financial stress, the municipal government tried to rationalise procurement procedures, restrain corruption and wasteful management, while it took serious efforts to attract European funding for a wide spectrum of social services that could absorb the severe effects of the crisis on less privileged groups. At the same time, other measures of the national government, such as new reporting obligations and new monitoring and support mechanisms (e.g. the OFALG) were forcing the municipality to further rationalise financial management and develop anticipatory capabilities that were introduced by OFALG.

All in all, City B proved able to cope with the crisis, not primarily because of anticipatory capacities, but simply because the level of slack was so high that rationalisation of municipal management, in combination with top-down imposed stabilisation measures, was good enough to counterbalance most of the financial pressures caused by the crisis. However, some signs of adaptation mainly through the attraction of European funds are evident.

This does not mean, however, that the city would be able to buffer another economic downturn. After all, the City B had already been shaken by successive shocks caused by unpredictable outcomes of massive litigations triggered by former employees and unsatisfied suppliers, while the municipal management had not found a way to timely estimate and record provisions for such risks. City B is not implementing modern systems of internal monitoring and performance indicators. According to the interviewees, this is partly due to the fact that leading posts are still occupied by older municipal servants who tend to be more passive and mistrustful towards management innovation and new technologies. On the opposite younger employees would be more aware of the possibilities offered by such systems. In summary, City B has shown significant buffer capacity, it has rationalised some internal procedures and improved its awareness for financial risks and chances, but the crisis has not been systematically dealt with as an opportunity for improvement of municipal operation. The City's perception of resilience is based on low levels of indebtedness and prudent management, while the interviewees highlighted narrow margins for municipal governance flexibility and strong dependence on central government decisions and funding.

City C

City C is a rather large working class city of approximately 140,000 inhabitants that used to have negative financial results until 2010 and, paradoxically, from 2011 onwards shows positive ones (measured under accrual accounting). However this surprising result can be explained. Until the crisis having a positive budgetary position was not a political priority and this is why deficits were reported. Showing surpluses was not considered wise from a political point of view as excess spending signalled that the city was devoting plenty of resources on service provision to citizens. Nevertheless this stance changed, when the financial environment drastically altered and City C faced the severe decline in state subsidies from 2011 onwards. More specifically subsidies decreased by 27% from 2011 to 2014.

Nevertheless, the first shock in 2011 has been well managed in this city that was very prudent with spending decisions at that year. This attitude was a clear indication of anticipatory capacity. Financial management adopted a conservative stance and authorises the execution of expenditures only when the necessary liquidity is available. Realism in revenues estimation is considered the cornerstone in financial management. Due to the crisis, taxpayers started delaying their payments which had as an effect a constant rise in the value of receivables on a yearly basis. At the same time, citizens' needs for city services augmented. On the other hand, operating costs went down mainly due to the decrease of employees and the salary cuts across the board. However, the quality and the breadth of services were not impaired. This was achieved thanks to the adequacy of infrastructure and the commitment of municipal personnel. Prior to the crisis, City C had heavily invested in land, infrastructure, machinery and vehicles. Municipal leadership prioritised investment spending in order to upgrade the position of the city within the wider area of major Athens. Thus after the crisis outbreak the city had already installed adequate capacity for service provision. Thus new investments were not needed, just operating expenses for their maintenance. These are rather indications of anticipatory capacities in the sense that the City C had invested in infrastructure instead of devoting resources in operating expenses. However, these actions are highly unlikely related to the ability of the City C to forecast the impending situation. The city has also showed adapting capacity and successfully exploited available European funding more intensively than before.

As for human resources management, the city prioritises coordinated action and good relations between employees and management. This has paid back. The Mayor of City C is in office since 2002 and this leadership stability has contributed to the creation of trust which decreases vulnerability. Being in office for such a long time, is not common for Mayors in Greece. Even the opposition seems to be supportive and approves the majority of financial management decisions. This facilitated consensus building for necessary budget reallocations. The city did not get any new loans after 2008 and debt servicing is uninterrupted. Thus the city was able to buffer the shock and recover to a great extent.

City C had also used some other out of the box ways of adaptation. The city has built a good reputation among suppliers and invested in building trust relations with them. These relations could be used as a buffer in periods of constrained liquidity. Furthermore, the city uses short-term employment schemes when possible, in order to relieve the heavy work load of permanent personnel. These are indications not only of adaption to the crisis but of transformation towards successful business practices, since this attitude is not typical for Greek public sector management. In this case, the crisis was a window of opportunity to learn under pressure and change formal and informal routines and priorities in city management.

While accrual accounting has been implemented since 2002, everyday financial management is made on the basis of cash data and budget related ratios. The financial management team is staffed by professional accountants with long-term experience in public sector accounting. Most of the ratios used are relevant to the formal oversight procedures initiated by the OFALG. They are reviewed on a systematic basis and they are monitored to be compliant with oversight obligations. Financial and non-financial indicators are not monitored in parallel, but the money City C spends on services to citizens (e.g. kindergartens, sports etc.) is related to a predefined negotiated volume of output. Therefore there is a very rough performance measurement system in place that according to the interviewees seems to work.

City C has successfully copied with other vulnerability sources prior to the crisis. The most important ones had to do with the abolition of earmarked grants which were then included in a general grant that drastically decreased afterwards. While this settlement was applicable to all LGs, City C was highly influenced as it was dependent on earmarked grants. Another vulnerability source refers to litigations from former employees that were fired because of national laws. Therefore, the origin of both past and future vulnerability sources is mainly found in central government decisions. As City C is heavily reliant on state subsidies, its fate is to a great extent dependent on the situation of the national economy.

After the crisis, City C increased social services. But an important part of these actions is financed by private sector donations and does not burden the budget. Social innovation was triggered and the city developed initiatives, apart from common ones dealing with poverty, that have to do with the support of young mothers and their infants as well as with students that study far from home. The role of the city towards poverty relief demonstrates significant coping and transformation capacities.

For the interviewed municipal actors, resilience is related to being careful, informed, well prepared and forward looking. Flexibility is also a parameter that corresponds to resilience. The fact that the city managed the crisis is not only due to sound financial management but also to an effective human capital management culture.

City D

City D is a medium-sized LG of approximately 70,000 inhabitants that shows a steady financial position of around zero for the last 10 years with minor exceptions. The crisis was seen as an opportunity for the LG to improve cost management and become efficient in registering citizens' tax obligations in a timely manner. As a result, the registration of higher revenues, thanks to their timely recognition, slowed down the negative effect due to the citizens' difficulties in repaying their obligations. Prior to the crisis, the city did not have any problems in collecting revenues. Its reliance on loans was and remained very low. Financial problems, albeit not intense ones, started after the crisis where several shops closed resulting in lower city taxes, while state-ordered abolition of municipal police nearly eliminated revenue from parking tickets. The city uses legal ways for tax collection but it avoids extreme measures in order not to cause social resentment.

City D provides an extensive array of services. Its sound financial condition even allowed service expansion after the crisis and several new social services aiming at the most vulnerable ones (e.g. social grocery, social pharmacy) were introduced.

City D was one of the first to apply accrual accounting and it is staffed with professional accountants. Financial statements are produced on time and financial ratios accompany the discussion of the financial statements. However, financial management is made, mainly, on cash information related to the budget execution. New norms imposed after the crisis by central government (e.g. monthly information about the execution of the budget, reporting to the OFALG etc.) are linked to reports that are also used for internal, managerial purposes. The city did not develop any other, customised, systems for financial management purposes and relies only on these centrally imposed systems. In parallel, City D does not set any non-financial targets.

The city had not experienced any memorable shocks before the crisis. The implications of the crisis were significant and stopped its growth as a prosperous part of major Athens. The interviewees pointed out that they tried to maintain a good level of social services, avoid measures against citizens who were unable to pay their taxes and they refrained from beginning new big investment projects. Nevertheless, some investments went on being financed by European funds. Moreover, part of the effects of the shock on revenues was counterbalanced by the decrease in the payroll cost.

The uncertainty about the development of the national economy is the main vulnerability source faced by the city. Decreasing subsidies, rigid procedures, new laws imposing tax burdens on LGs can easily impair the financial health of the city. These threats are difficult to predict and constitute important vulnerability sources.

There is also another vulnerability source that is related to the willingness of the city personnel to work towards improvement as the city follows the general rules governing public sector remuneration and promotions. Extensive red tape in everyday routine, successive salary decreases and the public sector promotion scheme that is based on years of service and education qualifications, do not really motivate people to do their best. Nevertheless, there are some dedicated employees that work towards improvement despite the unfavourable working conditions. However, in general the city does not seem to have developed any important anticipatory capabilities after the crisis nor has the crisis contributed towards transforming City D.

For City D, resilience is related to enduring capacity, being well prepared and forward looking and with the ability to recover quickly. Moreover, it is related to the financial health. The financial management of the city has situation awareness, but most of its actions are related to buffering capacities.

The city has set as a goal for the future to straighten the internal control mechanisms, to try to introduce better human resources management systems and become more accountable by disclosing financial information to citizens. Therefore, it seems that the crisis had increased the capacities – anticipatory and coping – of City D. City D understands that it has to be careful now, not only because it cannot take the level of state subsidies for granted (as it did in the past) but also because citizens' awareness has increased. Public spending is much more critically assessed by the citizens, compared to a rather relaxed attitude in the past.

DISCUSSION AND CONCLUSIONS

In this chapter we presented four case studies of Greek local government financial resilience. An overview of the distinct resilience dimensions is found in Table 2. The common denominator of the analysis is that all cities do not show significant anticipatory capabilities. This might be due to several shocks related to central government policies that are not only difficult to predict but also quick to introduce, and to the ambiguity of the financial condition in the country. Local governments do not possess sophisticated tools to anticipate crises. According to the interviewees the cash-based accounting information seems sufficient for monitoring and control while the accrual accounting information is used only to a limited extent in practice. In any case, the budgeting and accounting systems have not flagged the financial shocks coming and therefore their anticipatory capacity was low. This is not surprising as they do not have a meaningful medium to long-term orientation and above all the financial condition at central level was difficult to predict.

The empirical findings have shown that all investigated cities have demonstrated impressive buffering capacities. An explanation could be the high level of over-spending before the crisis that left a lot of space of manoeuvre for dealing with the shocks. Furthermore, centrally imposed and top-down implemented austerity measures reduced the level of spending and especially staff costs.

New principles and methods (e.g. zero deficit, debt break, continuous reporting and controlling) of budgeting and financial management introduced through national legislation considerably improved efficiency, transparency and accountability while the LGs, on their part, proved to be particularly flexible and open towards social innovation. All investigated LGs were not over-indebted and seem to have avoided taking new loans. Moreover, the shock of the crisis and the unprecedented decrease in municipal budgets seem to have triggered a cultural shift towards prudent management and parsimony. Anticipatory capacity of the cities stood at low levels before the crisis, but it considerably improved afterwards. Out of the four cities, City B and City D could rather be described as cases of contented fatalism, while City A and City C are reactive adapters. It might be that City A has started embarking on a path of self-regulatory/proactive adopter resilience but it is too early to conclude. More generally, across the cases reviewed there was adaptation but very limited transformation of LGs. Although partial changes in internal procedures and rationalisation of operation were introduced in several parts of the municipal machinery, it is obvious that most changes were responding to government decisions and were concentrating on financial management. Out of the four cities, City C is the only one implementing a rough system of performance control that is bridging financial indicators with service operation. As far as accounting systems are concerned, it has to be noted that while accrual systems are in place and financial statements are produced, cash basis accounting information prevails as a basis for decision making and financial management. This might be explained by the fact that oversight controls are solely based on budget execution abiding by specific rules. This finding is in accordance with earlier evidence regarding local governments in Greece even before the crisis (Cohen, Kaimenakis, & Venieris, 2013). Moreover, the same conclusion can be drawn as far as central government accounts are concerned. The Troika has only been interested in monitoring the implementation of the budget and in reviewing the variance between budgeted and actual expenditure and revenue. The modified cash accounting numbers produced since 2011 by the central government have not ever been discussed in periodic reviews by either the IMF or the EU, nor have they ever been used for target setting. Therefore, it would be concluded that the system that prevails is the one used for performance measurement and compliance assessment, in our case the cash-based budgeting system.

These findings show that Greek LGs are still vulnerable to future shocks and especially to a further deepening of the on-going crisis. Interestingly, no examples of LGs partnerships with private sector companies existed in any of the four analysed cases. On the contrary, there were several cases of partnerships with the civil society and a few cases of partnering with public bodies through 'programmatic contracts'. While efforts to balance the budget and sustain an acceptable level of service provision were successful, reform and modernisation of municipal operation was rather neglected and path-dependency of long-established centralist patterns is slowing down or even discouraging mobilisation of local reform capacities. Therefore, fiscal decentralisation and empowerment of local government seems to be the proper way to increase political accountability of local leaders for financial management and service performance and provide strong incentives for rationalisation and modernisation of municipal operation. The success story of social innovation after the crisis has revealed impressive capacities of local communities that were overlooked before and should therefore be the subject of further research for local resilience. In the same realm, it would be interesting to study why LGs did not proceed in partnerships with the private sector in order to build sustainable business collaborations.

NOTES

1. Expenses cannot exceed the levels of the approved budget and they have to be pre-audited for accuracy, legality and regularity by the Court of Audit. Salary expenses, rents, recurring expenses for utilities and low value expenditures are not subject to pre-audit. The ex-ante audit performed by the Court of Audit is to abolished from 1/1/2019.
2. However, while the number of permanent employees is low, there are some thousands of additional employees on contract basis (mostly during the summer and especially in tourist areas).
3. These figures are based on cash basis data.
4. The accrual accounting financial statements present the net surplus or net deficit of the year. This measure is important as it reflects the net result of LG operations during the year. It reflects the consumption of the necessary resources (including depreciation) for service provision and the recognition of accrued revenues that correspond to the year. This amount is deflated by total revenues (i.e. own revenues and subsidiaries) in order to account for LG size.

REFERENCES

Barbera, C., Jones, M., Korac, S., Saliterer, I., & Steccolini, I. (2015). Bouncing back and bouncing forward − Applying an alternative perspective on European municipalities' responses to financial shocks. EGPA Annual Conference, PSG VI: Governance of Public Sector Organizations, Toulouse, France, August 26−28.

Cohen, S. (2015). Public sector accounting and auditing in Greece. In I. Brusca, E. Caperchione, S. Cohen, & F. Manes Rossi (Eds.), *Public sector accounting and auditing in Europe: The harmonization challenge*. Basingstoke: Palgrave Macmillan.

Cohen, S., Kaimenaki, E., & Zorgios, Y. (2007). Assessing IT as a Key Success Factor for Accrual Accounting Implementation in Greek Municipalities. *Financial Accountability and Management, 23*(1), 91−111.

Cohen, S., Kaimenakis, N., & Venieris, G. (2013). Reaping the benefits of two worlds: An exploratory study of the cash and the accrual accounting information roles in local governments. *Journal of Applied Accounting Research, 14*(2), 165−179.

Dexia Credit Local Research Department. (2008). *Sub-national Governments in the European Union. Organisation, Responsibilities and Finance*. La Défense: Dexia Editions.

Dexia Credit Local Research Department. (2011). *Sub-national public finance in the European Union*. La Défense: Dexia Editions.

Hlepas, N. (2011). Impacts of local government reforms in Greece: An interim assessment. *Local Government Studies, 37*(5), 517–532.

Hlepas, N. (2015). *The quality of the national institutional environment of EU and neighbouring countries in comparative perspective.* In J. Albarracin (Ed.), SEARCH Research and Assessment on Euro-Mediterranean Relations, European Institute of the Mediterranean (IEMed.), Barcelona, pp. 193–230. Documents 10 IEMed.

L. 3845/2010. Measures for the application of the support mechanism for the Greek Economy by euro area Member States and the International Monetary Fund.

L. 3852/2010. Reorganization of Local Government – Kallikrates programme (in Greek).

L. 4093/2012. Approving the medium-term fiscal strategy 2013–2016 and introducing emergency measures implementing Law N° 4046/2012 and the medium-term fiscal strategy 2013–2016.

P.D. 315/1999. Sectoral accounting plan for municipalities (in Greek).

Sotirakou, T., & Zeppou, M. (2005), How to align Greek civil service with European Union public sector management policies: A demanding role for HR managers in the contemporary public administration context. *International Journal of Public Sector Management, 18*(1), 54–82.

CHAPTER 9

PATTERNS OF FINANCIAL RESILIENCE IN ITALIAN MUNICIPALITIES

Carmela Barbera

ABSTRACT

The 2008 economic and financial crisis has particularly hit Italy, forcing governments to cope with unprecedented shocks affecting their financial conditions. Drawing on the resilience concept, the chapter aims to investigate what capacities are deployed and developed by Italian local governments to respond to such shocks. Based on a multiple case study, it explores the role of organisational features and capacities, as well as the characteristics of the external environment, in affecting responses and the related results. From the analysis it emerges that different capacities have been deployed by Italian municipalities to anticipate and cope with financial shocks in recent years, leading to four main patterns of financial resilience: proactive and internally driven, fatalist, constrained and contented resilience. The contribution highlights that simply relying on (past) wealthy conditions, or accumulating resources, is not sufficient for coping with shocks. By contrast, it emphasises the importance of investing on anticipating the consequences of negative events.

Keywords: Resilience; local government; anticipatory capacity; coping capacity; crisis; austerity

Governmental Financial Resilience: International Perspectives on how Local Governments Face Austerity
Public Policy and Governance, Volume 27, 153–171
Copyright © 2017 by Emerald Publishing Limited
ISSN: 2053-7697/doi:10.1108/S2053-769720170000027009

INTRODUCTION

Italy has been particularly challenged in recent years as a consequence of the 2008 economic and financial crisis.

Di Mascio, Natalini, and Stolfi (2013), in contrasting Italy's responses to the 1992 and 2008 crises, point out that 'the 1992 crisis was mostly seen as an opportunity to innovate based on the principles of New Public Management (NPM), although it also produced a repertoire of cutback measures. Conversely, even though some of the managerial elements have been kept alive, the responses to the 2008 crisis have emphasized the cutback repertoire' (Di Mascio et al., 2013, p. 17).

Italy represents a particularly interesting case in the study of financial management during crises and times of austerity. Its public debt-GDP ratio ranges among the highest in the world (132.1% at the end of 2014, Banca d'Italia, 2015). The country experienced an increase of unemployment rates after 2009 (it was 12.7% in 2014, compared to an average of 7.4% of the OECD countries[1]) and its real GDP growth per capita was the weakest of all OECD countries between 2008 and 2011 (OECD, 2013, p. 13).[2]

In Italy there are three levels of government: central, regional and local (i.e. provinces and municipalities). Municipalities have been particularly stricken by the economic crisis (Barbera, Guarini, & Steccolini, 2016), both through the reduction of their tax base and an increased demand for welfare services. They also experienced a general reduction of revenues (e.g. transfers from the central government, revenues from building permits) that is posing increasing challenges in relation to their capacity to continue to provide services and make investments. According to the Financial Framework Report of Municipalities published by IFEL in 2014 (IFEL, 2014), between 2008 and 2012 total revenues remained almost stable (−0.6%), with current revenues increasing by 7.1%, also through a higher fiscal pressure on citizens, and revenues collected to fund investments[3] decreasing by 29.1%. On the expenditure side, there was a reduction of current expenditure by 0.3% and of expenditure for investment by 25%. These data should be read keeping in mind that, as a consequence of the crises, citizens' needs increased and municipalities appeared to be the only institutions to which they could address. This chapter presents a multiple case study analysis of four Italian medium-sized municipalities. It adopts an organisational focus, exploring the role of organisational features and capacities, as well as the characteristics of the external environment, in affecting responses and the related results. The empirical analysis emphasises that different capacities have been deployed by Italian municipalities to anticipate and cope with financial shocks in recent years. Based on different dynamic combinations of managerial capacities and environmental aspects, four main patterns of financial resilience emerge: proactive and internally driven, fatalist, constrained and contented resilience.

The chapter is structured as follows. The next section presents the context of the analysis while the section 'Methods' specifies the methods. In the section 'Patterns of Financial Resilience: The Italian Perspective', the results are presented, and Italian local governments' patterns of financial resilience are discussed. The section 'Discussion and Conclusion' draws conclusions and implications for practice and research.

CONTEXT

In Italy there are 8,092 municipalities, with a population ranging from 36 inhabitants (Pedesina) to about 2.8 million (Rome).[4] The governing bodies of the municipality are the legislative body, that is the Town Council, the executive body, that is the Cabinet, and the Mayor. The Mayor and the Town Council are elected by resident citizens. The Cabinet is chaired by the Mayor, who appoints the members (i.e. Aldermen).

Municipalities are in charge of all the administrative functions that concern the population and the municipal territory, in particular services related to individuals and the local community, for example social services, public transportation, waste collection, street lighting and road maintenance. Moreover, they provide services related to land use and economic development. They are allowed to raise both local taxes (with property tax representing the major revenue source), and fees for the services they provide, within the legal limits set by the central government. Italian municipalities' average own-revenue ratio[5] was 60.8% in 2013 (ANCI, 2015), however, they lack any real power to regulate the most important aspects of taxes, including the tax bases and rates (Corte dei Conti, 2015).

The average per capita expenditure of Italian municipalities in 2013 was 995.1 euros (of which 772.9 euros was current expenditure and 222.1 euros capital expenditure) (ANCI, 2015).

Since 2008 centrally defined fiscal policies concerning municipalities have been continually changing, inspired by a new emphasis of central government scrutiny and constraints on local governments. Among these there are decisions on central transfers to local governments, but also on tax bases related to local taxes, as well as on fiscal and budgetary constraints. In particular, since 2012 decisions over the amount of transfers have suffered from significant uncertainty as well as delays. Moreover, central government has repeatedly and significantly modified the regulations concerning local property taxes, increasing uncertainty over the revenue base and fiscal targets (Corte dei Conti, 2014).

Finally, constraints related to the Domestic Stability Pact[6] have been strengthened in recent years, to enhance the contribution of local government to fiscal consolidation. Indeed, past measures appear to have produced limited results in terms of current expenditure reduction, compared to the intended central policy (Corte dei Conti, 2014; see also Cepiku et al., 2013). By contrast, recent cutback measures and spending reviews affected municipal finances and their functioning. These polices have been claimed to represent an invasion of central fiscal policy into the sphere of the competences attributed to the municipalities, adding to their already worsened financial situation due to reduced and delayed transfer payments (Corte dei Conti, 2015).

In parallel to the above developments, recent years have also witnessed significant public sector accounting reforms.

Italy has traditionally adopted a cash-commitment basis of accounting, where budgeting was viewed as the most relevant phase of the accounting cycle. Since the mid-1990s accrual-based reporting was introduced in municipalities, though with an ancillary and marginal role (see Anessi Pessina & Steccolini, 2007).

In 2009, various laws were passed with the aim of harmonising Italian public sector accounting systems and intensifying control over public finances, confirming the role of the traditional commitment-based system and strengthening the requirements towards the adoption of accruals accounting.

METHODS

Case Selection

In line with other chapters, the case selection in this study followed a theoretical sampling approach (Eisenhardt, 1989; Eisenhardt & Graebner, 2007; Patton, 2015). The analysis was focused on medium-sized municipalities with a population of more than 40,000 inhabitants. This allowed identification of authorities subject to similar institutional and environmental pressures (Eisenhardt, 1989). The final reference population, therefore, included 184 units (among the 194 municipalities with population above 40,000 inhabitants, 10 big cities, defined as metropolitan cities, were excluded due to their size and as they are subject to different regulations).

Among these, four cases were identified. In particular, first, a meaningful and comparable measure of financial performance over the long term was selected. The budgetary position, and its 10-year volatility (2003–2012), were used for this purpose, as governments are expected to keep their actual budgetary positions around zero in the medium and long term, avoiding both excessive deficits and surpluses (see Barbera et al., 2016; Bretschneider & Gorr, 1992; Hendrick, 2006; Rose & Smith, 2011).

Second, the average budgetary position over 10 years (2003−2012) was normalised by total annual revenues. The budgetary position measure was calculated as the variation in the commitment-based surplus/deficit position[7] as follows:

In terms of volatility of the budgetary position, its standard deviation over the 10-year period 2003−2012 was calculated. Table 1 contains some information about the selected municipalities, with details about their financial performance between 2003 and 2012, and the 2003−2012 average budgetary position and volatility.

Third, the municipalities were classified in terms of their combination of normalised average budgetary position and volatility.[8] Different cases were selected representing the most common combinations of budgetary position and related volatility, for a total of four cases, resulting in different patterns of financial data over the period taken into consideration. In particular, most cases showed an around zero budgetary position, or a positive budgetary position combined with a medium volatility. What emerged was a significantly lower presence of cases displaying a negative budgetary position, mainly in Southern Italy Municipalities, and of cases with positive budgetary position associated to low or high volatility.

Collection of Data and Analysis

Financial data were collected through the use of the *AIDA PA* database[9] (2003−2012 data).

For each municipality, up to four semi-structured interviews were conducted (Bailey, 2007), resulting in a total of 15 interviews. In particular, the General Secretaries (acting also as CEOs),[10] the Directors of Finance and two Service Department Directors (one for Social Services and one for Public Works) were selected as key actors in the analysis, in order to ensure triangulation of views, and provide detailed information, related to (i) the financial situation of the municipalities, (ii) key events, and specifically shocks, undergone and (iii) how the responses to shocks affected specific relevant departments such as social services and public works. In two cases during the interviews with the Director of Finance, the Responsible for the Budget[11] was also present. The interviews included open-ended questions exploring the financial health of the municipality, its main financial and non-financial goals, the main risks and shocks that the municipality had faced over the 10-year period and the related Municipality's responses.

The interviews were conducted between March and June 2015. Each interview lasted between 50 and 90 minutes, was recorded and transcribed. Transcriptions were then returned to the interviewees for validation.

Table 1. Municipalities' Financial Performance (2003–2012).

Municipality	Financial Performance[a] (%)										Mean (%)	Volatility (Std. Dev.) (%)
	2003	2004	2005	2006	2007	2008	2009	2010	2011	2012	2003–2012	2003–2012
Lissone	11.75	9.67	2.18	2.62	1.21	−5.38	16.49	3.36	8.77	1.31	5.20	6.37
Piacenza	−1.31	0.64	1.83	−4.61	2.82	23.85	−25.21	0.37	−0.84	5.10	0.26	11.86
Rozzano	−9.37	−0.41	0.98	−1.02	−0.11	7.33	−8.22	4.05	5.84	−2.29	−0.32	5.44
Sesto San Giovanni	−0.02	0.66	−0.26	0.30	1.03	0.79	0.53	−1.21	−0.40	−0.90	0.05	0.74

[a]Financial performance refers to the normalised budgetary position, calculated as (Surplus/deficit t − Surplus/deficit $t − 1$)/total operating revenues. Surplus/deficit = (cash + revenues to be recovered-commitments to be paid) (see Methods section).

PATTERNS OF FINANCIAL RESILIENCE: THE ITALIAN PERSPECTIVE

Based on Barbera et al. (2015), the cases were analysed using the following dimensions: *(financial) shocks, vulnerability, anticipatory capacity and coping capacity.*

In addition, what emerged is that the combination of vulnerability and capacities characterizing the municipalities in the past seemed to affect the way in which they *perceived* financial shocks and their capacity to cope with them (see also Table 2).

The 2008 economic crisis and related national government austerity measures were considered to be the major shocks affecting municipalities over the 10-year period. The specificities of the other dimensions are reported, for each case, in the following sub-sections.

The relationships and dynamic interaction of the above-identified dimensions over time gave rise to different patterns of financial resilience, that is proactive and internally driven resilience, resilience as powerless fatalism, constrained resilience and contented resilience.

In particular, the level of vulnerability is not only dependent on shocks and external conditions, but is also influenced by the existence, scope and quality of the different internal anticipatory and coping capacities. Moreover, the combination of vulnerability and capacities affected the way in which the shocks were perceived and interpreted, determining the attention they received, and the level and timing of responses.

Sesto San Giovanni: Proactive and Internally Driven Financial Resilience

From 2008 to 2012, the Municipality of Sesto San Giovanni experienced a reduction of current transfers from the central government of about 85%[12] and capital revenues decreased by almost 90%. To maintain the budgetary balance, taxes were increased by 60%.

This Municipality appears to strongly rely on its own capacities and to continuously strive to become financially autonomous. The latter attitude is reflected in an average budgetary position that stays around zero and volatility that is generally relatively low, both before and after the crises. This mirrors a strong attention towards maintaining a stable financial position over time, even after adjusting for shocks, and is accompanied by low vulnerability and high anticipatory and coping capacities, both before and after the crises.

In particular, internal competences, planning capacity, control mechanisms and the adoption of risk management systems (especially within the department of public works) were well developed. Together with low debt and political stability, these aspects contributed to a lower level of vulnerability, thus a higher

Table 2. Comparison of Resilience Dimensions (Factors) across Cases.

	Sesto San Giovanni	Rozzano	Piacenza	Lissone
Budgetary position	*Zero*	*Zero*	*Zero*	*Positive*
Volatility	*Low*	*Medium*	*High*	*Medium*
Shock/ impact	Financial crisis, grant reduction, higher demand for services, tightening of fiscal targets, re-centralisation of decisions and financial controls	Financial crisis, grant reduction, higher demand for services, tightening of fiscal targets, re-centralisation of decisions and financial controls	Financial crisis, grant reduction, higher demand for services, tightening of fiscal targets, re-centralisation of decisions and financial controls	Financial crisis, grant reduction, higher demand for services, tightening of fiscal targets, re-centralisation of decisions and financial controls
Perception of shocks	Threat/opportunity	Threat	Threat	Threat
Vulnerability (before)	*Low/medium*: Low debt financing, strengths related to external networking, political stability, difficulties in revenues collection (social housing), rigidity (personnel costs)	*High*: High debt financing ('externalized to subsidiaries'), reliance on external subsidiaries but low control on them, reliance on external funding, weaknesses in revenues' collection	*Low*: Good economic conditions (presence of industries), low debt level, high monitoring level of subsidiaries (good financial results), strengths related to the exploitation of the private sector support	*Low/medium*: Good economic conditions (flourishing housing market and increase of population), low debt level, accumulation of slack resources, difficulties in revenues collection (social housing)
Anticipatory capacity (before)	*High*: Strong planning, monitoring and control processes	*Low*: Weak planning and monitoring processes, limited monitoring of revenues collection	*High*: Strong planning, monitoring and control processes	*Low*: Weak planning and monitoring processes
Coping capacity	*High*	*Low*	*Medium*	*Low*
	Buffering: Cost cuts, prioritising	*Buffering*: Increase in fees and charges, selling of assets, selling assets, deferring investments and maintenance, brake on debt	*Buffering*: Cost cuts, deferring investments (based on external funding)	*Buffering*: Increase in fees, selling of assets

Adapting: Restructuring and reorganisation of services, improving internal competences, greater networking with external stakeholders	*Adapting*: Re-targeting service users, informatization (only recently)	*Adapting*: Rationalisation, restructuring and reorganisation of services, improving internal competences, greater networking with the private sector (project financing, leasing)	*Adapting*: Rationalisation, restructuring and reorganisation of services, increasing networking (aim: cost cut and avoiding duplication)
Anticipatory capacity (after) *High*: Strong planning, monitoring and control processes	*Low*: Weak planning and monitoring processes, limited monitoring of revenues collection	*High*: Strong planning, monitoring and control processes	*Low/increasing*: Weak planning and first attempt to introducing monitoring and control systems
Vulnerability (after) *Increasing*: Low debt financing, political stability, unstable revenue sources, strict fiscal constraints	*High*: Uncertainty on revenues sources, weaknesses in revenues' collection, low control on subsidiaries, debt level decrease	*Increasing*: Low debt financing, unstable revenue sources, strict fiscal constraints, greater risks associated to alternative solutions (e.g. project financing)	*Increasing*: Low debt financing, inability to spend the surplus accumulated, strict fiscal constraints, unstable revenues sources
Pattern of resilience Proactive adapter	Powerless fatalist	Constrained	Contented

capacity to respond to shocks. The existence of problems such as the difficulties in the collection of revenues from social housing and the rigidity of some expenditures were considered as critical issues but, on the whole, as aspects that traditionally characterize all local governments.

> [We have] a strong control over expenditure. (Social Services Department Director)

To cope with the crisis, on the one hand the Municipality enhanced existing approaches, tools and capacities, on the other hand new solutions and alternatives were adopted. In particular, control mechanisms, and responsibility in contributing to the identification and achievement of financial goals, were strengthened, resulting in an improvement of anticipatory capacity.

The Municipality used near-term buffering capacities, but was also inspired by a long-term perspective. Reduction of expenditure and focus on priorities were seen as essential responses for the maintenance of existing services without compromising their quality. More substantial changes were, then, introduced, such as the restructuring and reorganisation of services, the improvement of internal competences and greater networking with private actors.

> The organization has tried to handle shocks through (...) the adoption of spending review processes and services' reorganization. (Director of Finance)

> We are carrying out a project (...) where the Municipality will supervise the service, contributing to the design and participating to calls for funding, but the service will be managed in partnership with the private sector. (Social Services Department Director)

These kind of responses reflect the perception of shocks as an opportunity for improvement, and thus responses were more proactive and wide-ranging, incentivizing adaptation in order to reduce expenditure. In short, this Municipality was shown to be able to internally develop, over time, capacities that allow it to more successfully cope with shocks. Reactions are, thus, based on existing competences and resources as well as exploring new alternatives (e.g. services' innovation, networking).

Rozzano: Powerless Fatalism

In the Municipality of Rozzano, current transfers from the central government decreased by 92% between 2008 and 2012. To offset this reduction, taxes where increased. Capital revenues decreased by almost 80%.

The Municipality showed a budgetary position around zero and a medium volatility. It had limited planning and monitoring mechanisms, reflecting low levels of anticipatory capacity when the crisis hit.

> Internally, culture over revenues' collection is not yet well developed; by contrast, the offices [i.e., people working within offices] are very likely to spend. (Responsible for the Budget)

This contributed to high vulnerability. Another source of weakness is the number of subsidiaries of the Municipality that is particularly high, causing difficulties in the control over their expenditure, according to the interviewees. The subsidiaries also showed a high level of debt that negatively affected the municipal budget. In addition, according to the interviewees, the Municipality has always tended to rely mainly on external funding to finance services and investments. For example, at the end of the 1990s urban regeneration programs were implemented, funded by regional and European resources. Since 2000, most investments were financed through urban plans that, relying on the flourishing housing market, allowed the Municipality to collect high levels of revenues that were used to requalify the town areas where social housing is developed.[13] These resources were also used on the current side, despite their exceptional nature. However, this proved a misjudgment when the housing bubble burst.

Between 2008 and 2011 [the high surpluses] were definitely related to urban plans that guaranteed extraordinary revenues (…). (Public Works Department Director)

Another aspect of vulnerability of the Municipality was associated to its 'conservative' approach adopted in the past with reference to the hiring policies of employees (i.e. hiring much fewer people than it could have been feasible). Paradoxically, while this can be attributed to the need to bring expenditure under control, it became a weakness after the shocks, when centrally imposed hiring freezes did not allow the Municipality to cope with the increased demand for services and central government criteria for defining governmental transfers to municipalities have been based on their previous years' expenditure. This implies that part of the solution to past financial issues contributed to ongoing problems.

The Municipality was, thus, particularly unprepared when the shocks arrived and a sense of powerlessness prevailed. Anticipatory capacity was still weak. Indeed, the absence of culture towards monitoring prevailed within the municipality. Furthermore, external pressures (e.g. central government impositions) affected municipal capacity to plan activities.

The timing for the approval of the budget is both related to law and to organizational difficulties that prevent us from making adequate planning. (General Secretary)

Responses were limited and a passive behaviour oriented towards relying on buffering capacities (e.g. increasing taxes and fees, selling assets, transforming superficies rights to properties,[14] selling assets, deferring investments) prevailed within the Municipality, not willing (or unable) to take ownership of the changes and deflecting issues back onto national governments. Adapting capacities were limited and consisted in the re-targeting of service users and improving internal efficiency through greater reliance on ICT (only recently).

> On the revenues side, we are forced to increase rates at the maximum level (...). In the past, we partly used some reserves, i.e. selling assets... (Public Works Department Director)

> Now we tend to limit investments to the most deteriorated sections [of roads] or we only repair the potholes. (Public Works Department Director)

While representing a way for responding to the shocks and dodging the central government constraints, the short-term-oriented buffering capacities deployed, together with a persistent low anticipatory capacity, seem to have contributed to the maintenance of a high level of vulnerability. Uncertainty over external resources and the Stability Pact also affected municipal autonomy and margins for manoeuvre, leaving the Municipality with a sense of inability to react to the shocks.

> (...) the continuous change of rules [due to external impositions], even those related to how the budget should be managed... these are the main issues, because we do not know what's coming. (Social Services Department Director)

In sum, a fatalist approach characterises this Municipality, where a day-by-day approach to managing emergencies prevails.

Piacenza: Constrained Resilience

The Municipality of Piacenza, like the other cases, experienced a reduction of current transfers from the central government, amounting to about 97%. Capital revenues decreased by 86% while taxes increased by 84%.

The Municipality of Piacenza displayed an around zero budgetary position but high volatility, and was not financially vulnerable before the crisis. This was mainly due to its good economic conditions, dependent on the presence of many industries at the local level that guaranteed high revenues, reducing the need for the Municipality to access borrowing. Municipal subsidiaries were made responsible for their financial performance. This guaranteed positive financial results, thus representing another major strength. Reliance on the exploitation of the private sector support was found to further contribute to low vulnerability.

> The presence of industries brings resources [to the municipal budget], including the building permits: this has reduced the need to access borrowing (...). (General Secretary)

Anticipatory capacity was high, characterised by on time approval (at least until 2012) and good administering of the budget, strong monitoring and control.

> We have a reporting system and specific indicators (...) We also have an internal evaluation system (...) and a series of external controls (e.g., by users, on services' provision). We use questionnaires of customer satisfaction (...). We have constant and daily monitoring. (General Secretary)

The increasing uncertainty on revenues from the central government has impacted on the approval times of the budget, which have been postponed since 2012. However, after the shocks, anticipatory capacity remained high. Indeed, efforts were made oriented towards an improvement of internal monitoring and control, although this was also partially dictated by external constraints.

> While, in the past, (...) subsidiaries were managed by different municipal offices and departments, based on their field of competence (education, social services, economic development, etc.), now monitoring, management and control over them have been centralized. (Director of Finance)

With reference to coping capacity, the Municipality had relied heavily on its favourable economic conditions in the past; after the shocks, it was necessary to defer investments due to the lack of availability of external funding. Reliance on competencies developed in the past (e.g. a greater understanding of, and capacity to answer to, local needs by social services had improved this service before the crises) allowed the Municipality to initially absorb the shocks without a strong investment in new capacities. Only recently has the Municipality recognised the need to differently address emerging challenges, through rationalisation, the restructuring and reorganisation of services and the improvement of internal competences. Also greater networking with the private sector (i.e. project financing, leasing) started to be taken into consideration. These tools were not considered in the past and they were not particularly appreciated also after the shocks, as they require specific skills – that traditionally do not characterize local governments – to be developed within the Municipality.

> The positive aspect [of the crisis] is that we had to review and reconsider our expenses through processes aimed at enhancing efficiency. I do not know whether we would have put them into practice in the absence of this storm. We are now more efficient than we were before crisis. (Social Services Department Director)

> This is a period in which you can provide resources by using innovative systems of project financing; we are currently taking into account leasing procedures (...). [However,] we lack internal competences able to deal with these tools. This implies significant risks. (Public Works Department Director)

The development of strong coping capacities was postponed (approximately between one or two years later) compared to the timing of the crises hitting local governments and this was due to its initial favourable economic conditions. This may have contributed to an increase in vulnerability after the crisis. The high level of revenues collected due to the presence of industries allowed the Municipality to rely on bearing resources in the past but, after the economic crises, these resources started to decrease.

Despite its anticipatory capacity and the deployment of both buffering and adapting coping capacities (although the adoption of adapting capacities were postponed, compared to other cases and specifically the case of Sesto San Giovanni with which it shares some similarities), this Municipality, thus, appeared to perceive that external constraints and financial shocks limited its capacity to cope with external challenges and lead to the identification of temporary responses.

> We run the risk of not being able to find structural responses to the problem of expenditure reduction (...) The answer we are brought to give could be extraordinary. (...) (Director of Finance)

Lissone: Contented Resilience

The Municipality of Lissone witnessed a reduction of current transfers from the central government of 96%. The decrease of capital revenues (39%) was less severe than the other three cases. Both taxes and fees increased, respectively by 53% and 4%.

In Lissone, the budgetary position was positive with medium volatility.

Financial vulnerability was quite low before the shocks. This was mainly due to the good economic conditions that it had been experiencing in the previous years, when the housing market flourished as well as local population. Moreover, the Municipality was characterised by a low debt level and the accumulation of slack resources. Indeed, it experienced huge surpluses during the 10-year period under study (with peaks in 2011 and 2012). Some difficulties were related to the collection of revenues from social housing.

> I think that Lissone was very cautious, with regard to investments (...). In fact, we found a huge surplus (...). So we were able to cushion the crisis. We can say that Lissone did not see the crisis. (...) Probably we are now witnessing it. (General Secretary)

The low level of vulnerability may have contributed to the presence of weak anticipatory capacities, included a lack of medium term financial planning, also after the shocks, although the interviewees declared to have started a collaboration with a software house, for the introduction of a monitoring and control system. Apart from some interventions of rationalisation, restructuring and reorganisation of services, and networking with local associations in order to avoid services duplications (cost cutting), coping capacities mainly relied on buffering.

> [We need to] plan, at least adopting a medium term perspective, because it is not good to focus only on the single financial year. (Director of Finance)

> Let's say that our monitoring, until this year, has been like homemade. This is a critical issue. (General Secretary)

> We have been buffering, in recent years. Yes, we rationalized expenditure but we adopted many extraordinary, non-consolidated, measures (...) e.g., you make agreements with associations just because this is the only solution that you have (...). We find year by year solutions. (Director of Finance)

This contented-like approach, based on buffering capacity and the downplaying (at least until 2015) of the adoption of anticipatory capacities, led to an increase of the vulnerability perceived by the interviewees. In addition to unstable revenues sources, strict fiscal constraints reduced decision-making power over the municipal finances, impeding the Municipality to use the surplus accumulated in previous years. In addition, like in the case of Rozzano, a 'conservative' approach adopted in the past with reference to the hiring policies of employees represented a major weakness after the crises, as retirements and the need to answer emerging needs clashed with the inability to hire new personnel.

> According to the ministerial decree that identifies the proportion between population and municipal employees, we should have 420 employees. Instead, they are 200 (...). (General Secretary) The Municipality did not hire people when it was able to... (Social Services Department Director)

DISCUSSION AND CONCLUSION

As anticipated in the results section, the Municipalities appeared to be hit by similar shocks. However, the letter can be perceived and interpreted in different ways within organisations (Weick, 1988). In three cases, they were perceived as a threat, given the potential impact on financial resources, the effects on the local economy and society and, in turn, on the increasing complexity of services demanded.

In one case, that is Sesto San Giovanni, while recognising the negative consequences of shocks, perceived the crisis period as an opportunity to question the status quo, leading to changes in organisational activities and design just after shocks and in a proactive and wide-ranging way.

A range of external and internal factors were seen to contribute to the vulnerability of municipalities, that is dependence on uncertain revenue bases, rigidity of expenditure, uncertain or reducing resource transfers from higher governmental levels, external networking, political stability, high levels of debt. In two cases the lack of slack resources, in terms of human resources and current expenditure for services' provision, was considered as a source of vulnerability, as this made it harder to address the growing citizens' demand for welfare services after the crises and the reduction of the expenditure imposed by the central government.

Anticipatory capacities included good strategic and financial planning, internal monitoring processes, risk management.

The analysis revealed that dealing with shocks required municipalities to rely on two main *coping capacities*, that is *buffer capacity* and *adaptive capacity*. *Buffering capacity* was present within all cases both before and after the shocks and relied on cost cutting, prioritising, increasing taxes and fees, selling assets, deferring investments, collecting dividends by the subsidiaries and selling assets to absorb short-term, one off and minor financial shocks. This was mainly managed at a service level and in some cases on a day-to-day basis. A*daptive capacity* did not characterize all municipalities before the shocks, but it started to be developed in some cases after. It consists in the improvement of internal competences, the adjustment of organisational activities, rationalisations, the reorganisation or restructuring of services, the re-targeting of services users, while not fundamentally changing the modus operandi/aims and objectives of the municipality.

It is important to note that the two types of coping capacities are not mutually exclusive and can be used in conjunction with one another, or even overlap. Indeed, some municipalities used both types of coping capacities while others, initially, limited themselves to rely on buffering capacities.

The diversity of financial resilience patterns found in this study seems to rely on both the types of capacities deployed – that is the prevalence of buffering or adapting capacities – and on the timing of deployment.

The analysis also highlights that, in Italy, the external pressures due to the unstable legislative framework in which the municipalities operate, with the central government increasingly encroaching on local level decision-making sphere, has led most recent years to a widespread increased level of vulnerability. This can be interpreted according to what has already been emphasised in literature, that is that the burden of consolidation in some countries, like Italy, has been shifted to sub-national units. This has been accompanied by higher levels of expenditure required for providing services, due to new demands and the need to address much more complexity, without corresponding revenue power (in practice) (OECD, 2015b, p. 82).

This does not imply that investing in anticipatory and coping capacities is not relevant; by contrast, from those cases that relied almost exclusively on their wealthy conditions in the past, lessons can be learned. In particular, a greater focus on anticipating the consequences of the shocks, adopting the already existing (or improving/developing new) capacities, would probably have implied minor difficulties in facing the shocks. This can also represent a reminder for municipalities that accumulating resources (i.e. rainy day funds) in times of stable or developing economic environment may not be sufficient for avoiding or minimising the consequences of unexpected crises. Other factors, such as external constraints imposed by the central state, may interfere on the ability to manage the budget (Wolkoff, 1987).

The contribution, thus, highlights that the policies adopted by central governments are not necessarily perceived in the same way at the local level, depending on existing capacities and vulnerability.[15] At the same time, as responses to shocks depend on these dimensions, central government decisions may not have the desired effect, according to the same direction, on local governments' reactions. Only in those contexts where resilient behaviours are predominantly based on a proactive approach, adaptation processes seem to prevail.

The study conducted on Italian municipalities showed that these organisations have been experiencing diverse shocks affecting their finances, at least since the 1990s. The financial crisis, however, represented an unprecedented challenge: some municipalities felt that it was particularly threatening while in other cases it was also seen as an opportunity to change. From this perspective, one possible question arising from the analysis which may deserve attention in further studies may be related to the extent to which recent crises have represented an opportunity for learning for public organisations.[16] This becomes an even more important point considering the findings that prior responses to a crisis determine the way municipalities face following shocks, as has been pointed out in the study by Di Mascio et al. (2013) based in Italy, comparing the measures adopted to cope the 1992 and the recent crises.

NOTES

1. OECD (2015a).
2. The average GDP per capita was 26,400 euros in 2013, compared to 27,000 euros for the EU28 countries. ISTAT (Italian National Statistic Institute): http://noi-italia2015.istat.it/index.php?id=7&L=0&user_100ind_pi1%5Bid_pagina%5D=91&cHash=fdd73a1b23d68030a42ffa4a6353cc95
3. It specifically refers to revenues collected through the disposal of assets and grants from upper levels of government (e.g. Regions, the State) or from private entities.
4. 2013 data.
5. The own-revenue ration is calculated as [(Tax revenues + Revenues from service fees and tariffs)/Current revenues]. Current revenues consist of tax revenues, current grants and transfers from other public sector sources and revenues from service fees and tariffs.
6. The Italian 'Domestic Stability Pact' has been in place since the 2000 and it involves local governments in the effort to reduce the general government deficit, with the aim to comply with the EU fiscal rules. Each financial year, local governments are required to achieve specific fiscal targets, that is expenditure cutbacks or increase in cash surpluses (for further details, see Barbera et al., 2016).
7. More information about the budgetary position under budgetary accounting in Italian municipalities can be found in Bellesia (2002), Anessi Pessina, Sicilia, and Steccolini (2012), Ministero dell'Interno (2013).
8. The normalised budgetary position was defined as negative when below −0.5; around zero when between −0.5 and +0.5; positive when over +0.5. For volatility the standard deviation of each local government was divided by the range of volatility of all the reference population (i.e. the difference between the highest and the lowest volatility, excluding outliers). When this ratio was below 0.25 volatility was considered low, whereas it was considered as high when higher than 0.75. Volatility between 0.25 and 0.75 was described as medium.
9. Aida Pa is a database of financial data of Italian local public authorities.
10. The General Secretary shall cooperate with, and assist from a legal point of view, municipal bodies, that is he/she is responsible for the compliance of administrative activity to Law. He/she also oversees the actions performed by directors and coordinates their activities, in case no CEO has been appointed within the municipality. This means that in Italy some municipalities may have two distinct people, that is the General Secretary

and the CEO, while those municipalities where there is only the General Secretary, the letter also acts as a CEO.

11. Directors of Finance are generally in charge for strategic planning, budget preparation, financial reporting, internal and external audit, etc. The department that he/she coordinates is divided, thus, in different offices/services corresponding to the various functions, each of which is managed by a responsible.

12. Financial data were retrieved from Aida pa.

13. Looking at financial data, which are available only since 2001, it can be noticed that between 2 million and 15.8 million euro of revenues were collected, every year, from 2001 and 2011, through the tax on building permits (associated to the new urban plans), with a reduction of about 80% in 2012. The amount of regional funds was not constant between 2001 and 2009 but it was between 7,000 and 4.3 million, while no funds were received between 2010 and 2012.

14. The transformation of the superficies rights consists of the sale of municipal properties involving areas already granted as surface rights. This allows municipalities to inject funds to municipal budgets.

15. This is also in line with previous literature, as scholars have already pointed out that 'capacity and response repertoire affect crisis perception' (Weick 1988, p. 311).

16. According to Christianson, Farkas, Sutcliffe, and Weick (2009), organisations learn not only 'from' but also 'through' rare events.

REFERENCES

Anci. (2015). *Ifel, I Comuni italiani 2015 – Numeri in tasca*, Ifel Fondazione Anci, Roma, SER Società Editrice Romana. Retrieved from http://www.fondazioneifel.it/studi-ricerche-ifel/item/3109-i-comuni-italiani-2015-numeri-in-tasca. Accessed on February 21, 2016.

Anessi Pessina, E., Sicilia, M., & Steccolini, I. (2012). Budgeting and re-budgeting in Italian Local Governments: Siamese twins? *Public Administration Review*, *72*(6), 875–884.

Anessi Pessina, E., & Steccolini, I. (2007). Effects of budgetary and accruals accounting coexistence: Evidence from Italian local governments. *Financial Accountability & Management*, *23*(2), 113–131.

Bailey, K. (2007). *Methods of social research* (4th ed.). New York, NY: Free Press.

Banca d'Italia. (2015). Relazione Annuale sul 2014. Retrieved from https://www.bancaditalia.it/pubblicazioni/relazione-annuale/2014/rel_2014.pdf. Accessed on February 21, 2016).

Barbera, C., Guarini, E., & Steccolini, I. (2016). Italian municipalities and the fiscal crisis: Four strategies for muddling through. *Financial Accountability and Management*. Retrieved from http://papers.ssrn.com/sol3/papers.cfm?abstract_id=2616193

Barbera, C., Jones, M., Korac, S., Saliterer, I., & Steccolini, I. (2015). Bouncing back and bouncing forward – Applying an alternative perspective on European municipalities' responses to financial shocks. Paper presented to the 2015 EGPA annual conference, Toulouse, France, PSG VI: Governance of Public Sector Organizations, August 26–28.

Bellesia, M. (2002). Analisi di bilancio. Dai dati contabili alle valutazioni di efficacia e di efficienza, Ipsoa (Milan).

Bretschneider, S., & Gorr, W. (1992). Economic, organizational, and political influences on biases in forecasting state sales tax receipts. *International Journal of Forecasting*, *7*(4), 457–466.

Cepiku, D., Jesuit, D. K., & Roberge, I. (2013). *Making multilevel public management work: Stories of success and failure from Europe and North America*. (1st ed.). CRC press, Taylor and Francis Group. ISBN: 978-1-46-651380-8.

Christianson, M. K., Farkas, M. T., Sutcliffe, K. M., & Weick, K. E. (2009). Learning through rare events: Significant interruptions at the Baltimore & Ohio railroad museum. *Organization Science*, *20*(5), 846–860. doi:10.1287/orsc.1080.0389

Corte dei Conti. (2014). *Rapporto 2014 sul Coordinamento della Finanza Pubblica*. Delibera n. 5/ 2014/RCFP. Retrieved from http://www.corteconti.it/export/sites/portalecdc/_documenti/ controllo/sezioni_riunite/sezioni_riunite_in_sede_di_controllo/2014/rapporto_2014_coordina-mento_finanza_pubblica.pdf. Accessed on February 21, 2016).

Corte dei Conti. (2015). *Rapporto 2015 sul Coordinamento della Finanza Pubblica*. Retrieved from http://www.corteconti.it/export/sites/portalecdc/_documenti/controllo/sezioni_riunite/ sezioni_riunite_in_sede_di_controllo/2015/rapporto_2015_coordinamento_finanza_pubblica. pdf. Accessed on February 21, 2016).

Di Mascio, F., Natalini, A., & Stolfi, F. (2013). The ghost of crises past: Analyzing reform sequences to understand Italy' s response to the global crisis. *Public Administration*, *91*(1), 17–31. doi:10.1111/j.1467-9299.2011.01970.x

Eisenhardt, K. M. (1989). Building theories from case study research. *The Academy of Management Review*, *14*(4), 532–550.

Eisenhardt, K. M., & Graebner, M. E. (2007). Theory building from cases: Opportunities and challenges. *Academy of Management Journal*, *50*(1), 25–32.

Hendrick, R. (2006). The role of slack in LG finances. *Public Budgeting and Finance*, *26*(1), 14–46.

IFEL. (2014). *Il Quadro finanziario dei Comuni. Rapporto 2014*. Studi e Ricerche. Retrieved from http://www.fondazioneifel.it/studi-ricerche-ifel/item/2175-il-quadro-finanziario-dei-comuni-rapporto-2014. Accessed on March 4, 2016.

Ministero dell'Interno. (2013). Decreto 18 Febbraio 2013. Individuazione degli enti strutturalmente deficitari sulla base di appositi parametri obiettivi per Il triennio 2013-15, Rome.

OECD. (2013). *OECD economic surveys: Italy 2013*. Paris: OECD Publishing. doi:10.1787/eco_sur-veys-ita-2013-en

OECD. (2015a). *OECD employment outlook 2015*. Paris: OECD Publishing. doi:10.1787/empl_out-look-2015-en

OECD. (2015b). *Institutions of intergovernmental fiscal relations: Challenges ahead, OECD fiscal federalism studies*. Paris: OECD Publishing. doi:10.1787/9789264246966-en

Patton, M. Q. (2015). Qualitative research & evaluation methods. *Integrating theory and practice* (4th ed.). London: Sage.

Rose, S., & Smith, D. L. (2011). Budget slack, institutions, and transparency. *Public Administration Review*, *22*(2), 187–195. doi:10.1111/j.1540-6210.2011.02491.x

Weick, K. E. (1988). Enacted sensemaking in crisis situations. *Journal of Management Studies*, *25*(4), 305–317.

Wolkoff, M. (1987). An evaluation of municipal rainy day funds. *Public Budgeting and Finance*, *7*(2), 52–63. doi:10.1111/1540-5850.00743

CHAPTER 10

FINANCIAL RESILIENCE: HOW DUTCH CITIES HAVE BUFFERED AND ADAPTED TO THE FINANCIAL CRISIS

Tom Overmans

ABSTRACT

Since 2010, Dutch local authorities (LGs) have been coping with fiscal stress and austerity. Restoring fiscal balance is difficult for Dutch LGs as they have very limited abilities to increase the level of local income. Fundamental choices regarding policy priorities and public services are required to reduce fiscal deficits. An in-depth case study of four carefully selected LGs revealed three typical financial shocks in the Netherlands: the reduction of national transfers to LGs, the decentralisation of national tasks to LGs without corresponding budgets and the declined value of municipal assets (construction land). The perceived vulnerability for financial shocks is relatively high in Dutch LGs due to their undiversified and uncertain revenue sources. This chapter illustrates that while the anticipatory capacity initially was low, many efforts have been made since 2010 improving risk management and medium-term financial planning. Dutch LGs have typically deployed short-term and long-term responses to cope with austerity. Regarding the short-term, two types of responses were commonly used to balance the budget: cutting costs and postponing investments. Long-term responses were deployed to realign actual operational outputs with strategically desired outputs. Sticking to strategic plans was not easy as financial shocks evolved

Governmental Financial Resilience: International Perspectives on how Local Governments Face Austerity
Public Policy and Governance, Volume 27, 173–186
Copyright © 2017 by Emerald Publishing Limited
ISSN: 2053-7697/doi:10.1108/S2053-769720170000027010

quickly. An important long-term response in the Netherlands was the 'transition of the role of government in society', moving from a proactive self-organising type of government towards a more passive, coordinating type of government. No evidence was found for radical changes of the financial system.

Keywords: Coping with austerity; local governments; Netherlands; cutback management; resilience

INTRODUCTION

Many public sector organisations in the Netherlands have been coping with shocks since 2008. At the national level, for instance, the government identified and responded to three types of shocks (Kickert, 2012). Firstly, the government saved and supported banks to deal with the financial crisis. Secondly, they took economic recovery measures to deal with the economic crisis. Thirdly, serious austerity management was needed to tackle the fiscal crisis.

Although these shocks did not noticeably influence local policies until 2010, Dutch cities have been facing austerity ever since (Overmans & Noordegraaf, 2014). Restoring the equilibrium between income and expenditure is difficult for local authorities. Not only are they partly responsible for the implementation of nationally imposed cuts, they also have limited abilities to increase the level of local income. Local authorities in the Netherlands have limited financial autonomy; they are heavily dependent on transfers from the national government. Because of these restraining determinants, local authorities need to make fundamental choices regarding policy priorities, performance and public services.

A growing number of studies focus on the effects of shocks and crises for public sector organisations. The emphasis in this chapter is on the long-term consequences of financial shocks in local authorities in the Netherlands. This is important as crises have had significant effects on the Dutch public sector and the role of government in society. Either forced by philosophical or financial motives, politicians have introduced numerous policies that contributed to the shift from *welfare state* to *participation society*. Consequently, local authorities must not only anticipate and absorb short-term fiscal gaps; they must also react strategically in order to safeguard their organisational-environmental fit (cf. Morgan, 1998).

This chapter is structured as follows. Firstly, the context of Dutch local authorities is introduced. In the methods parts, the case selection and research process are elaborated. Subsequently, the results section provides the empirical findings regarding the patterns of financial resilience. Conclusions are drawn in the final section.

CONTEXT

Main Features of Local Government and the Financial System in the Netherlands

The Netherlands is a constitutional state and has a parliamentary system (Breeman & Van Noort, 2008). There are four levels of government: national government, provincial authorities, local authorities and regional water authorities. Unlike some other countries there is only one type of local authority in the Netherlands.

The governance of Dutch local authorities consists of three elements. Firstly the *City Council* (CC), the main role of which is to provide guidelines for the local policies and to exercise oversight over their implementation. The size of the CC depends on the number of inhabitants, but is maximised to 45 members in the largest cities, such as in the cities of Amsterdam and Rotterdam. Members of the CC are chosen by the general populace. Decisions are made by simple majority. Secondly, there is the *Council of Mayor and Aldermen* (CMA), which is the executive board of the city and implements policy. The CMA has the proactive duty to inform the CC on policy and budgetary issues. The size of the CMA might vary across cities. Typically, a CMA varies from two (part time) aldermen in the smallest cities up to 5,000 inhabitants, to six full timers in cities with over 100,000 inhabitants. Members of the CMA have their own portfolio; they cannot be a member of the City Council at the same time. The CMA operates as a collegial body and decisions are made by consensus. Thirdly, there is the *Mayor*. In contrast to many other countries, the mayor in the Netherlands is not elected, but crown-appointed. The mayor is responsible for public order and safety and has a minor policy setting role. The mayor chairs the CC as well as the CMA in which he or she operates as *primus inter pares*.

In the Netherlands, local authorities are an important branch of government. More than 25% of the government's spending is accounted for by local authorities (Allers & Steiner, 2014). This contribution increases as national tasks, such as youth care, have been decentralised in recent years. The budgets spent by local authorities cover around 9% of GDP. The large contribution of local government spending indicates the wide range of public services provided by Dutch municipalities: social care, housing, infrastructure, environment, promotion of local economy, primary education, culture, sports and maintenance of public space (cf. Leisink & Bach, 2014).

There are three principal sources of income for Dutch cities. Firstly, the Municipality Fund (MF). Municipalities get most of their budget from the central government, around two-thirds of total budget. Although some transfers are ring-fenced, there is a movement towards more generic budgets with local autonomy for spending the budget. Secondly, local authorities charge users for specific services, such as garbage collection and sewage. Although this might be around 25% of total budget, it has to be spent on the specific services of the charge. No other policy can be financed with these monies. Thirdly, there are the local taxes, such as a property tax for homeowners. Around 8% of a city's budget comes from locally collected taxes (Overmans & Timm-Arnold, 2015).

As a result of NPM-thinking, many financial management practices were changed in the 1980s and 1990s. For instance, the decentralisation of financial authority to lower level managers increased the need for financial skills and professional controllers and accountants. Furthermore, accrual-based accounting standards were introduced in Dutch municipalities in 1985. Accrual accounting recognises transactions in the accounting period where transactions occur, regardless of when the payments or receipts are made or received (Bandy, 2014). It provides executives and managers with a fuller picture of actual costs and benefits of municipal services. Dutch cities must balance their budget yearly and multi-year forecasts have to provide a convincing picture of the long-term finances with matching income and expenditure. The financial sustainability is overseen by the provincial authority. Budgets for investments, such as new municipal buildings, have to come from previously collected reserves or borrowings.

Local Authorities and the Aftermath of the Financial Crisis

According to the OECD, the Netherlands suffered severely from the financial crisis and the economic consequences exceeded the average of Western countries. The period of moderate continuous growth ended. At first, the downturn was considered as a temporary slowdown; later it became obvious that the decline was severe and Dutch public organisations moved into an era of long-term fiscal stress and austerity.

Since municipal budgets depend strongly on transfers from national government, local finances were seriously affected by the crises. However, analyses of municipal budgets and austerity plans show that there were no significant concerns for the effects of the crisis until 2010. Since then, municipalities have been coping with serious levels of fiscal stress. On average, Dutch cities have had to restore a gap of approximately 250 euro per capita (Allers, 2009; Overmans & Timm-Arnold, 2015). However, there are large variations between cities. For instance, the challenge was more pressing in the city of Amsterdam (531 euro per capita) than in Haarlemmermeer, the city hosting Schiphol Airport (436 euro per capita).

METHODS

On the basis of a multiple case study, this chapter provides insights on four levels: types of financial shocks in Dutch local authorities, the perceived level of vulnerability, the level and types of anticipatory capacity and the level and types of coping capacities.

Case Selection

In line with the comparing aims of the broader research project and the other chapters in this book Barbera, Jones, Korac, Saliterer, & Steccolini, 2017), the selection of cases in the Netherlands followed the same logic and steps. Four local authorities, with maximum variety on two dimensions, were selected in order to examine the global phenomenon of *financial resilience* in the Netherlands. For reasons of comparison, only cities with more than 50,000 inhabitants qualified for the study. In the Netherlands, 75 municipalities had more than 50,000 inhabitants in 2014 (around 20%). Municipalities that had recently been involved in merges were excluded, resulting in 67 cities that were potentially appropriate for this study.

Two criteria were used to select cases: financial performance and volatility. A city's *financial performance*, in this study, refers to the 10-year average of its budgetary position. Local authorities have to balance their budget every year. In the case of an (imminent) deficit, cutbacks in expenditure are required, or unallocated reserves have to be used. The size of the movement in the latter reflects the budgetary position of the municipality. If reserves are being used to cover expenditures, the budgetary position can be characterised as being negative. If benefits exceed expenditures and money is being added to reserves, the budgetary position is positive. If expenditures and benefits are more or less equal the budgetary position is around zero. Using data of Statistics Netherlands (CBS) the budgetary position was calculated for 67 municipalities between 2005 and 2014. The second criterion is *volatility*, the rate at which the budgetary position goes up and down. Volatility is an important criterion as maintaining a stable financial position is a basic challenge for governments (Hou & Moynihan, 2008). Similar to the budgetary position, volatility was determined again using data between 2004 and 2015. Using standard deviations, a municipal's volatility was labelled low, medium or high.

In line with the other chapters, four types of cities were selected which were at the outer ends of the dimensions (see Table 1). Ede was selected as it had negative budgetary position (−2.59%) and medium volatility (1.66%). Hoorn was selected as it had a budgetary position around zero (−0.12%) and high volatility (2.18%). Zwolle was selected as it had a budgetary position around zero (0.17%) and low volatility (0.69%). Hengelo was selected as it had a positive budgetary position (1.43%) and medium volatility (1.35%).

Table 1.   Selected Local Authorities.

Budgetary Position Volatility	Negative	Zero	Positive
High		Hoorn	
Medium	Ede		Hengelo
Low		Zwolle	

Table 2.   List of Respondents.

Ede	Zwolle	Hengelo	Hoorn
City Manager	Head of finance department	Head of staff and finance	Head of planning and control
Head of services and operations	Financial manager	Senior policy advisor	Concern controller
Concern controller	Financial policy advisor	Policy advisor	Senior policy advisor

Data Collection and Interpretation

In line with the aims of this chapter, information about responses to budgetary shocks had to be uncovered as well as elements of financial resilience. Therefore, 12 qualitative interviews have been conducted with key players in each of the four local authorities (see Table 2). Among the interviewees were financial specialists, such as a chief financial officer or a concern controller. However, we have also spoken to generic officials, holding positions as city manager or policy advisor. Most respondents have long track records within their organisation. Many have been working there for over 10 years and were able to provide us with detailed information about the event. All interviews were semi-structured around five parts: introduction (personal and organisational introduction, financial aims), context (risks and shocks in the last decade), responses (actual responses, determinants, inhibitors), financial resilience (meaning and expressions), and open ending (additional information). Interviews typically took one hour. Interviews were recorded and elaborated in detailed transcripts. In order to write the case studies, these transcripts were encoded and analysed.

RESULTS

City of Ede

The city of Ede (110,000 inhabitants) is a local authority in the centre of the Netherlands. Presenting a balanced budget during the crisis years was not a sinecure; Ede has overspent its income in several years. While balanced budgets are required for Dutch local authorities, the city repeatedly had to use its reserves to restore the gap between income and expenditure. The city has a significant debt level (136% of total budget, worsening since then) but also has substantial general reserves. According to the respondents three external shocks have brought the city to a fiscal squeeze. Firstly, the decentralisation of national tasks without corresponding budgets. Not only was the provision of inadequate levels of money considered a problem, but also the modification of variables that are used for dividing national budgets over the cities caused major concerns. Secondly, the reduction of grants from the Municipality Fund (MF) which directly affected the level of income. Thirdly, the income from selling construction land has dropped significantly as land prices have declined. These factors have put a true burden on the city's finances. In 2009, the city of Ede was relatively vulnerable to financial shocks. The city was strongly dependent on ring-fenced and generic transfers from the national government, and there were limited abilities to diversify the nature of their income. Moreover, the vulnerability was increased by the high level of debt financing. However, the debt level was not perceived as a main problem. As one respondent noticed:

> Yes, our debt is relatively high. But large parts of it in fact concern debts of local housing corporations. If you look more closely, we only have a financial issue with our land stock and depreciation of its value. But we knew what risks could occur at the time we bought the land.

Although crisis management was picked up relatively fast after 2009, the anticipatory capacity at that time was average. Respondents state that despite swift political responses to fading incomes, the city might have been a little optimistic regarding the consequences and severity of the financial crisis. Besides multi-year forecasting and budgeting, the use of early-warning systems for uncovering potential financial instabilities was not typical. However, risk management has seriously improved the anticipatory capacity in the city, especially the capacity of the local financial managers and executives. The city has become more careful and cautious. Or, as one of the respondents argued,

> We have developed a new control paradigm, covering a longer time frame than the political cycle of four years. [...] All proposals for new policies or projects now have to come with a solid risk analysis. Because this procedure is new and people are not used to it, the role of the controller becomes more important.

Also, the annual participation of the city in a series of benchmarks and stress-testing programs generates additional insights in the long-term financial performance of the city. The interviews uncover two dominant coping capacities. Firstly, the short-term impact of the crisis was absorbed by using reserves, cutting operational costs, selling more land and ceasing or postponing investments. There was a strong agreement on the use of reserves to restore the fiscal gap. One respondent stated:

> Reserves are not primarily meant for the internal organization, it is public money. Therefore, instead of saving and keeping the money to ourselves, we used it to create value in times of poverty.

Secondly, incremental changes were implemented to deal with the long-term effects of the crisis. For instance, to increase the level of efficiency, the level of financial transparency or the quality of partnerships.

City of Zwolle

The city of Zwolle (125,000 inhabitants) is a local authority in the centre of the Netherlands. It has a relatively young, rich and growing population. It is the economic heart of the region and home to many industries and service providers. Despite the economic prosperity, Zwolle suffered a major adverse impact during the austerity period. In Zwolle, the crisis originated mainly from two external elements. Firstly, the national cutbacks on the MF which generated a severe drop in income. Secondly, the significant losses on construction lands. However, also the decentralisation of tasks from central government without adequate budgets increased budgetary pressure. Although the financial situation was better than average, the city was relatively vulnerable to financial shocks. The city strongly depends on uncertain national transfers and has little options for generating income through additional sources. However, due to sound financial management in pre-crisis years, the city found itself in a comfortable position when the crisis occurred. There was a balanced budget, the level of debt was relatively low (80%, improving since then) and the city had comfortable levels of reserves.

> In Zwolle, the budgetary process always was about dividing the extras. There was no need to discuss the budgetary base, let alone a need to cut back expenses. [...] We have always been a financially healthy city. Our solid and reliable financial base was a great advantage when we needed to adjust our expenses.

When the crisis occurred, the anticipatory capacity in Zwolle was moderate. Although there definitely were risk management activities in pre-crisis years, this financial shock happened unexpectedly to Zwolle. Or, as one respondent argued:

> We never realized that periods of great wealth could turn around so quickly.

Public finance was managed solidly, but besides some basic multi-year forecasting, no important forecast activities were deployed. Since 2010, therefore, a number of developments have been introduced to increase the capacity to recognise and manage financial vulnerabilities. For instance, tighter risk policies were introduced to identify potential risks, and financial procedures were optimised for better insights in the long-term consequences of new policies. Although the crisis was not foreseen, the response in Zwolle was hands-on.

Once the consequences of the crisis were identified, we acted immediately. We made the necessary decisions and implemented them.

Two coping capacities were evident in Zwolle. Firstly, the city used a number of buffering strategies to cope with immediate shortfalls, such as cutting costs, tapping additional income sources (e.g. co-sponsoring of investments and services by the provincial authority or other partners), terminating optional services or postponing investments. Also, organisational changes were realized, for instance to increase the level of efficiency and the quality of partnerships.

City of Hengelo

The city of Hengelo (80,000 inhabitants) is a local authority in the eastern part of the Netherlands, close to the German border. It is the second largest city in the robust economic region of Twente and was, in the past, home to many industries and large companies. Before 2010, Hengelo was a relatively healthy authority, according to the respondents. There was a balanced budget, decent levels of reserves, and frequently the budget was underspent. On the other hand, it is noticeable that – referring to the financial position of the municipality – none of the respondents refers to the extraordinary debt level of Hengelo (255%, worsening). The prosperous situation changed dramatically when the crisis hit.

We had no experience at all with axing personnel. Everybody of course knew stories of people who got fired, but not here. Not in our own organization. Everybody felt that the crisis was nearby.

The severe levels of fiscal stress were mainly caused by three shocks. In particular, the decentralisation of tasks without appropriate budgets caused large problems in Hengelo. National services, such as the provision of youth care, were passed down, combined with budget cuts of up to 25%. Furthermore, the deficit was caused by the consequences of national cuts on the Municipality Fund and depreciation of construction lands. In 2009, Hengelo was definitely vulnerable to financial shocks. Not only because a large part of the city's income is derived from one single source, but also because of its extraordinary level of debt. This decreases the financial autonomy of the city, as a substantial part of the yearly budget has to be spent on interest. Initially, the anticipatory capacity was medium. Although risk management did exist in pre-crisis years, austerity and fiscal stress were not foreseen and real cutbacks were uncommon before 2010. However, this improved as the crisis evolved. Since the crisis, the controlling and monitoring of finances have become more accurate.

> The advisory process is tighter and has improved a lot. Instead of solving financial issues along the way, we now clarify problems immediately. Apart from calculating precise deficits, we also uncover the consequences of specific proposals. [...] It is our job to provide our executives with a good advice, even if they sometimes want to hear another story.

Furthermore, risk management techniques have significantly improved to better identify potential risks. Austerity management in Hengelo takes the form of two coping capacities. Firstly, shocks were absorbed by terminating services, ceasing and postponing investments, and cutting expenditure. In first instance merely across-the-board cuts were used, later the cuts became more targeted based on savings reviews. Also, some incremental changes were found such as organisational reforms and shared services to improve the efficiency and effectiveness, and to increase the level of transparency.

City of Hoorn

The city of Hoorn (70,000 inhabitants) is a local authority in the north-western part of the Netherlands. Although this city is home to many commuters in the Amsterdam area, it also has a central economic and cultural role in the region. Traditionally, Hoorn always was a relatively rich city.

> There were gigantic surpluses in the long-term budgets and everything was focus on growth, growth, growth.

In recent years, however, the city has been coping with financial challenges, up to 10% of the total budget. In the first place, fiscal stress was caused by the usual suspects: decreased transfers from the MF, large losses on construction lands and decentralisation of tasks without proper budgets. However, in Hoorn also an additional *fourth shock* affected the budget, that is the physical collapse of the *Toneeltoren*. This refers to a local event of a brand-new theatre building that collapsed even before it was completed. The aftermath (legal settlement, rebuilding) put a major burden on the local finances; finances that already were affected by the other shocks. Although the city of Hoorn had relatively low levels of debt financing before the crisis (82%; improving), they were vulnerable to financial shocks due to undiversified income sources. This vulnerability is likely to increase as one important source of income, that is the selling of construction land, evaporates as Hoorn literally touched its spatial borders.

> We are reaching the limits to growth. We don't have any new lands to build on. If we want to build something new, we must demolish old buildings and build new ones.

The anticipatory capacity to respond to the crisis was relatively low and, especially during the early stages of the crisis, the authority had some problems to calculate the financial dimension of the event.

Already in 2010 we knew that major cuts were likely. We prepared an initial austerity package worth 18 million. However, the challenge turned out to be only 12 million. This caused a
series of unnecessary political debates about spending or saving 6 million. This distracted the
attention from the challenge itself.

However, the anticipatory capacity grew as the event evolved. Growing
awareness about the city's financial vulnerability created a platform for
improvements, such as the introduction of a professional risk management system, the appointment of risk officers, and improved monitoring and forecasting
efforts following the basic principles of project management. Responses to the
financial shocks in Hoorn took the form of two coping capacities, buffering
and adapting. Buffering, because many of the responses merely absorbed the
fiscal squeeze, such as terminating optional services, cutting costs or postponing
investments. Adapting, because also reforms were implemented that contributed to the long-term improvement of organisational efficiency and the changing relationship between community and authority.

CONCLUSIONS

The consequences of the financial and economic crises have been visible in all
the municipalities in our sample (Table 3). Before the crisis, municipal circumstances can be characterised by continuous moderate growth with 'plenty of
money' for locally desired policies. Then, the attention for fiscal stress and austerity management exploded onwards from 2010. More than once, respondents
in our sample entitled the encounter as the largest financial challenge in their
personal careers. Besides its severity, also the suddenness of the crisis was mentioned often in the interviews. Although respondents regarded the crisis as a
serious issue with many consequences for the organisations and society, also
many interesting positive effects can be extracted from the interviews. In this
sample, local authorities also used the crisis as opportunity, for instance, to
improve their level of transparency, to introduce organisational innovations, to
reduce organisational slack, or to stimulate team spirit and pride ('together we
were fighting the dragon'). These examples of reform-oriented responses are similar to other studies in the Netherlands (e.g. Overmans & Timm-Arnold, 2015).

Buffering and Adapting to the Crisis

One aim of this chapter was uncovering responses that were used to deal with
the shocks. We distinguish between short-term responses and long-term
responses. Regarding the short-term, two types of responses are commonly
used: cutting costs and adjusting investments. There were many responses
aimed at cutting costs. These concern reductions in staff, reductions in

Table 3. Patterns of Financial Resilience in Dutch Cities.

	Ede	Zwolle	Hengelo	Hoorn
Financial shocks	Grant reduction, declined value of assets (construction land), decentralised tasks without adequate budgets	Declined value of assets (construction land), decentralised tasks without adequate budgets, grant reduction	Decentralised tasks without adequate budgets, grant reduction, declined value of assets (construction land)	Local event, grant reduction, declined value of assets (construction land), decentralised tasks without adequate budgets
Perceived vulnerability levels and sources before the shock and their/evolution over time	*Initially high, stable over time* Undiversified and uncertain revenue sources, dependence on grants, high debt financing, budget deficits/increasing debt, uncertain grants	*Initially medium, stable over time* Undiversified and uncertain revenue sources, dependence on grants, budget deficits, low debt, solid financial position/decreasing debt	*Initially high, stable over time* Undiversified and uncertain revenue sources, dependence on grants, high debt financing, budget deficits, increasing debt	*Initially low, increasing over time* Low debt financing, healthy financial reserves, volatile budgets/increasing dependence on grants due to growth limitation
Level and types of anticipatory capacity before the shock and their/evolution over time	*Initially medium, increasing over time* No early-warning system, quick response/stronger risk management, more benchmarking and stress testing, stricter budgeting	*Initially medium, increasing over time* No early-warning system, basic risk management/tighter risk management and other monitoring tools, financial reviews	*Initially medium, increasing over time* Medium-term financial planning, response/stronger risk assessment, more advises, more transparency, more strict budgeting	*Initially low, increasing over time* Medium-term financial planning/stronger risk assessment, more strict budgeting
Levels and types of coping capacity	*Selective* *Buffering:* Cut costs, cancel investments, prioritisation *Adapting:* Efficiencies, transparent budgets, partnerships *Transforming:* –	*Selective* *Buffering:* Cut costs, cancel investments, postpone investments, prioritisation, alternative resources *Adapting:* Efficiencies, layoffs, partnerships *Transforming:* –	*Selective* *Buffering:* Cut costs, cancel investments, postpone investments *Adapting:* Efficiencies, transparent *Transforming:* –	*Selective* *Buffering:* Cut costs, cancel investments, postpone investments, deferring maintenance *Adapting:* Efficiencies, thematic working *Transforming:* –

maintenance levels, or the ending of public services. Cost cutting activities were deployed across-the-board as well as targeted. Furthermore, many investments on capital and projects were evaluated and then continued, ceased or cancelled. Although a great many projects have been cancelled or postponed, cutting investments was done carefully to avoid a lock down of the city. In contrast to many other countries, increases of local taxes were absent in Dutch cities. This is most likely to be caused by the financial arrangements in the Netherlands and the limited financial autonomy of the local authorities. As only an insignificant part of their budget comes from taxes, even the smallest contribution to the restoration of the fiscal squeeze would require an extraordinary rise of local taxes.

Besides short-term responses to restore immediate fiscal deficits, also long-term responses were deployed to realign actual operational outputs with strategically desired outputs. Sticking to strategic plans was not easy as financial shocks evolved so quickly. One long-term response is evident in the Dutch cases, namely the transition of the role of local government in society. The interviews indicate a transition from a proactive self-organising type of government towards a more passive, coordinating type of government. This transformation was driven by two elements. Firstly, governments operate in a broader web of stakeholders, or as one respondent said:

> A municipality always needs other organizations to realize goals. Thinking that we can do everything on our own is a bit old-fashioned.

Secondly, many issues nowadays are not regarded as an exclusive governmental problem.

> Having a deficit is not a problem of the municipality, it is a societal problem. The society therefore has to be involved, from the beginning, to solving it.

In the Netherlands, no evidence is found for radical changes of the financial system. However, since the end of 2015 a political debate has started to reform the financial arrangements in the Netherlands. This debate is likely to result in larger financial autonomy for cities to collect a higher level of taxes, at the expense of lower nationally imposed taxes.

ACKNOWLEDGEMENTS

The findings in this chapter are based on a secondary analysis of data gathered by Fien de Koning MSc, who in 2015 investigated the financial resilience of five Dutch local authorities as part of her master's thesis at the Utrecht University School of Governance. The author is very grateful for the provision of the research data.

REFERENCES

Allers, M. (2009). Rijksbegroting 2010: Gemeenten moeten bezuinigen, maar niet allemaal even veel. *Tijdschrift voor Openbare Financiën, 41*(5), 282–292.

Allers, M., & Steiner, B. (2014). *Gemeenten in perspectief 2014–2018*. Groningen: Groningen University.

Bandy, G. (2014). *Financial management and accounting in the public sector*. Abingdon, UK: Routledge.

Barbera, C., Jones, M., Korac, S., Saliterer, I., & Steccolini, I. (2017). Governmental financial resilience under austerity in Austria, England and Italy: How do local governments cope with financial shocks? Public Administration, forthcoming.

Breeman, G. E., & Noort, W. V. (2008). De Bestuurlijke kaart van Nederland. Het openbaar bestuur en zijn omgeving in nationaal en internationaal perspectief (4e druk).

Hou, Y., & Moynihan, D. P. (2008). The case for countercyclical fiscal capacity. *Journal of Public Administration Research and Theory, 18*(1), 139–159.

Kickert, W. (2012). How the Dutch government responded to financial, economic and fiscal crisis. *Public Money & Management, 32*(6), 439–443, doi:10.1080/09540962.2012.728784

Leisink, P., & Bach, S. (2014). Economic crisis and municipal public service employment: Comparing developments in seven EU Member States. *European Review of Labour and Research, 20*(3), 327–342.

Morgan, G. (1998). *Images of organization*. Thousand Oaks, CA: Sage.

Overmans, J. F. A., & Noordegraaf, M. (2014). Managing austerity: Rhetorical and real responses to fiscal stress in local government. *Public Money and Management, 34*(2), 99–106. (8 p.).

Overmans, J. F. A., & Timm-Arnold, K. P. (2015). Managing austerity: Comparing municipal austerity plans in the Netherlands and North Rhine-Westphalia. *Public Management Review*. doi:10.1080/14719037.2015.1051577

CHAPTER 11

FINANCIAL RESILIENCE: THE SWEDISH CASE

Niklas Wällstedt and Roland Almqvist

ABSTRACT

In this chapter, the development of financial sustainability and resilience in Swedish local governments is analysed. We analyse four Swedish municipalities, where we have interviewed top managers and co-workers. As a complement, we have examined the municipalities' strategic plans, budget documents and annual reports. We also contextualise this analysis with other findings from local government research during this time, as well as with central government initiatives. In summary, we examine why Swedish municipalities in general remained strong after the financial crisis by showing how they strengthened their anticipatory and coping capacities over time — something that, in the cases of this chapter, was achieved before the 2008/2009 crisis in response to previous crises, rather than because of it. We also show that this is not the only reason. As Swedish finances were comparatively stable, and the problems of the banking sector relatively small, the financial shocks to the municipalities could be overcome relatively easily.

Keywords: Sweden; local governments; financial sustainability; resilience; financial crisis; accounting

In 2008, the problems of the world economy gained attention in Swedish municipalities. Forecasts from the Swedish Association of Local Authorities and Regions (SALAR) on rapid tax-base erosion due to an industrial sector

Governmental Financial Resilience: International Perspectives on how Local Governments Face Austerity
Public Policy and Governance, Volume 27, 187–205
Copyright © 2017 by Emerald Publishing Limited
ISSN: 2053-7697/doi:10.1108/S2053-769720170000027011

crisis and the subsequent increase of the unemployment rate were issued, as well as unpromising social subsidies figures. This situation raised questions among practitioners and researchers on the municipal economy in Sweden. The main question was how to promote financial sustainability and resilience in the Swedish municipal sector?

The question spurred a national research programme in Sweden, in which different municipalities were investigated and analysed. The financial crisis provided opportunities to investigate financial sustainability and resilience within the municipal sector in Sweden. This chapter on financial resilience in Swedish local governments is based on findings from the research programme, and uses the resilience framework developed for this book (Barbera, Jones, Korac, Saliterer, & Steccolini, 2017).

Consequently, we analyse four Swedish municipalities. We also contextualise this analysis with other findings from the national research programme. In summary, we examine why Swedish municipalities in general remained strong after the financial crisis by showing how they strengthened their anticipatory and coping capacities over time − something that, in the cases of this chapter, was achieved before the 2008/2009 crisis in response to previous crises, rather than because of it. We also show that this is not the only reason. As Swedish finances were comparatively stable, and the problems of the banking sector relatively small, the financial shocks to the municipalities could be overcome relatively easily.

The chapter starts with an overview of the Swedish system of government, followed by the methods. Subsequently, four cases are presented and the chapter concluded.

THE CONTEXT

In Sweden, there are three government tiers: the first is the central government, the second is the county or regional government and the third is the primary municipality level. In this chapter, the focus is on the primary municipality level, albeit in the context of the central government's efforts to alleviate the financial crisis impact.

In total, there are 290 primary municipalities in Sweden with populations ranging from 2,500 to 900,000 citizens. The Swedish municipal sector has a long-standing tradition of autonomy from the state, especially regarding organisational structure and taxation. However, they are required by law to prepare a yearly budget, and to issue an annual report. That is, each municipality is allowed to form its own organisational structure and internal control systems, whether centralised or decentralised.

However, there are three practical options to form decentralised bodies. The first option is the district council, whose decentralised structure is built on the basis of geographical closeness and serves the citizens in a particular geographical area. The second option is the specialized council, which is built on functions such as schooling, elderly care or infrastructure. The third option is the municipal corporation (commonly regarding water, energy or real estate management), which is different in that it is legally subject to the Swedish Companies Act. Because the municipality owns the company as a majority shareholder, the municipality normally demands that the company delivers value to the citizens according to the stipulations of the Local Government Act. These bodies are governed by the Municipal Council and the municipality's executive board, that is, the political majority ruling the municipality. Moreover, a Swedish municipality can choose to provide services itself, act as a purchaser and buy services from private providers, or act as both purchaser and provider.

Each municipality has full freedom to impose taxes on the municipality population. About two-thirds of the municipality's revenues derive from income taxation (Larsson & Bäck, 2008), the remainder coming from state grants and direct fees to the customer (e.g. parents utilising kindergartens. Such direct fees account for an average of about 20% of the total income for a municipality). State grants can come in the form of a compensation scheme that equalizes differences between municipalities, municipalities with high costs and/or low incomes being compensated. Consequently, some municipalities may have negative grants (see Table 1).

As such, most municipal revenues emanate from taxation and only to a lesser extent from customer fees. Moreover, state grants are decided by external actors, whereas the municipality decides the income tax and the fee rates. As there is competition between the municipalities when it comes to attracting citizens (i.e. revenue contributing taxpayers), the differences between tax rates are rather small among municipalities. The possibilities for municipalities to manage their incomes are limited – both because the above-mentioned competition and the central governments legal demands for maximum fees (see below) – despite the formal autonomy in decision making. Consequently, their revenues depend primarily on the size and average wage of their populations.

The municipality is legally required to perform its core functions (e.g. child care, compulsory schooling, social services and elderly care). It is also allowed to execute voluntary services (e.g. maintaining cultural activities and sports facilities). Each municipality decides whether tax money or fees finance voluntary services and if the municipality or its corporations perform them. The possibilities to manage costs and revenues in an organised and structured way may seem rather significant but are practically restricted. This is due to the competition between municipalities, for institutional reasons (e.g. the maintenance of sports facilities is regarded as something that every municipality 'should do') and, in some cases, because of central government imposed regulations regarding maximum fees for most required activities, such as child care (for child care, the maximum fee the municipality can charge parents were 1,313 SEK per month in 2016).

Table 1. Data from the Four Municipalities.

	2004	2005	2006	2007	2008	2009	2010	2011	2012	2013
S1										
Number of inhabitants	61,564	61,743	62,342	63,427	64,355	65,295	66,211	67,320	68,210	69,167
Unemployment (%)	3.9	4.4	4.3	3.3	2.9	3.6	5.6	5.3	5.7	6.9
Income tax level (%)	19.13	19.13	19.13	18.98	18.80	18.63	18.63	18.63	18.63	18.98
Tax income/inhabitant (SEK)	34,042	34,081	35,492	35,681	36,632	35,986	36,011	36,953	37,667	39,022
Income from state grants/inhabitant (SEK)	−2,609	−1,341	−864	349	993	2,318	4,507	4,876	5,528	6,371
Financial position	Positive	Positive	Positive	Positive	Zero	Positive	Positive	Zero	Positive	Positive
Equity ratio (%)	9	14	15	9	10	10	11	7	9	16
S2										
Number of inhabitants	40,830	40,873	40,943	40,961	40,902	40,860	40,892	40,942	41,078	41,278
Unemployment (%)	9.0	9.8	8.5	6.1	4.9	7.2	9.1	8.4	7.9	7.5
Income tax level (%)	22.03	22.03	22.03	22.03	22.03	22.03	22.03	22.03	22.03	22.25
Tax income/inhabitant (SEK)	31,157	32,089	33,932	35,211	37,262	37,820	38,313	39,689	40,649	41,794
Income from state grants/inhabitant (SEK)	5,179	5,829	5,705	6,238	5,927	6,065	7,121	6,689	6,382	6,965
Financial position	Zero	Positive	Positive	Positive	Positive	Positive	Positive	Positive	Positive	Positive
Equity ratio (%)	26	27	27	24	26	23	25	23	25	24
S3										
Number of inhabitants	71,786	71,910	71,966	72,090	71,862	71,770	71,641	71,580	71,774	71,988
Unemployment (%)	7.8	8.0	7.5	5.3	5.0	8.1	10.1	8.4	8.2	7.7
Income tax level (%)	22.40	22.40	22.40	22.40	22.40	22.40	22.40	22.40	22.40	22.60
Tax income/inhabitant (SEK)	30,904	31,845	33,758	35,196	36,809	37,451	37,929	39,258	40,181	41,143
Income from state grants/inhabitant (SEK)	7,942	8,792	8,907	9,308	9,966	10,415	11,819	11,173	11,086	11,735
Financial position	Positive	Positive	Positive	Positive	Positive	Positive	Positive	Positive	Positive	Zero
Equity ratio (%)	24	26	27	25	28	28	31	30	33	30

S4

Number of inhabitants	765,044	771,038	782,885	795,163	810,120	829,417	847,073	864,324	881,235	897,700
Unemployment (%)	4.5	4.7	4.4	3.7	3.0	4.0	5.3	5.1	5.0	5.4
Income tax level (%)	18.08	18.08	18.08	17.78	17.58	17.48	17.48	17.48	17.48	17.33
Tax income/inhabitant (SEK)	33,657	33,476	34,743	35,305	36,460	36,500	36,641	37,605	38,785	39,954
Income from state grants/inhabitant (SEK)	-1,568	-54	-51	247	48	-205	1,629	1,531	820	124
Financial position	Zero	Zero	Negative	Positive	Positive	Positive	Positive	Positive	Positive	Positive
Equity ratio (%)	63	58	49	51	55	60	59	55	55	54

Source: www.kolada.se, municipal benchmark database.

In early 2000 and onwards, the central government tightened regulations of and control over the municipalities, both in terms of financial responsibility and service quality. The municipalities' accounting framework is based on the International Public Sector Accounting Standards, and hence on accrual accounting (in contrast to the central government's cash-based accounting method). This has consequences when it comes to financial responsibilities: Since the year 2000 there has been a legislated 'balanced budget requirement'. This requirement states that a municipality has to have an in-year income statement surplus (revenues have to exceed expenses, or at least be equal in the income statement) at the end of the fiscal year (the fiscal year is always from 1 January to 31 December) in order to meet future financial demands. However, this has been rigidly interpreted; even if a municipality has a high equity ratio[1] (e.g. S4 in Table 1) and a considerable financial buffer, a negative result in the income statement would still require cost cuts, as the buffer cannot be used to cover deficits according to the interpretation.

As such, a Swedish municipality may find itself in fiscal distress, even if it has a strong balance sheet. This is a consequence of accounting regulations (i.e. the balanced budget requirement and its rigid interpretation) imposed by the central government. We, however, show that at least one municipality (S1) has worked to override this limitation and created a financial buffer in the balance sheet, which was subsequently used to cover deficits post crisis. In connection with the crisis, the requirement has received heavy critique, and from 2013, it is possible for municipalities to build and utilise financial buffers (Proposition 2011/12:172, 2011).

On service quality, the increased control came later – mostly implemented by the right wing government taking office in autumn 2006. The central government has increased governmental control by employing new standards and rules, and increased surveillance by deploying more inspections in areas such as schooling and elderly care (Proposition 2012/13:20, 2012; SOU 2007:101, 2007).

Summing up, the Swedish municipal system is characterised by high autonomy and freedom of choice, but is also constrained by inter-municipal competition, institutionalized ideas built on expectations of what a municipality 'should do', and increasing central government control and issuing of rules and regulations. These constraints, in combination with the above-mentioned levelling out of costs and income by state grants through the compensation system, make the Swedish case one where organisational structuring and control are very important.

METHOD

The empirical material in this chapter is collected within The Swedish National Research Program on Local Public Management (NatKom) established with the intention of analysing how municipalities cope with financial and organisational stress. As such, the aim of the research programme corresponds with the analytical framework of this book: the empirical material was collected with the aim of understanding how financial resilience is developed.

The first round of the research programme included 47 out of Sweden's 290 municipalities. The first phase was an initial study in 2010 in which the 47 participating municipalities were visited and 195 interviews conducted. This initial phase focused on exploring the municipalities' financial situation and historical development, with the aim to generate further research questions for the next phase of the programme. The second phase was a series of thematic studies conducted in 2011 and 2012. Funding, demographic challenges, local democratic development, infrastructure, internal management control, competence development, and collaboration with civil society and industry were investigated. This first round ended in 2013 with a final report (Brorström, Donatella, & Wänström, 2013).

In 2014, a second round was started, this time including 27 municipalities (NatKom 2), ending in 2016. Among these 27 municipalities there were both 'old' municipalities from NatKom 1 and some that had not been part of the first round. The aim of the second round was to examine how the municipalities adapt and adjust their resource allocation to changing conditions (e.g. growth or decline), and how they develop their organisational structures, management control systems, and collaborations with the environment accordingly.

At the time of writing, some 400 interviews have been conducted in the two research programs by researchers from four research institutes (Gothenburg University, Linköping University, Lund University and Stockholm University). Additionally, statistical data, document analysis, surveys, and literature reviews have been used to build the cases. Hitherto, 34 research reports have been published on the research programme's website, along with two peer-reviewed articles (Wällstedt & Almqvist, 2015; Wällstedt, Grossi, & Almqvist, 2014).

Because the national research programme forms the empirical foundation of this chapter, the selection of municipalities is slightly different than in other chapters. There have been two criteria for selection. The first is that the municipalities are representative of the Swedish case: they are medium to large-sized municipalities, and they have a neutral to positive financial position with low volatility[2] and they suffer from similar vulnerabilities to most Swedish municipalities. This can be compared with the overall situation in Sweden between 2004 and 2013, where around 20 out of 290 municipalities had budget deficits each year and only about five of these had deficits for more than two years in a row. All of the municipalities with recurring financial problems are small and often far from large cities.

The second criterion is that the analysed municipalities are well known by the authors. Because we wanted to go in depth in our cases, we chose the municipalities where we made most of our interviews: because the research programme spanned so many organisations, most researchers made in-depth interviews in only four or five municipalities. The downside is that we are not able to show examples of municipalities with financial problems. We are, however, thanks to the extensive work within the research programme, aware of those municipalities, and try to incorporate a discussion about them in the conclusions section.

We made document studies and interviews in all four organisations. We have looked at budget documents, annual reports, and other relevant documents, and we have interviewed top managers in all municipalities where we asked structured questions about their historical developments of management control, and how it relates to crises over time. CEO and Director of Finance have been interviewed in all four municipalities, together with relevant actors in each municipality's top management groups. Subsequently, we interviewed and observed staff and middle managers to understand how management control is operationalized. In total, we have conducted over 100 interviews and observations within the four municipalities.

RESULTS

The reaction of the Swedish municipalities during the 2008/2009 financial crisis should be considered in light of the comparatively stable financial Swedish situation: the crisis affected Sweden less than most of the EU and the United States (Sveriges Riksbank, 2011). Among the reasons is the sound financial position of the central government that has been hard-fought and accomplished through several reforms aimed at stabilizing the financial management of the Swedish state (e.g. the introduction of a budget ceiling). Another reason is that Swedish banks, although troubled, were not as exposed as other banks around the world. The consequence was that the central government could intervene with subsidies and loan guarantees, to both banks and municipalities, while using the downturn to make cheap investments (e.g. infrastructure). Overall, the situation was one of comparative stability in the Swedish system: the sound finances of the state made Sweden feel safe and secure, leading to few bankruptcies, limited investment decrease, and only a small but noticeable increase in unemployment (see Table 1).

The impact on the Swedish municipalities varied; most municipalities were not affected significantly, whereas a few (those with high concentration of jobs in the export industry) faced difficulties. As a response to the forecasted decrease in municipal income (a consequence of the increase in unemployment), the central government increased grants to the municipal sector in 2010 with 17 billion SEK (i.e. an increase in total income for municipalities with about 3%), and 3 billion SEK in 2011. This was announced in autumn 2009, and because most municipalities had already made their budget decisions for 2010, funds were unused, the increase in grants roughly corresponding to the total surplus of the municipal sector (Konjunkturinstitutet, 2012).

Instead of covering deficits, the 2010 surplus was used predominantly for investments in 2011, which probably helped maintain the Swedish economy (Konjunkturinstitutet, 2012). This is the context of the four municipalities in the chapter and, although different, they came out strong after the crisis, nevertheless with some negative changes in unemployment (Table 1).

Before the Crisis

All four municipalities were affected by public sector reforms and restructuration during the 1980s and early 1990s. These represented cost cuts in the beginning and introduction of competition and privatisations in the later period. A common explanation for cost cuts was that the public sector had grown more inefficient, and there were needs for investments following a growth in population, and that the public support for raising taxes was diminishing. Together with a demand for more efficient public sector organisations, a demand for the introduction of competition and privatisation appeared on both the central government and municipal agendas. As a consequence, both municipalities and central government had to cut several policy programmes, leading to lay-offs of public sector employees all over the country, at the same time as state grants diminished. The negative effect was hence doubled for the municipalities. Moreover, the severe financial crisis of 1991[3] put even more pressure on the public sector organisations in Sweden.

S1 used state grants to employ people during the 1970s in order to accommodate a growing population. This came to an abrupt ending in 1982, when it had a significant budget deficiency. In the coming decade, 'finance' became the focus of S1; taxes were raised in the beginning, and there was significant cost cutting, which included both lay-offs and cuts in services. Officials refer to this period as a 'chain saw massacre', being strong in the organisational memory of S1. The reliance on a strong budget process, based on a 'salami strategy', where appeals from the operational areas were never fully granted, a move of the budget decision from autumn to spring — which made the operations aware of next year's budget already in summer — was coupled with an ambition to create a financial buffer by fiscal year surplus: because the fiscal year ends the 31 December, the operations now had more than six months to adapt to next year's budget.

S2 was affected by the 1980s central government cost cuts, because the most important municipality employer was a state owned mental hospital and its closure lead to the unemployment of almost 500 people — a significant blow to the income tax base for S2. However, S2 decided to buy the property and turn it into a business park, to attract new companies and be able to employ the same

number of people within five years. Because of the 1991 financial crisis, the
accomplishment was delayed by five years. This accomplishment showed S2 that
self-sufficiency was important, and that they could affect things themselves.

In the beginning of the 2000s costs were increasing, especially with regards
to S2's ageing population: given the low turnover of inhabitants and non-
existent population growth, the population was ageing, creating future costs,
such as elderly care and pensions. This trend had been visible for years, and
there was much talk and no action. In order to move from talk to action, the
management, led by the financial director who later became the new CEO,
made efforts to communicate this, appealing to carefully prepared forecasts in
order to pedagogically convince operations and citizens that cost cuts were
needed despite the 'good times'. Before the 2008 financial crisis, S2 established
a capability for forecasting and communicating future changes and a positive
budget position by cutting costs.

Before the crisis of 2008/2009, S3 had stable finances and the municipality
had not been forced to change the organisation significantly for many years.
The municipality had a tradition of strong financial control – something that
has existed as long as every respondent can remember. The municipality is also
the sole owner of a successful energy company (founded in 1906 by the municipality), earning an extra 500 million SEK (i.e. about 10% of the annual turnover) each year. Historically, the municipality has had a high equity ratio and
never been forced to take loans for investments. Furthermore, it had a higher
tax compliance compared to other municipalities in the region, which contributed to financial stability. However, much of the capital is in fixed assets, which
requires securing loans for future investments.

Since funds were readily available the municipality has, historically, had a
high degree of self-financing, with funds being spent on, for example, social
services. There have been no cutbacks; in fact, the municipality has developed its different activities. This historically positive situation has caused
issues for the management. First, the organisation has become too
comfortable and changes are difficult to implement. Second, the municipality
appears rich because of the substantial fixed assets in the balance sheet.
However, a positive balance sheet does not automatically generate a good
cash flow, which is difficult to communicate to citizens and employees.
Consequently, S3 has been working to develop a new control system, a balanced scorecard that would help communicate the need for organisational
change.

S4 was slow to react to the changes in the 1980s. Instead, the 1991 financial
crisis was a shock: excess slack in the organisation became evident as unemployment skyrocketed. Cost cuts – both in terms of service delivery and staff
lay-offs – were needed and budget discipline became the order of the day.
Subsequently, it was time for a politically motivated reform: a decentralisation
of the organisation. Consequently, a new management control system that

could handle a diverse, decentralised organisation was needed: S4 introduced a form of balanced scorecard that has been in use since.

This system is based on visualising financial and non-financial performance targets for the whole organisation. Every operational unit formulates targets, achievement plans, resource use, and development plans in a web-based version of the system. Moreover, several arenas for dialogue in the organisation were created, and quantitative measurement and communication were at the heart of the system. Additionally, S4 worked with their anticipatory capacities: their finance office was charged with forecasting every possible issue, even macroeconomic predictions.

Table 1 shows the pre-crisis situation for each municipality, as well as how things changed during and after the crisis. We have selected the indicators that show the (often non-existent) financial crisis impacts, such as number of inhabitants, unemployment, incomes, tax level changes, and the annual financial position. For comparability, we display the monetary indicators per inhabitant. However, state grants are difficult to compare as they contain a mixture of central government grants, deficits, and surpluses from the municipal compensation scheme. In these schemes, municipalities with high employment, building costs, etc., are compensated by those with low costs, and high income municipalities (i.e. higher tax income per inhabitant) compensate those with inhabitants with low incomes (lower tax income per inhabitant)[4]. Consequently, S1 and S4 have occasional negative values.

Vulnerability and Shocks

All Swedish municipalities suffer from similar vulnerabilities: being dependent on income taxation, they depend on their inhabitants' incomes. It is also important to have many working age inhabitants: if a high proportion of inhabitants are retired and/or elderly in need of care, the ratio between income and cost lowers. This is an issue for Sweden, and definitely for S1, S2, and S3. S4 has a slightly better position as a big city with a heterogeneous population and a large inflow of young people.

Existence of jobs is also important, and as such so is the general business climate in each municipality's region. All four municipalities have worked hard during the last decade to secure a business climate that would appeal to a variety of industries. Much focus is on attracting not only traditional production industry businesses, but also services and businesses that can take advantage of the digitalization of the society. The Swedish central government investments in broadband have been important: municipalities in rural areas, such as S2 and S3, are able to invest in good conditions for high-tech businesses and can attract knowledge intensive companies despite being located far from major cities. Generally, the management of the four municipalities emphasise the importance of their respective region; if it is possible, through collaboration with other municipalities and business actors in the region, to keep up a constructive business climate, much of the Swedish municipality's traditional vulnerabilities may be overcome.

The shocks of the 2008/2009 financial crisis were not as anticipated. As per Table 1, there was no need for raising income taxes in any municipality, and rises in 2013 in S2 and S3 seem politically motivated. Additionally, the income from taxes increased throughout the analysed decade. There was an increase in unemployment in all municipalities, although with some lag, mostly because the shock waves from the international crisis took some time to reach Sweden. Mostly low-salaried blue-collar workers were laid off. Consequently, there was little (if any) effect on taxable income. The vulnerability of state grants dependence was reduced by the good central government financial situation. Moreover, central government grants saved several jobs in the municipal sector, which further diminished the shock (Konjunkturinstitutet, 2012).

Perceiving the Crisis

Because the municipalities were well prepared − S1's well-oiled budget process, S2's previous cost cuts, S3's successful energy company, and S4's control system − they were capable of weathering the crisis. All of them worried, but there were no signs of fatalist feelings of helplessness. S4, who had a strong financial position (an equity ratio of 55% in 2008) (Table 1) saw the crisis as an opportunity to take advantage of lower market prices while boosting the economy by making needed investments ahead of schedule. Because the demand for services in the private sector decreased, it became possible to utilise the lower price level for investments. S3 felt comfortable during the crisis due to the energy company, and changed focus on organisational development through the new management control model. S1 saw the crisis as a threat: because of the budget process focus, lower income and a budget deficit were expected. In summary, S1 saw the crisis primarily as a threat, S3 saw an opportunity to change the organisation, and S2 and S4 saw the opportunity to make investments and thereby maintain a sound business climate in their respective regions.

Anticipatory Capacity

When it comes to anticipatory capacities, the Swedish public sector relies heavily on two actors: the Swedish national bank and SALAR. Both make macroeconomic forecasts, which they distribute several times per year. SALAR's is more adapted to their clients (the municipalities) and includes forecasts on for example the development of income taxes in different regions.

S2 and S4 also worked extensively to develop their own in-house anticipatory capacities. S2 did this to convince the organisation and its citizens that cost cuts were needed: the ambition was to create an organisation that could assemble all possible future 'facts' that could be used to change the organisation if needed. S4 saw itself as a macroeconomic actor, and, therefore, took responsibility for forming its own forecasting capacity. Both S2 and S4 argued that their in-house systems gave them 'a feeling' of something being 'off' in the world economy already in the autumn 2007 and spring 2008 because their macroeconomic forecasts looked a bit different than both SALAR's and the Swedish national bank's forecasts. Because of these discrepancies in forecasts, they were not taken by surprise by the US crash, although they were not fully prepared either.

As such, S1 and S3 have not developed any own anticipatory capacities: they 'only' routinely use SALAR forecasts, while relying on their coping capacities – their budget processes and strong financial controls. However, because of the in-house capacities and the SALAR forecasts, all four municipalities had developed a clear picture in the autumn of 2008 that the Swedish economy would be affected by the US banking crisis and could start taking precautions.

Coping Capacity

As per Table 1, S4 had a good buffering capacity because of a high equity ratio, whereas S1, S2, and S3 were in more precarious situations. S1, however, had much of its equity as a financial reserve: the surplus from earlier years had been placed in this reserve. That is, when the crisis occurred, they had reserve funds to cover the deficits in 2008. This reserve was also used in 2009 – despite the rigid interpretation of the balanced budget requirement – and the idea was to not cut any costs in 2009 to give the organisation an opportunity to plan for the cost cuts in 2010. However, the early budget decision regarding 2010 had effects in 2009 and as such, the deficit that needed to be covered in 2009 was much lower than expected. Hence, both the budget process and the buffer were sufficient.

Both S2 and S4 started to prepare for the crisis as soon as it became clear for them that the US banking crisis would have effects also on the Swedish economy: S2 balanced demands for cost cuts with a promise that no one in the organisation would be laid off if the cost cut targets were achieved, while S4 used their control system to communicate the negative forecasts. S2 reached its target through 'everyday restructurings' in the operational units, whereas S4 never had to realise their cost cuts, mostly because the level of taxable income did not decrease as much as feared (see Table 1). The interviewed actors in S4 argue that due to the forecast communication, they could have realized cost cuts as high as 5% of the municipality's total operational costs. S3 relied on income from the energy company, while feeling confident because of its high equity ratio, but it also took the opportunity to develop its financial control. Even if the new management control model was introduced to signal organisational development both externally and internally, management claimed that financial control processes within the organisation are still important, the city council using the expression 'means go before ends'. So, the attitude was that the financial control processes in the end were the most important.

When it comes to adaptive capacity in the four municipalities, communication and channels of communication are important: clear lines of communication lower uncertainty for managers and co-workers in the organisation and makes clear what to expect in terms of adaptation and change.

The focus regarding how to communicate, and what to communicate, was however different in the municipalities. S1 had few channels of communication when it comes to things other than the financial budget: there are quick responses within the organisation when it comes to adapting to cost cuts, but there are difficulties changing other things. For example, when the manager of the social service department tried to communicate the need to combat increasing unemployment, it was only when he used a financial question (he commissioned a report from PwC that could be used as hard evidence of increased costs) the top management listened and introduced a labour market division in the organisation.

S2 made use of what they called their 'informal system' that built on 'talk in the corridor': when they understood the possible crisis impact, they formalized it more, and gathered all middle management and held seminars on 'what would you do if you were part of the top management'. As such, they implemented a sense of urgency for staff, and could make incremental changes that lead to lower costs. S4 made use of their control system, and made sure that every unit understood the severity of the situation. Tough targets, both as costs and quality measures were communicated to signal that the organisation was ready to cut costs while keeping up the standards of operations. The message was that the 'buying bonanza' was over (implying that the operations were over financed), and that everyone in the organisation needed to help, in order for things to be business as usual. There were no specific directions for the subordinate units from the top management on how to achieve the cost cuts: the top management instead counted on the function of the control system, and the loyalty of subordinates to achieve the targets.

S3 changed focus on activities and organisational improvements through the new balanced scorecard. The most important thing was that the organisation implemented a new customer perspective, which became anchored in the organisation, and a new view on the citizen as a customer emerged. This led to increased quality for citizens and users (customers), gave the organisation an opportunity to 'go in one direction, instead of several', and helped the municipal board and the municipality's special councils – the subordinate units – to better understand the management control processes.

When it comes to transforming capacity, all four municipalities aimed for 'business as usual' during the crisis. Although they prepared for extensive shocks, little had to be done. One reason was that all four municipalities were prepared and needed transformations were already done. All these changes helped during and post the 2008/2009 crisis, and, therefore, there were limited – if any – transformations during the crisis (see Table 2).

CONCLUSION

The responses of the Swedish municipalities to the financial crisis are difficult to understand without the big picture. Owing to the comparatively good financial position of Sweden, many municipalities had fewer problems than expected. The municipalities are dependent on the environment and, to some degree, on the central government, not primarily for financial grants but for the stability the state can provide. The long-standing tradition of autonomy from the state, however, makes the Swedish municipalities both vulnerable and self-sufficient: most municipalities are used to taking matters into their own hands, and, in the four cases, they had worked hard before the crisis to transform their organisation, an important part of the successful outcomes.

It should be noted that this was not the case for all municipalities in Sweden; our cases represent a majority, but there are a few municipalities facing problems as demonstrated by the NatKom research project. Some of them are small countryside municipalities that suffer from ongoing urbanisation: they are losing population, and therefore income, while costs are rising because inhabitants are ageing, losing income, and require care. Even though there is a scheme for financial compensation, the ongoing depopulation in a municipality leads to feelings of helplessness and fatalism in the political and administrative management: such feelings were not encountered in the four analysed municipalities.

These problems were not caused, but rather intensified by the crisis, as urbanisation has been happening for a while. A few municipalities, especially in the west of Sweden where the exporting industry has been the traditional focus, were hit by the crisis when important industries had to lay off staff. For them, the extra state financial grants were integral in order to be able to cope with the situation.

The ongoing urbanisation, together with the crisis, has highlighted the importance of collaboration – not only between public sector organisations, but also between public sector organisations, the civil society, and the business world. Efforts were made in all our four municipalities; however, in varying degrees and in different forms, to be active in the society. Whereas for example

Table 2. Comparison of Resilience Dimensions (Factors) across Cases.

SWEDEN	S1	S2	S3	S4
Budgetary position	*Positive*	*Positive*	*Positive*	*Positive*
Volatility	*Low*	*Low*	*Low*	*Low*
Shock/impact	Higher unemployment, increased state grants, higher social subsidies	Higher unemployment, increased state grants	Higher unemployment, increased state grants	Higher unemployment, increased state grants
Filtering	Threat	Threat/opportunity	Threat/opportunity	Threat/opportunity
Vulnerability (before)	*Low/medium:* Strong budget process, good business climate, low equity ratio, low taxable income	*Medium:* Precarious position in northern Sweden, ageing population, low operations costs	*Medium:* Strong balance sheet but precarious position in northern Sweden, ageing population	*Low:* Strong balance sheet, heterogeneous population, strong business climate
Anticipatory capacity (before)	Low/medium	Medium/high	Medium	High
Coping capacity	*Medium*	*High*	*High*	*High*
	Buffering: Financial reserves, strong budget process, early budget decisions	*Buffering:* Cost cuts, trust in management	*Buffering:* High equity ratio, strong financial control, income from owned company	*Buffering:* High equity ratio, well-implemented control system
	Adapting: Good communication regarding financial issues	*Adapting:* Informal communication, issue selling	*Adapting:* Communication through the balance scorecard, strong financial control	*Adapting:* Communication of tough budget targets, issue selling
	Transforming: Not needed during the crisis	*Transforming:* Not needed during the crisis	*Transforming:* Not needed during the crisis	*Transforming:* Not needed during the crisis
Anticipatory capacity (after)	*Low/medium:* Similar to before	*Medium/high:* Similar to before	*Medium:* Similar to before	*High:* Similar to before
Vulnerability (after)	Low/medium: Similar to before	Medium: Similar to before	Medium: Similar to before	Low: Similar to before
Pattern of resilience	Reactive adapter	Proactive adapter	Reactive adapter	Proactive adapter

S4 focused on collaboration with businesses and other organisations in the region by constructing business opportunities, S2 and S3 made an effort to shape the regional environment in a way beneficial to different actors.

The main conclusions are summarised in Table 2. As per Tables 1 and 2, the preconditions for the municipalities were good: the budget positions were positive, and there was limited volatility. Moreover, the municipalities had done a lot of work before the crisis that helped them weather it. The reasons for these changes were historical in the cases of S1 and S4: there were responses to earlier problems and an effect of a realisation that the organisation needed an overhaul. The forms however differed considerably: where S1 focused on financial management and a strong budget process, S4 took a more multidimensional and proactive approach. However, when the crisis arrived, both the reactive approach developed by S1, and the proactive approach developed by S4, worked well.

S2, on the other hand, had their arguments for change in the future: they saw an unsustainable cost structure and made efforts to make their operations more efficient and effective. Although S2 suspected an economic downturn, this was not the reason for their reforms – it was a general trend, together with the initiative from the current Financial Officer that spurred action while the economy was still positive. This is probably a good strategy, because a good financial situation will make cost cuts in the municipal organisation less noticeable for citizens. We, however, came to understand from our respondents in S2 that the pedagogical efforts needed to convince members of the organisation and citizens that cost cuts are needed when the budgetary position is positive are considerable. To accomplish this, new and more effective channels of communication were needed, as well as a capacity to construct images that included the possibility of a harsh financial future: such channels and images could be used to communicate expected economic and societal changes. This makes S2 a proactive adapter – a municipality with their own anticipatory capacities and a 'formalized informal' system devised to communicate and effect change.

S3 had its successful energy company and focuses on management control improvement instead. The balanced scorecard project was described as a 'cultural trip' to change procedures, routines, and working style, and the overall focus has changed towards 'for whom does the municipality exist'. This helped the organisation focus on organisational development rather than the financial crisis. However, this was combined with a strong financial control. As such, S3 shows signs of being a reactive adapter: it focuses on financial stability and strong financial controls, albeit with an ambition to widen their communication capacities to include other dimensions.

In summary, we consider the financial stability in Sweden as a main reason for the success of the Swedish municipalities to weather the 2008/2009 financial crisis. Moreover, the long-standing tradition of municipal autonomy meant municipalities were used to acting on their own, but also in conjunction and collaboration with their immediate environment: they know that they will not be 'bailed out' by anyone else. Therefore, the four municipalities in this study were prepared for the crisis, and, thus, the strategy during the crisis was to 'sit tight' and aim for 'business as usual'. Consequently, there were little or no changes within the studied municipalities during the crisis: they made use of the capacities they had constructed before the crisis. Whereas we argue that the autonomy and self-sufficiency of the Swedish municipalities is an overall strength because it leads to proactive and reactive adaptive capacities, there is also evidence from other municipalities that when negative trends are becoming too strong, tendencies towards powerless fatalist behaviours exist.

NOTES

1. The equity ratio is used extensively in Sweden to evaluate an organisation's long-term financial position. It uses information from the balance sheet and is calculated as equity divided by total assets.
2. In Table 1, the financial position of each municipality is indicated as positive, negative or zero (neutral), in accordance with the framework of the book. The calculation that underlies the indication is on the traditional measure used to evaluate the financial result in Swedish municipalities, which is the 2% target. The aim for each municipality is to have a financial result that is 2% of the income from taxes and state grants. If the financial result is between +2% and −2% of the income from taxes and state grants, the indication in Table 1 is 'zero', and if it is below, it is 'negative', and above, 'positive'. If the fluctuation between positive and negative is low over the years, the municipality has low volatility (see Table 2).
3. The financial crisis in 1991 was a combined real estate, banking and governmental crisis − probably the worst since the 1930s, from a Swedish perspective, and definitely worse than the 2008/2009 crisis. For an overview of the 1991crisis (and others), see Haugh et al. (2009).
4. The calculations used in the scheme are detailed and disaggregated, and therefore too complicated to account for here, but these are the main principles of the scheme.

REFERENCES

Barbera, C., Jones, M., Korac, S., Saliterer, I., & Steccolini, I. (2017). Governmental financial resilience under austerity in Austria, England and Italy: How do local governments cope with financial shocks? Public Administration, forthcoming.

Brorström, B., Donatella, P., & Wänström, J. (2013). *Hur kommuner hanterar besvärligheter: resultat och insikter från det nationella kommunforskningsprogrammet.* NatKom-rapport no. 25.

Haugh, D., Ollivaud, P., & Turner, D. (2009). *The macroeconomic consequences of banking crises in OECD countries.* OECD Economics Department Working Papers No. 683.

Konjunkturinstitutet. (2012). *Effekter av de tillfälliga statsbidragen till kommunsektorn under finanskrisen.* Fördjupnings-PM no. 16.

Larsson, T., & Bäck, C. (2008). *Governing and Governance in Sweden.* Studentlitteratur AB.

Proposition 2011/12:172. (2011). *Kommunala utjämningsreserver.* Regeringens Propositioner.

Proposition 2012/13:20. (2012). Inspektionen för vård och omsorg − en ny *tillsynsmyndighet för hälso- och sjukvård och socialtjänst.* Regeringens Propositioner.

SOU 2007:101. (2007). *Tydlig och öppen — förslag till en stärkt skolinspektion.* Statens Offentliga Utredningar.

Sveriges Riksbank. (2011). Finanskrisens effekter på arbetsmarknaden — en jämförelse av Sverige, euroområdet och USA. Penningpolitisk rapport februari 2011.

Wällstedt, N., & Almqvist, R. (2015). From 'either or' to 'both and': Organisational management in the aftermath of NPM. *Scandinavian Journal of Public Administration, 19*(2), 7–25.

Wällstedt, N., Grossi, G., & Almqvist, R. (2014). Organizational solutions for financial sustainability: A Comparative case study from the Swedish municipalities. *Journal of Public Budgeting, Accounting & Management, 26*(1), 181–218.

CHAPTER 12

FINANCIAL RESILIENCE AT THE ROOT OF THE CRISIS – MICHIGAN, U.S.

Sanja Korac, Iris Saliterer and Eric Scorsone

ABSTRACT

The United States (U.S.) has been described as the root of the global financial crisis. The events of the financial, sovereign debt, and Euro crisis and the accompanying economic turmoil that have spread throughout most of the Western world have been traced back to the excessive consumer borrowing, sub-prime mortgage lending and ultimately the housing bubble in the United States. Its burst in 2008 created a shock that overshadowed prior recession and fiscal stress of governmental entities in the United States. Deriving over 90% of their own tax revenues from property taxes, local governments in Michigan have been hit even more excessively. However, the cases analysed in this chapter not only tell a unique story of deep shock and legacy costs, but also of creative ways of surviving the crisis, exerting different patterns of financial resilience. In general, state regulations restricted buffering the impact, and some cities additionally suffered from their geographical vicinity to and economic dependency on Detroit, a city that stands for the turbulence of the U.S. automobile industry. After first deploying buffering capacities that still existed, two cases saw the crisis as an opportunity to address their vulnerabilities (reactive adapters), an opportunity that was not recognised in the case of a constrained adapter. In contrast, one case showed strong anticipatory and coping capacities that have been built up in the past, equipping

Governmental Financial Resilience: International Perspectives on how Local Governments Face Austerity
Public Policy and Governance, Volume 27, 207–227
Copyright © 2017 by Emerald Publishing Limited
ISSN: 2053-7697/doi:10.1108/S2053-769720170000027012

*the local government to operate in a lean and efficient way, and to proac-
tively adapt to arising shocks.*

Keywords: U.S.; Michigan; financial resilience; financial crisis; property
taxes; legacy costs

INTRODUCTION

This chapter analyses local government resilience in a national context that has
been described as the root of the global financial crisis, or in the American
vocabulary the *Great Recession* (Shiller, 2008). Between the 1970s and 2000s,
U.S. states (e.g. Massachusetts, California, Texas), but also big cities (e.g. New
York, NY; Miami, FL; Pittsburgh, PA), smaller municipalities (e.g. Flint, MI;
Hamtramck, MI; Bridgeport, CT) and counties (e.g. Jefferson County, AL;
Breathitt County, KT; Grant County, NM) experienced severe fiscal stress.
However, these crises have been described as being a result of long-term issues
in their respective economic context, excessive borrowing in capital projects, or
mismanagement (see Ebel, Petersen, & Vu, 2012; Hendrick, 2011; Honadle,
2003; Reschovsky, 2003). The financial crisis in 2008–2009 differed in that first,
local governments experienced it as an external shock, and second, its magnitude overshadowed prior recession or economy-related fiscal stress (see Ebel
et al., 2012).

Considering the diverse structure of U.S. local governments, the setting
for the investigation has been narrowed to one state, Michigan. Local governments in Michigan have been significantly affected by the economic
recession following the financial crisis, and their characteristics tell a unique
story of legacy costs, deep shock, and creative ways of surviving the crisis.
The presented cases show that coping with such a crisis requires a set of
capacities that goes beyond the intra-organisational fiscal toolbox investigated in earlier studies (see Hendrick, 2011). In this context, a financial resilience perspective (see introduction) appears to be viable for exploring these
aspects.

The chapter is organised as follows. The next section presents the national
as well as regional context, highlighting the main features of the U.S. local
level, the local government accounting system and recent challenges. The section 'Method' introduces the method including case selection, data collection
and analysis. Subsequently, we present and discuss the results from the case
analysis before we discuss across-case findings and draw conclusions in the last
section.

MAIN FEATURES OF THE U.S. LOCAL LEVEL

The U.S. government landscape is highly diverse. Its sub-national level consists of 50 highly autonomous states and nearly 90,000 local governments, and covers a plethora of political and fiscal arrangements. State governments control the structure, financing possibilities and procedures of local governments (see *Dillon's Rule*, Grumm & Murphy, 1974) in their territory (National League of Cities, 2013). However, the so-called *Home Rule* enables devolution of state power to local governments and hence allows greater structural, functional, personnel and financial autonomy of the local level (Haider-Markel, 2009, 791 f., Ebel & Petersen, 2012). The level of power and autonomy granted to local governments varies strongly between the 50 U.S. states, as either Dillon's Rule, or Home Rule, or both rules may apply at the same time.

The local level is divided between general-purpose governments, school districts, and special purpose governments. The latter provide urban services such as water, sanitation, and fire protection, are less politically visible and not directly accountable to voters. School districts are mainly independent bodies governed by an elected board. General-purpose governments comprise counties (subdivisions of the state) and municipalities (cities, towns, villages, townships), that are self-governed (Ebel & Petersen, 2012). Municipalities cover a spectrum of services of public interest, such as streets and roads, economic development, parks and recreation, libraries; police and fire services, and emergency medical services (often in combination with a fire or police department), but also water, sewer, leaf pick-up, snow removal, as well as waste and recycling, if not provided for by special purpose units.

The main revenue sources of local governments are property tax (ca. 30%), user fees and charges (ca. 23%) sales tax (ca. 7%) and personal income tax (ca. 2%). The volume of intergovernmental transfers however is considerable — more than a third of total local revenues are from state government payments (ca. 36%) (see Tax Policy Center, 2014). U.S. local governments are able to issue own debt obligations in form of municipal bonds. The basis for municipal bonds are either general obligation bonds, where bondholders have the right to establish a tax levy, or revenue bonds that are repaid from revenue collected from a specific project, for example a toll road, or an airport (Fortune, 1991). The municipal bond market plays a significant role in U.S. local government financing, and rating agencies are essential and highly influential when it comes to the terms and conditions of issuing debt. Almost all state governments (47 out of 50) limit however the amount of debt issued via their constitution or statutory provisions (Spiotto, 2013).

LOCAL GOVERNMENT ACCOUNTING SYSTEM AND RECENT CHALLENGES

Local government accounting and financial reporting in the U.S. integrates modified accrual accounting with government-wide financial statements (GASB Statement No. 34, 1999). While budgets are not standardized, local government financial reports are comparable due to stringent legal standards set by the state governments. Many of them mandate standards and principles brought forward by the Government Accounting Standards Board (GASB). The financial reports are audited by private sector firms (certified public accountants) that are selected by the local governing board (e.g. the city council) (Giroux et al., 2002).

Local governments have to follow balanced budget requirements, that is the basic rule that revenues must be equal or greater than expenditures. However, the rigidity of these requirements varies across the states as in some, deficit spending up to the fund balance is allowed, and in others, like Michigan, deficit is prohibited for the general fund (operating fund of the local government) and all special revenue funds (revenue sources for specific purposes, e.g. water and sewer) (Dillon, 2012; Giroux et al., 2002). In times of serious fiscal stress, states can deploy a financial control board or so-called emergency financial managers in their local governments (CBO, 2010; Kasdan, 2014). As a last resort, U.S. local governments can also default on their debt and file for bankruptcy (Chapter 9, CBO, 2010; Lewis, 1994; United States Courts). This allows them to continue operating without liquidation of assets while adjusting or refinancing creditor claims (Spiotto, 2013).

Pension and health care obligations to employees place a huge burden on U.S. local governments. In the past decades, generous pension and health care benefits have been negotiated in order to compete for the workforce while not placing a burden on the present budget with higher wages (since these benefits are excluded from the balance sheets and shown in footnotes only). Federal and state laws generally also do not require local governments to make annual contributions to the employees' pension and health care funds (CBO, 2010). In times of fiscal stress, payments to these funds therefore are often deferred. As the number of retirees increases, these *other post-employment benefits* (OPEB) take a major part of the general fund revenues (see Kellogg, 2014), and will affect the local governments as *legacy costs* for years to come (Shoulders & Freeman, 2012). This is also the reason why the GASB pushes towards including economic condition/fiscal sustainability and especially the unfunded actuarial accrued pension liabilities and OPEB in the government-wide financial statements (Shoulders & Freeman, 2012).

METHOD

In line with the other chapters in this book (Barbera, Jones, Korac, Saliterer, & Steccolini, 2017), a purposive sampling strategy (Patton, 2015;

Barbera et al., 2017) was applied in the selection of the setting and the cases. In order to level out immediate factors of the crisis epicentre, we attempted to capture the financial resilience of local governments that were strongly affected by the developments in the housing market but were neither located in one of the local housing bubbles (see Martin, 2011), nor in close proximity to US financial capitals like New York City, San Francisco or Washington, DC. The state of Michigan has been selected as the study setting for two reasons: first, it meets the initial criteria of easing out crisis epicentre effects. Second, the state had introduced several policies that limit local financial autonomy in order to prevent or alleviate fiscal emergencies several years before the global financial crisis (CRC, 2000). Michigan is one out of six U.S. states with ongoing legislation for the fiscal monitoring of cities, and its laws for the financial control of cities are described as having 'real teeth' (Weikart, 2013, p. 395). Its regulative framework therefore presents a particularly interesting context for investigations of local government financial resilience.

The case selection was first based on the size of local governments. Michigan consists of 1,240 townships, 258 villages and 275 cities (Michigan Manual, 2010). Up to a population of 10,000, those are classified either as villages, towns, or townships, and their functions and responsibilities can be compared only to a limited extent. Large municipalities on the other hand tend to be inhomogeneous from a demographic and economic perspective (Hendrick, 2011) and hence are likely to exhibit a higher variety in functions and service provision. We therefore selected cities within the population range of 10,000–25,000, resulting in a total of 48 cases included in the subsequent step of the sampling process. Based on the published financial statements of local governments between 2008 and 2013, we use two criteria to select the cases: normalised financial performance (annual changes in increase/decrease in net assets) and volatility (standard deviation of the normalised financial performance over the period).[1] In a next step, local governments were classified in terms of their combination of financial performance and volatility. This allowed to identify main groupings of cases. The four selected local governments represent different combinations of financial performance and volatility along the spectrum, ranging from negative financial performance and high volatility (M1) to positive performance and medium volatility (M5). M1 was selected as it shows negative financial performance (−1.43%) and medium volatility (6.6%). M2 was selected as its financial performance is around zero (−0.05%) and it shows lower levels of volatility (5.1%). M3 was selected as a case of high negative financial performance (−2.91%) and high volatility (10.0%), and M4 as one of positive financial performance (1.12%) and lower levels of volatility (5.2%). Fig. 1 shows the patterns of normalised financial performance for the selected cases between 2008 and 2013. Moreover, we present the development of the annual financial performance (increase/decrease in net assets/ revenues) for each case.

Case	Normalized financial performance	Financial Performance
M1	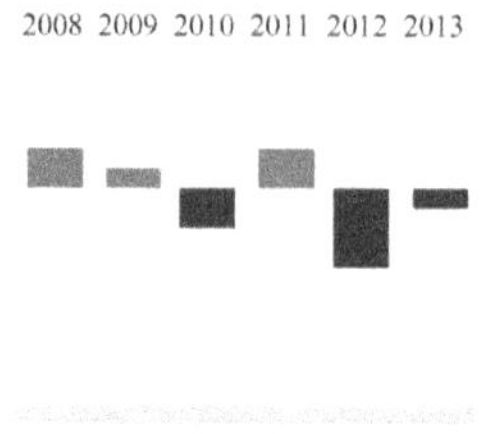 2008 2009 2010 2011 2012 2013 Negative: −1.43% Volatility: 6.6%	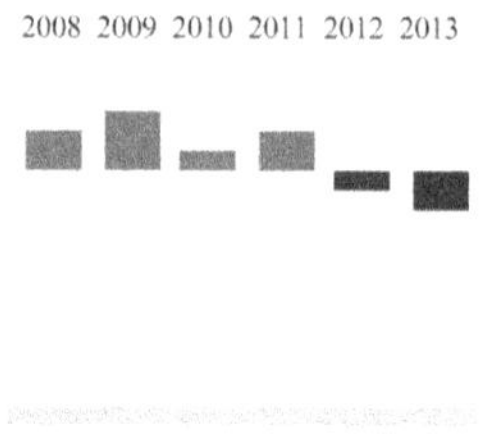 2008 2009 2010 2011 2012 2013
M2	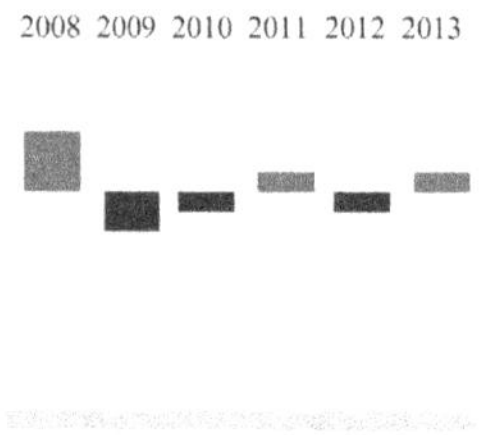 2008 2009 2010 2011 2012 2013 Around zero: −0.05% Volatility: 5.1%	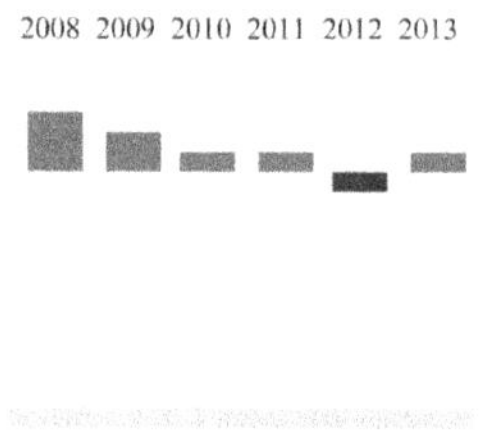 2008 2009 2010 2011 2012 2013
M3	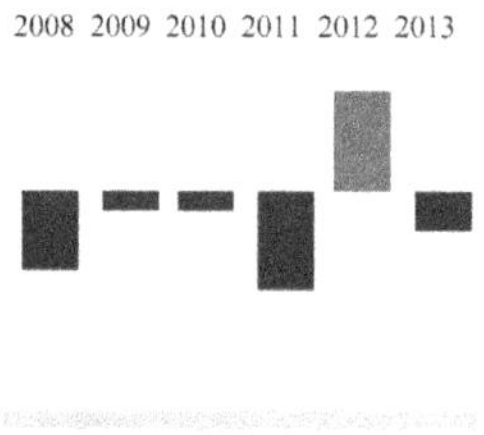 2008 2009 2010 2011 2012 2013 High negative: −2.91% Volatility: 10.0%	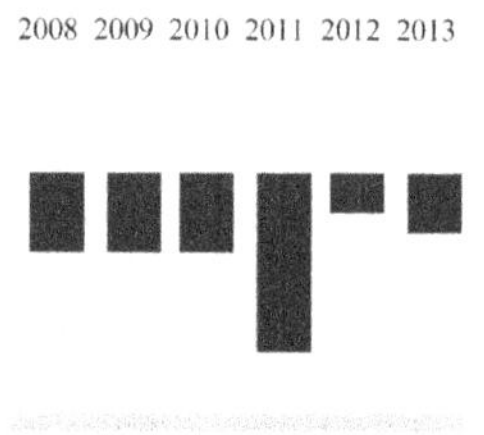 2008 2009 2010 2011 2012 2013
M4	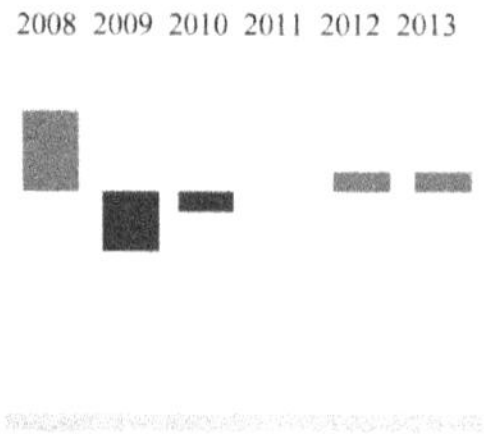 2008 2009 2010 2011 2012 2013 Positive: 1.12% Volatility: 5.2%	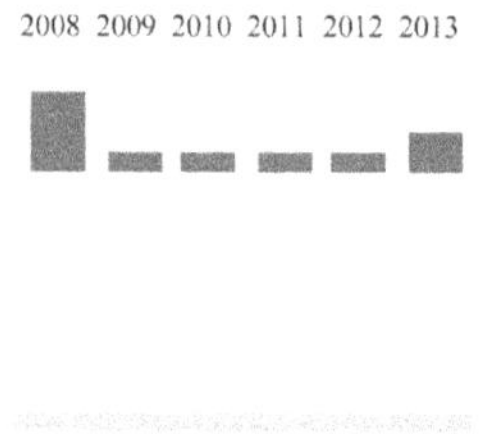 2008 2009 2010 2011 2012 2013

Fig. 1.   Basic Financial Data of the Selected Cases.

The qualitative analysis comprised semi-structured interviews as the corner-stone of the case study (Yin, 2009), but triangulation of data using document analysis was applied to provide stronger 'substantiation of constructs' (Eisenhardt, 1989). To ensure triangulation of views, interviews were conducted with the chief executive officers (CEOs), that is city managers, and chief finan-cial officers (CFOs), that is financial directors of the local governments. The interviews included open-ended questions about the financial condition of the local government, financial and non-financial goals, financial and political sta-bility, strategy and goals, main shocks experienced within the last 10 years, and the local government's responses to them. In order to ensure a more open dis-cussion, the questions were not designed to operationalise any one theory or construct (Woodside, 2010). Two researchers conducted the interviews on-site and in one case by phone in February 2015, with one leading the discussion based on the interview protocol and the other taking notes and asking addi-tional questions (Eisenhardt, 1989). The interviews lasted between 60 and 75 minutes, were recorded, transcribed and used for qualitative content analysis. The within-case analyses allowed the identification of distinct resilience patterns of the four local governments.

RESULTS

In the following, we introduce the more general crisis context that all local gov-ernments included in this study had to face. Results on the perceived shock(s) and the respective impact on the local government, the perceived financial vul-nerabilities, and anticipatory and coping capacities are first presented from a within-case perspective. The combination, or dynamic interplay of these dimen-sions gives an understanding of the resilience pattern that can be identified in the respective cases. A subsequent across-case analysis allowed tracing out the similarities and differences between the different local government financial resilience patterns (Table 1).

The Michigan Context

The financial crisis and its aftermath had a substantial impact on local govern-ments in the U.S. Michigan local governments, which are in the focus of this chapter, seem to have been affected even more than most of the other countries and regions covered in this book. Several aspects of the context in Michigan help in understanding this considerable impact. From a legal perspective, U.S. local governments have high financial autonomy. However, their strong finan-cial ties to the states – through revenue shares and regulations limiting the type and level of taxes local governments can raise – suggest otherwise. Revenue

Table 1. Resilience Patterns.

	M1	M2	M3	M4
Context	*Institutional* Low financial autonomy, high dependency on property tax	*Institutional* Low financial autonomy, inhibiting regulations	*Institutional* Dependence on property values, inhibiting regulations	*Institutional* Regulation allows no deficit
	Economic Favourable location (proximity to capital), local government has assets (land), urban development confined	*Economic* Favourable location (distance to Detroit), agricultural community, landlocked	*Economic* Unfavourable location (proximity to Detroit)	*Economic* Undiversified economy, landlocked
	Socio-demographic Young, low to medium-income population	*Socio-demographic* Perceived older and higher income population — objective data contradicting	*Socio-demographic* Working-age, medium-income population	*Socio-demographic* Demographically diverse, well-educated, working-age high-income population
Shock/impact	Financial crisis, bad investment (urban renewal) Drop in taxable value (25%), loss of big employer	Financial crisis Delayed impact, decrease in property taxes, decrease in revenue shares	Financial crisis, housing bubble, recession Double dip (housing bubble, recession), huge decrease in property taxes (50%), decrease in revenue shares, functional bankruptcy	Financial crisis Recession, increasing unemployment, decrease in property taxes, decrease in revenue shares
Filtering	Threat, opportunity	Threat	Threat, opportunity	Threat
Perceived vulnerability levels and sources before the shock and their evolution over time	*Medium*: High debt resulting from bad investment, pension plan overfunded *Increasing*: Constant erosion of property taxes, low financial reserves, high debt, deferred maintenance and improvement,	*Low*: Good financial reserves, low debt, revenue gap in water and sewer system (designed for larger city) *Slightly increasing*: High financial reserves, low debt, constant gap in revenue shares,	*Low/medium*: Good financial reserves, high property taxes, property values did not mirror fair value, legacy costs, old infrastructure *Increasing*: Deficit, no financial reserves, debt manageable,	*Low*: Good financial reserves, constant decrease in debt, efficient operations, old infrastructure, dependence on undiversified economy *Slightly increasing*: Good financial condition, low and

	legacy costs, only core services delivered	decreasing control over revenues due to regulation, legacy costs, unfavourable location in the long term (transportation)	legacy costs unmanageable, recovery of revenues impossible, ongoing lawsuit, old infrastructure, inter-fund liabilities, bad investment of local government, crime rate	constantly decreasing debt, old infrastructure, legacy costs, accounting regulations will formally increase debt
Level and types of anticipatory capacity before the shock and their evolution over time	*Medium*: Awareness of early warning signals, expenditure cuts as preparation, monitoring of drop in taxable values *Increasing*: Cost-benefit analyses	*Medium*: Low awareness of early warning signals, cautious borrowing, citizen co-finance in investments, monitoring and control, purchasing procedures *Increasing*: maintenance as prevention, monitoring, internal cost accounting, internal control, operational procedures, cost-benefit analyses, awareness of regulations that will affect local governments	*Low*: Negation of early warnings, disbelief in magnitude of financial crisis, reluctance to personnel and service cuts as preparation, operation by crisis *Increasing*: Increased demand for information, monthly/quarterly budget monitoring, constant monitoring of pension fund, forward-looking, long-term financial planning, cost-benefit analyses, predictions, high individual awareness, sense-making of developments	*Low/medium*: Monitoring of automotive industry, awareness of early warning signals but crisis as a surprise *Increasing*: Medium-term financial planning, frequent and timely information of political actors, monitoring of regional economy/spending/revenues/revenue collection/media/state regulations, cautious/transparent/participative decision-making, long-term task-related plans
Levels and types of coping capacity	*Selective* *Buffering* *Adapting*	*Selective* *Buffering* *Adapting*	*Comprehensive* *Buffering* *Adapting* *Transforming*	*Selective* *Buffering* *Adapting*
Pattern of resilience	*Reactive adapter (retrenchment)*	*Constrained adapters*	*Reactive adapter (repositioning)*	*Proactive adapter*

shares, mainly coming from state sales taxes, are a significant financial source for Michigan local governments (Gross, 2011). During the last decades, these revenue shares have decreased constantly as a consequence of a weakened automotive industry that dominates Michigan's economy (Skidmore & Scorsone, 2011).

The little diversified economy also amplified the fiscal impact on local governments once the economic recession started. Massive lay-offs in the already shaken automotive industry caused unemployment spill-over effects in other industries, which led to a wave of foreclosures across local governments, depriving revenues from property taxes. Michigan local governments rely heavily on tax revenues derived from property values (more than 93% of own tax revenues, which is about 20% higher than the U.S. average) (Tax Policy Center, 2015). Despite the experiences of severe fiscal stress in U.S. local governments in general and in Michigan municipalities in particular (Hendrick, 2011; Mallach & Scorsone, 2011), property values were seen as a relatively stable source of revenues (CBO, 2010). However, the roots of the latest financial crisis in the housing market caused a bullwhip effect (Chernick et al., 2011; Lutz, 2008): property values plummeted from 2008 to 2010 and the main tax base for numerous local governments eroded. In the following, Michigan's specific state regulations inhibited the recovery of local government revenues. Introduced in times when property values increased faster than the rate of inflation and the tax burden for citizens thus grew rapidly, the regulations ensured that tax rates automatically rolled back to the rate of inflation or were capped at 5% if inflation was higher. While property values recovered in the last years, the property tax revenues – capped by these regulations – did not recover to a similar extent.

M1

M1 represents an old city located in some distance to the city of Detroit. The geographic location was considered an advantage during the financial crisis and the economic recession. However, the city's urban development possibilities are highly restricted as one institution extents over a major part of the city's land. M1 has a young, left-wing, low to medium-income population. The major financial shocks experienced in the last 10 years were a failed investment project and the financial crisis. During the following economic recession, the local government lost a big employer and was hit by a drop in taxable value of about 25%. These shocks to the local government finances amplified the already high debt level (the highest per capita debt level of the four cases included, and about 19% long-term debt as a percentage of taxable value in the local government[2]) resulting from the failed investment in urban renewal mentioned above. The latter was also considered M1's biggest vulnerability source.

> The city decided to do this massive urban renewal project, they bought a huge property in downtown. [The] downtown was junky, and it was bringing the city down, so they decided this renewal, [they decided to] buy all the property, clean the infrastructure, clean it environmentally, and redevelop it. This started 15 years ago, but only a small part has been sold so far. Now the urge is to sell it, as the debt has been delayed. (CEO)

Nevertheless, M1 was also the only one case out of the four included in the study where the pension fund was overfunded in the past (about 103% in 2007 and 2008), thus legacy costs were not considered a vulnerability source. Interestingly, the former CEO seems to have identified early signals of the unfolding threat of the financial crisis by monitoring the drop in taxable values. In order to prepare for what was expected to hit the local government, M1 cut back personnel expenditure to be ahead of the game.

> The previous city manager did see it coming to a certain degree. He decided to cut back city workforce, put aside every possible dollar. This is a basis for the city manager to do the things he does, so he does not run out of money before refinancing the debt. [...] [I think] the former city manager did a very good job. (CEO)

> [I] saw it coming when experienced a huge drop in taxable values and therefore property taxes in 2007/2008. [It fell] from [xxx] million to [xxx] [3%], now it is down to [xxx] million [10% lower than in 2007]. (CFO)

When the crisis hit, the city buffered by pushing a retrenchment strategy, that is refinancing debt, selling assets, cutting overhead costs, and cutting services to a minimum. Having outsourced most of its personnel with the aim to reduce personnel expenditure before the crisis, only few personnel measures were feasible however. More recently, the local government also faced a change in administrative leadership (2013). The new CEO reported that innovations were needed for the local government to adapt and recover. M1's main strategy was a redevelopment of the city, that is creating commercial real estate, but adaptation was also based on negotiation in the investment of the local government's money where the CFO managed to obtain a 0.5–1% instead of 0% interest rate, selling local government services to other agencies, and utilisation of efficiencies.

> Let me give you an example: employee benefits insurance – the city found a Medicare plan that offers actually better insurance and is subsidized by federal government, and the costs went down substantially. The city constantly tries to innovate, constantly pushes the envelope. You have to put certain amount of work and resources to it, but you try to spend to save more in the future. (CEO)

New personnel was hired specifically in order to search for cutback and asset selling possibilities. Still, this measure of adaptation in fact seems to result in the exploitation of the local government's buffering capacity, especially as the staff was hired based on short-term contracts that will expire after cutbacks are implemented and assets are sold.

At this time, people are hired to search for cutbacks and to sell property – after that, the city workforce will fall back to [XX]. But now is the time to take advantage of the market to sell property – two years from now is too late. CEO

M1 is the only case out of four where, several years after the burst of the housing bubble and the financial crisis, property taxes still eroded. With low financial reserves, high debt, deferred maintenance and improvement, and growing legacy costs (drop from 103% to about 83% funded in pension fund), its vulnerability in fact further increased. Although the local government was perceived as recovering slowly, further efficiency gains seem unlikely and increase in the service level or in staff thus almost impossible. M1 therefore mainly shows a reactive and buffering-oriented pattern of resilience.

M2

M2 is located in some distance to Detroit and landlocked by two surrounding townships. Respondents described the city as a mainly agricultural, middle to higher income community with a population that is older than in comparable local governments. However the figures on median age (in M2, the median age was lower than in two other cases included in the analysis, and lower than in Michigan in general), as well as on median household income (rather low to medium-income population, comparable to M1) did not support this perception. The local government provided little incentives for younger people (e.g. it had no recreational facilities) or businesses (e.g. the infrastructure was perceived as inadequate), and the standard of living was expected to stagnate over the long term.

The major shock to local government finances in the last 10 years was the financial crisis that led to a huge drop in property taxes and a decrease in revenue shares. However, the respondents explicitly stated they did not experience the effect of the recession-induced unemployment and that M2 felt the crisis' impact only in the last five years before the study (about two years later than the other cases). The local government was in good financial condition before the crisis, its level of financial reserves was perceived high and the debt level as one of the lowest per capita debt levels in the state. However, the respondents identified two major vulnerability sources: the constant gap in revenue shares and the revenue gap in the water and sewer system. The system was built to serve a larger community, thus the collected revenues did not cover the expenses. M2 was cautious in increasing debt and invested in projects only where co-funding by citizens (through tax increases) could be achieved, implemented monitoring and control systems and purchasing procedures. The financial crisis was a surprise to the respondents, since indicators were suggesting the opposite from what actually unfolded. Despite some signals from the internet and housing bubble, and experience of two other financial crises in the past, the respondents' awareness seemed low. Prior crises were described as 'different' in their extent:

> No one saw the financial crisis coming. It blindsided everybody, because everything went so well. It is the third crisis in my career, but nothing was ever like this. Because in the ones before, you did not have these huge losses in property values, and not the cutbacks in shared revenues. (CEO)

When early warning signals were detected, the crisis had already hit. The CEO was reluctant in using financial reserves in the general fund to stabilise the local government's financial situation, and centralised any decisions on service and cost cuts. Since increases in taxes were considered unfavourable and non-affordable for the local government's population, M2 relied mainly on expenditure cuts – personnel cuts (25%), service cuts in police and public works as well as significant cuts in basic operations to buffer the impact.

> If you know your demographics and socio-economic status, you know that your taxpayers cannot afford much in additional taxes. (CFO)

The case showed however also some adaptive capacity in that it 'piggy-backed' (collaborated with other governments) in purchasing, thus maximising purchasing power and using efficiencies of scale. A master plan was developed to address the local government's vulnerability sources (e.g. revenue gaps) mentioned above. At the time of the investigation however, this was still in the development stage and did not allow further conclusions on M2's adaptive capacity.

After the crisis, the anticipatory capacity increased. M2 invested in maintenance, monitoring of services and staff time, enhanced the use of internal cost accounting, internal control, operational procedures, and cost-benefit analyses. Additionally, the respondents showed high awareness of currently discussed state regulations and their likely (negative) effect on local governments. Overall, M2 managed to cope with the crisis well, still exerting a high level of financial reserves and a low debt level. Having almost regained the financial situation as of before the crisis, the respondents claimed that the local government was prepared for further crises in the magnitude of the last one. However, while the respondents addressed vulnerability sources that could be controlled by the local government itself, they perceive the context and thereby arising vulnerability sources, that is the constantly decreasing revenue shares and the decreasing control thereof, as out of their hands. The perceived vulnerability increased slightly due to legacy costs and the geographical location, which, should prices for energy and transportation increase, is considered as a long-term vulnerability source. This seemingly non-controllable vulnerability sources are crucial in understanding the resilience pattern of case. While M2 successfully addressed internal vulnerability sources, the perception of not being able to influence 'external' vulnerability sources indicates a constrained resilience pattern.

M3

M3 was founded as a suburb of Detroit, which is why its inhabitants can be described as mainly medium-income blue-collar workers. The local government experienced the shock of the financial crisis as a double dip: through the drop in property values causing a tax loss of 50% in 2008, and through the increasing unemployment during the recession from 2010 to 2012. The additional significant loss in revenue shares and huge increase in legacy costs (double-digit increase in 3 years) left the local government in functional bankruptcy.

Before the crisis, M3 had good financial reserves and high revenues from property taxes, which accounted for seemingly low vulnerability. However, the property values did not mirror fair value, and this vulnerability source was also the major reason the local government was hit hard when the housing bubble burst. Other vulnerability sources were its unfunded OPEB plan that caused high legacy costs (see section on accounting system and challenges), as well as its old infrastructure.

In an early stage of the crisis, the county where M3 is located and professional networks had issued warnings pinpointing to the local government's specific vulnerabilities: being landlocked with no area for expansion, and having old infrastructure. This would have required capital investment for maintenance on the one hand and restricted possibilities to raise further revenues in times of austerity on the other hand. However, the prior CEO showed disbelief in the severity of the crisis and seemed reluctant to make 'hard' decisions regarding personnel and service cuts. Ignoring the signals, the latest crisis appears to have been a surprise, and the local government was operating 'by crisis'.

> My predecessor, who was a good city manager for 17 years, having gone through three dips in the economy, he really believed those developments were a temporary bump in the road. [...] I would say that the city operated by crisis. It appeared they would not make any changes until the crisis happened. (CEO)

Service cuts seemed to go against the council strategy, and even during the crisis, the local government kept its most costly service (leaf pick-up). Due to its old infrastructure, deferring maintenance was seen as a high risk and thus no option. Having exploited its rainy day funds in the past, buffering therefore consisted of personnel cuts (almost half of staff), which resulted in reduced service hours. M3 further changed its fee schedules and enforced building licences more aggressively. Changing its leadership right before (CFO in 2006) and during the crisis (CEO in 2011), the local government also pursued adapting measures, starting with the change from a self-administered pension and OPEB plan to a bought in larger system. This resulted in a more professionalized management and control and in efficiency gains. The new CEO built on networking, information sharing, advice-taking, and exerted high individual creativity in searching for additional revenue possibilities to avoid emergency financial management. Since M3's assets were low, this required a more innovative approach than in M1. The solution was an old act that allowed special tax increase for fire and police services. In order to implement the latter as a buffering measure, adaptation capacity was required in form of persuading the council and citizens. Attempts to collaborate and consolidate with more affluent neighbouring local governments were unsuccessful as, based on its crime rate, M3 was considered a weak partner. However, the city indicated the capacity to transform: the CEO induced a change from a conservative to an innovative culture and searched for new identity for the local government. At the time of the study, the transformation was still ongoing.

After the shock, the anticipatory capacity increased – not least due to the change in the leadership that increased the demand for information and the frequency of budget monitoring, as well as ensured a constant monitoring of the unfunded pension plan. The local government took a more forward-looking perspective, used long-term financial planning, cost-benefit analyses and predictions in decisions. The new CEO exerted high individual awareness, and high sense-making of general socio-economic developments, for example overestimated property values, accumulating health care costs. The increased anticipatory capacity however did not translate into a comparable decrease in vulnerability. M3 was still a deficit local government (the only one of the four cases), and did not manage to build up its financial reserves. With the local government still being in a trough, the vulnerability was perceived as high.

> It is definitely in the trough. [...] It would be nice not to have to move things around but to have something there to be able to address problems. (CFO)

> The city has climbed out of the cliff, and we are hanging now on the edge. I do not want to be totally pessimistic, but the city is in a delicate enough position that one disaster would force it into emergency management. (CAO)

Although the general debt level was considered reasonable and manageable, the legacy costs were perceived as unmanageable. They were expected to even increase in the short- to medium-term, since the counter-measures taken would be effective only in the long term. The respondents believed that the recovery of revenues to a level as of before the crisis was impossible. They also perceived the context and particular the U.S. 'culture of suing' as a source of vulnerability. The latter appears however to be related to the fact that at the time of investigation, the city had to deal with an ongoing lawsuit regarding its OPEB plan where the outcome was still uncertain. Other sources of vulnerability were present in the local government's aging infrastructure, and some also emerged during the crisis: inter-fund liabilities (from the general fund to other funds and between the refuse and the water and sewer funds), a prior investment in infrastructure (shopping mall) that turned into a liability as it could not generate the expected revenues, and crime were considered as problematic. A closer look at the crime rate revealed that the overall crime rate indeed was higher than the

Michigan average but comparable to M1. In particular, the problem seemed to be the crimes against property, which were almost double the rates in M1 and surmounted the other cases and the Michigan average by far. However, considering the various examples for its increased anticipatory capacity and the deployment of coping capacities, M3 seemed more long-term-oriented than M1. The local government embarked on a transformational path by searching for a new identity and changing its organisational culture. While the crisis was a threat to the local government survival (functional bankruptcy), it was also perceived as a trigger to build up and strengthen its capacities and as an opportunity to initiate necessary changes, thus indicating a reactive adapter resilience pattern.

M4

M4 is located in the Detroit metropolitan region. The CEO described it as a strong family community that is forward-looking, resourceful and moderate. Its population is perceived as demographically diverse, well educated, and medium-income. However, compared to Michigan in general and to the other cases in particular, M4's mainly working-age citizens show a relatively high median household income ($73,111 compared to $49,576 median household income in Michigan, data from United States Census Bureau, 2016).

> The people are very looking-forward, resourceful. They prepare themselves for tough times. When you drive around the city, you will not see a lot of mansions, the people live moderately, within their means, so we did not have as many people leaving the community. We did not have many people going through foreclosures, like some other surrounding communities. (CEO)

The major financial shock for the local government in the last 10 years was the financial crisis. The impact was felt during the economic recession that followed, resulting in increasing unemployment and the decline of property taxes of about 18–19%. However, compared to other local governments, M4 seemed to have only a low level of foreclosures. During the time of the financial crisis, the local government also experienced decreasing revenue shares. While this is true also for the other local governments, M4 is one of two cases (the other being M2) in the study where revenue shares were a considerable part of the general fund (about 15–16%). From 2011 to 2012, M4 experienced a drop in revenue shares to 9.6%. In the early 2000s, M4 had experienced serious financial stress that left the local government with almost no financial reserves. After taking office, the current CEO stabilized the financial condition before the financial crisis hit in 2008. At that time, M4's vulnerability was perceived low as it had good financial reserves (15–20% of annual budget), showed constant decrease in debt, and was described as lean and tight, providing only core services. However, its old infrastructure and the context, in particular its geographical location and thus the dependence on but weak control of the economy, were seen as the major sources of vulnerability. Decision-makers have been monitoring the developments in the automotive industry as the dominating factor in the economy, and although the respondents were aware of early warning signals coming from financial indicators, the extent of and reasons behind the financial crisis seemed to be a surprise.

> Yes, we saw it coming. The tax value declined, SEV^3 declined. I do a three-year-budget when projecting the general fund, so the data and information coupled with the information of auto industry, you start to measure how the auto industry is doing, [...] and it started to snowball. (CFO)

> Did we see it coming ... I do not think anyone saw it coming. Especially when we found out the reason behind it, it was a shock to all of us and I think that all of us were very surprised that the checks and balances that they required us were not there. It was very disappointing. Something like this? No. (CEO)

M4's first responses to the impact were concentrated on expenditure cuts through cutting capital improvements, cutting services and programs, pay freeze, and cutting employee benefits. It deferred investments in equipment and, after a proactive offer by its business partners, the local government deferred also various payments giving them some leeway right after crisis hit. This allowed an overall budget cut of 10–15% without having to lay off staff. Targeted revenue increases further contributed to buffering the crisis, and a citizen vote to override state regulations on property tax caps enabled raising own revenues. The latter was uncommon for Michigan cities (four out of 48 Michigan cities in the initial sample achieved such an override) and was considered 'a bold move' that required a well-functioning, well-informed council. The voter support for the override and thus the loosening of the cap on property tax was achieved through the information policy, prudence and persuasion ability of the local government actors at the apex. As such, this measure indicates adapting capacity that allowed the local government to deal successfully with more conflict laden fiscal measures. In addition, M4 adapted to the new situation by further pursuing its strategy of partnering – an approach that had been taken in the past where buffering proved insufficient in dealing with severe fiscal stress.

> [...] this was long before anybody did it, [...] we developed collaborations, worked with other communities. [...] So collaboration, the willingness to work with other businesses, besides other cities. The unions, they are very strong in this city, but they do too understood the situation. (CEO)

Partnering with the unions was essential as, at the time of the study, M4 also attempted to cap its OPEB in order to reduce an emerging vulnerability source. After the crisis, local government anticipatory capacity was increasing. Medium-term financial planning was applied to help identifying risks and to tackle the local government's main issues (e.g. infrastructure). The CEO implemented frequent and timely information for political actors, monitoring of the city's spending and its main revenue sources as well as the respective revenue collection. The respondents argued that since revenue sources became weaker after the crisis, more monitoring of the regional economy, the media, and the state regulations was needed in order to identify emerging vulnerabilities. Local government decision-making was considered cautious, transparent, and participative and its investments and equipment were planned long term.

Although vulnerability increased slightly after the crisis, M4 was perceived as, in a 'good enough' financial condition and recovering; its debt level was still low and constantly decreasing. While the vulnerability source of its old infrastructure remained, the legacy costs emerged as the main vulnerability source during and after the crisis. Since new regulations will probably require those liabilities to be included in the books, and thus formally increase local government debt, this vulnerability was considered as increasing in the future. However, the anticipatory capacity and the history of coping capacity in this case suggests that M4 was proactively adapting to financial shocks and managed to stay relatively stable over time.

DISCUSSION AND CONCLUSION

The investigation of cases in a context where local governments experienced the financial crisis very early and, due to the regulatory context, had to cope with an amplification of its impact provides an important puzzle piece to the comparative view of financial resilience pursued in this book. Different external (contextual) and internal factors contributed to the vulnerability of the local governments. All four cases in our study reported that the dependency on revenue shares and the state regulations restricted buffering as well as recovery in case of financial shocks. However, the financial crisis and the subsequent economic recession revealed another contextual factor as a latent vulnerability: the geographical location of local governments. Particularly the proximity to the perishing hub of the city of Detroit accounted for differences in the financial vulnerability of the cases. Two of the four cities included in this study (M3 and M4) are located in the Detroit metropolitan region. In general, they reported that the proximity to Detroit was an advantage in economically flourishing times, but converted to a liability once the crisis hit and the economic recession began. Unfunded pension plans and OPEB continue to be a major vulnerability in three of the four cases in the study. As federal and state laws do not require local governments to make annual contributions to these funds (CBO, 2010), local governments deferred payments in order to buffer financial shocks. These accumulated legacy costs were highlighted as vulnerability sources in two cases (M3, M4), but will challenge local government in the future in general (see McFarland & Pagano, 2014).

All four cases experienced the impact of the financial crisis as a threat. Its roots and causes were a surprise and its impact was described as unexpected. It seems that the disbelief in the magnitude of the shock prevailed, and one city even negated early warnings. The latter was also the case that exerted low *anticipatory capacity* in general (M3). While M3 did not have any financial reserves left to buffer the impact of the latest financial shock, its council was reluctant to cut even non-core and costly services. However, after first deploying buffering capacities that still existed, the city also recognised or learned to see the crisis as an opportunity for changes that concerned its major individual vulnerability sources, which in the long term probably would have been necessary even if no crisis would have emerged. While this characterised both cases that showed a reactive adapter pattern of resilience (M1, M3), M3 was the only case deploying comprehensive *coping capacities*, ranging from buffering to adapting as well as transforming.

In contrast, we find that a proactive adapter pattern of resilience does not necessarily require transforming in order to cope with a financial shock. In the case of M4, it was rather the combination of (previously) developed anticipatory and coping capacities that equipped the local government to operate in a lean and efficient way. Thanks to the city council, M4 had managed to build up financial reserves (buffering capacity) after a period of serious fiscal stress in the past. The fiscal stress encouraged the local government to concentrate on core services and to further enhance collaboration with external stakeholders (adapting), thereby strengthening its capacity to cope with the most recent financial crisis. In contrast, we find that in M2, although showing similar anticipatory capacities and deployment of buffering and adapting as M4, a perception of not being in control of vulnerability sources due to external factors indicated rather a constrained adapter resilience pattern. Thus, the analysis highlights that financial resilience is related to the perceived vulnerability sources that either were kept in control through anticipatory and coping capacities, or were perceived and/or slipped out of the local government decision-makers' control, thereby raising the local government's vulnerability or exposure to financial shocks.

NOTES

1. Normalised increase/decrease in net assets $=$ (Increase/Decrease t $-$ (Increase/Decrease $t - 1$)/Revenues).
2. The State Department of Treasury benchmark is 6%.
3. State equalized value, calculated as 50% of a property's true cash value.

REFERENCES

Barbera, C., Jones, M., Korac, S., Saliterer, I., & Steccolini, I. (2017). Governmental financial resilience under austerity in Austria, England and Italy: How do local governments cope with financial shocks? Public Administration, forthcoming.

CBO. (2010). Fiscal stress faced by local governments. Economic and Budget Issue Brief, Congressional Budget Office, December 2010.

Chernick, H., Langley, A., & Reschovsky, A. (2011). The impact of the Great Recession and the housing crisis on the financing of America's largest cities. *Regional Science and Urban Economics, 41,* 372–381.

CRC. (2000). Avoiding local government financial crisis: The role of state oversight. Citizens Research Council of Michigan, Report No. 329.

Dillon, A. (2012). Audit manual for local units of government in Michigan. Department of Treasury, State of Michigan.

Ebel, R. D., & Petersen, J. E. (2012). *The Oxford handbook of state and local government finance.* Oxford: Oxford University Press.

Ebel, R. D., Petersen, J. E., & Vu, T. T. (2012). Introduction: State and local government finance in the United States. In R. D. Ebel & J. E. Petersen: *The Oxford handbook of state and local government finance* (pp. 2–40). Oxford. Oxford University Press.

Eisenhardt, K. M. (1989). Building theories from case study research. *The Academy of Management Review, 14*(4), 532–550.

Fortune, P. (1991). The municipal bond market, Part I: Politics, taxes, and yields. *New England Economic Review,* September/October, 13–36.

Giroux, G., Jones, R., & Pendlebury, M. (2002). Accounting and auditing for local governments in the U.S. and the U.K.

Gross, E. (2011). National context: History of municipal financial crisis and policy. Urban Affairs, October 2011.

Grumm, J. G., & Murphy, R. D. (1974). Dillon's rule reconsidered. *The Annals of the American Academy of Political and Social Science, 416*(1), 120–132.

Haider-Markel, D. P. (2009). *Political encyclopedia of U.S. states and regions.* Washington, DC: Sage, CQ Press.

Hendrick, R. M. (2011). *Managing the fiscal metropolis. The financial policies, practices and health of suburban municipalities.* Washington, DC: Georgetown University Press.

Honadle, B. W. (2003). The states' role in U.S. local government fiscal crises: A theoretical model and results of a national survey. *International Journal of Public Administration, 26*(13), 1431–1472.

Kasdan, D. O. (2014). A tale of two hatchet men: Emergency financial management in Michigan. *Administration & Society, 46,* 1071–1091.

Kellogg, G. (2014). In the red – Drivers of local government debt in Michigan, Urban Affairs, June 2014.

Lewis, C. W. (1994). Municipal bankruptcy and the states authorization to file under chapter 9. *Urban Affairs Review, 30*(1), 3–26.

Lutz, B. F. (2008). *The connection between house price appreciation and property tax revenue. Finance and economics discussion series.* Washington, DC: Federal Reserve Board.

Mallach, A., & Scorsone, E. (2011). *Long-term stress and systemic failure: Taking seriously the fiscal crisis of America's older cities.* Center for Community Progress. Retrieved from http://community-wealth.org/sites/clone.community-wealth.org/files/downloads/paper-mallach-scorsone.pdf. Accessed on December 21, 2016.

Martin, R. (2011). The local geographies of the financial crisis: From the housing bubble to economic recession and beyond. *Journal of Economic Geography, 11,* 587–618.

McFarland, C., & Pagano, M. A. (2014). *City fiscal conditions 2014.* Washington, DC: National League of Cities.

Michigan Manual. (2010). Michigan Manual 2009-2010. Michigan Legislature. Retrieved from http://www.legislature.mi.gov/(S(udrihsoq1wjqrwp1wxpgt1pt))/mileg.aspx?page=PublicationHomePage&PublicationHomePage=16. Accessed on August 1, 2015.

National League of Cities. (2013). Local government authority. Retrieved from http://www.nlc.org/build-skills-and-networks/resources/cities-101/city-powers/local-government-authority

Patton, M. Q. (2015). *Qualitative research & evaluation methods* (4th ed.). Thousand Oaks, CA: Sage.

Reschovsky, A. (2003). The implication of state fiscal stress for local governments. Prepared for the conference: State fiscal crises. Causes, consequences, & solutions. The Urban Institute, Washington, DC, April 3, 2003.

Shiller, R. J. (2008). *The subprime solution: How today's global financial crisis happened, and what to do about it*. Princeton, NJ: Princeton University Press.

Shoulders, C. D., & Freeman, R. J. (2012). Government financial-reporting standards: Reviewing the past and present, anticipating the future. In R. D. Ebel & J. E. Petersen (Eds.), *The Oxford handbook of state and local government finance*. Oxford: Oxford University Press.

Skidmore, M., & Scorsone, E. (2011). Causes and consequences of fiscal stress in Michigan cities. *Regional Science and Urban Economics, 41*(4), 360–371.

Spiotto, J. E. (2013). The role of the state in supervising and assisting municipalities, especially in times of financial distress. *Municipal Finance Journal, 34*(1), 1–32.

Tax Policy Center. (2014). *Local general revenue by source*. Retrieved from http://www.taxpolicycenter.org/briefing-book/what-are-sources-revenue-local-governments. Accessed on April 16, 2015.

Tax Policy Center. (2015, January). *Local property taxes as a percentage of local tax revenue*. Retrieved from http://www.taxpolicycenter.org/. Accessed on February 18, 2016.

United States Census Bureau. (2016). *Michigan quick facts, Berkley city, Michigan quick facts*. Retrieved from https://www.census.gov. Accessed on February 18, 2016.

United States Courts. Retrieved from http://www.uscourts.gov/

Weikart, L. A. (2013). Monitoring the fiscal health of America's cities. In H. Levine, J. B. Justice, & E. A. Scorsone (Eds.), *Handbook of local government fiscal health*. Burlington, VT: Jones and Bartlett.

Woodside, A. G. (2010). *Case study research. theory, methods, practice*. Bingley: Emerald Group Publishing Limited.

Yin, R. K. (2009). *Case study research: Design and methods* (4th ed.). Thousand Oaks, CA: Sage.

CHAPTER 13

CONCLUSION

Ileana Steccolini, Martin Jones and Iris Saliterer

ABSTRACT

Ambitious though it is to summarise the richness of experiences emerging from the country chapters in a few lines, in this concluding chapter we attempt a short synthesis and interpretation, searching for different approaches to resilience and the underlying contextual and organisational explanatory variables. In doing so, we summarise what we have learned about the financial resilience of local governments across 11 countries and discuss possible developments and future research avenues.

While the financial crisis − in some way − impacted most of the countries included in this book, the effects on local governments were not uniform, with some being affected immediately and/or more substantially than others, partly due to the proximity of the crisis, the natural effects of pre-existing fiscal profiles and intergovernmental relations or national coping policies.

The analysis conducted across the 45 local shows that resilience can take different forms, but that important commonalities can be identified across countries. This reveals that there is no one single approach to resilience and that organisations have the choice, based on their latent capacities and how they perceive their vulnerability in the face of a crisis, over which pathway they follow.

The different patterns of financial resilience that emerge can be interpreted as the result of the dynamic interplay among the dimensions of anticipatory

Governmental Financial Resilience: International Perspectives on how Local Governments Face Austerity
Public Policy and Governance, Volume 27, 229−240
Copyright © 2017 by Emerald Publishing Limited
ISSN: 2053-7697/doi:10.1108/S2053-769720170000027013

capacity, coping capacity and financial shocks, as well as a local govern-
ment's associated vulnerability to them.

Keywords: Local government; austerity; resilience; anticipatory capacity;
coping capacity

The recent economic and financial crises have nurtured new attention towards
the related governmental financial responses among financial management
scholars, and to the role of management capacities in facing and absorbing
shocks among organisation scholars. This book suggests that looking at the
recent crises through the conceptual lens of resilience may help bridge the gap
between these two research streams and provide lessons of general and long-
term relevance on how governments face shocks that affect their financial conditions. Moreover, it highlights how the evolutionary and dynamic perspective
offered by resilience (Davoudi, Brooks, & Mehmood, 2013; Sutcliffe & Vogus,
2003) may contribute to enrich and integrate the insights coming from financial
management and organisational literatures on how governments deal with
financial shocks and disturbances.

The resurgence of scholarly interest towards governmental financial crises is
due to a number of factors, including not only the sovereign debt crises, but
also the increasing number of bankruptcies in local authorities and, more generally, the conditions of cutback management that are striking many public sector organisations. This has encouraged reflections on how to predict and detect
fiscal distress (Cepiku & Bonomi Savignon, 2012; Hendrick, 2004; Kloha,
Weissert, & Kleine, 2005; Maher & Deller, 2010; Trussel & Patrick, 2009), as
well as on how austerity is being tackled by governments (Baker, 2011;
Bozeman, 2010; Dougherty & Klase, 2009; Hendrick, 2011; Klase, 2011; Maher
& Deller, 2010; Pandey, 2010; Raudla et al., 2013; Scorsone & Plerhoples, 2010;
West & Condrey, 2011). However, this literature tends to overlook the organisational conditions, capacities and histories that may affect reactions to crises.
The adoption of a long-term, strategic view on the whole life cycle of public
organisations (Bozeman, 2010) requires exploring not only actions and reactions to crises and shocks, but also how pre-existing conditions and capacities
affect decisions and actions (see also Barbera, Jones, Korac, Saliterer, &
Steccolini, 2017). In the light of these considerations, authors contributing to
this book used the dimensions of the resilience framework (see Barbera et al.,
2017), that is financial shocks, vulnerability, anticipatory capacity and coping
capacity, to explore these aspects. The results show that the financial management arena appears to be particularly suited for studying resilience at a time
where fiscal stress and shocks are of particular significance.

'Though it may be too ambitious to summarise the richness of experiences emerging from the country chapters in a few lines, in this concluding chapter we attempt a short synthesis and interpretation, searching for different approaches to resilience and the underlying contextual and organisational explanatory variables. In doing so, we summarise what we have learned about the financial resilience of local governments across 11 countries and discuss possible developments and future research avenues.

COUNTRY SETTINGS AND THE ROLE OF THE EXTERNAL ENVIRONMENT

Across the world, countries have been affected by the global financial crisis differently, and thus have also responded to the related challenges in distinctive ways (Lodge & Hood, 2012; Peters, 2011). In order to account for this variety, our book takes into consideration local governments in 11 countries, which are characterised by different administrative systems (Meyer & Hammerschmid, 2010; Pollitt & Bouckaert, 2011), local government profiles (Wolman, 2014), as well as strategies in responding to the financial crisis.

While the financial crisis − in some way − impacted most of the countries included in this book, the effects on local governments were not uniform, with some being affected immediately and/or more substantially than others, partly due to the proximity of the crisis, the natural effects of pre-existing fiscal profiles and intergovernmental relations or national coping policies.

In this regard, the centrally defined policies for local governments, including fiscal arrangements (i.e. the structure, basis, and controllability of major revenue sources, debt rules, investment guidelines, monitoring systems, tax limits), appear to have influenced not only the impact, but also the range of possible fiscal responses to the financial and economic crisis. Local governments in several countries (e.g. France, England, Italy, Greece, The Netherlands, US) had to deal with national governments intentionally cutting back or delaying subnational transfers/grants. The latter was regarded as particularly problematic in contexts where the local level's fiscal autonomy (level of own revenues sources, tax base, tax scope) was described as low and strict spending limits as well as debt rules were in force, resulting in expenditure reductions putting great pressure on local governments. Indeed, local governments in most countries have limited financial autonomy (see Sweden and Greece as exceptions), with some of them (e.g. Austria, US) being (heavily) dependent on shared tax arrangements, where local governments suffer when tax revenues as a result of economic crisis decrease in general. The loss of flexibility in revenues through tax limits on or removal of local taxes mandated by upper government levels was also described as a great challenge, or even perceived as a shock (e.g. France, Italy, Australia and Germany).

While national policies constrained local governments' responses both on the revenue as well as the expenditure side, crisis-related factors (e.g. unemployment) automatically triggered expenditure increases in areas where local governments are directly responsible, such as social care services. Only in a few cases, increased expenditures were buffered through increased grants from the national level (e.g. Sweden), while in others they had to be carried by local governments themselves (Italy, Germany), even in a context of decreasing own revenues (e.g. local taxes) and/or transfers. In a number of countries, services were transferred from the central or regional government to the local level with inadequate or no funding support at all (e.g. Austria, Italy, England). It became also evident that in some contexts, regulations or guidelines seem to have fostered the institutionalisation of stronger capacities across cases, thus better equipping the investigated local governments to anticipate or to cope with possible shocks (England, The Netherlands, Victoria in Australia) while reverse effects are shown in others (Brazil, Greece, New South Wales in Australia).

Not unexpectedly, the role of the external environment, and especially of national policies, emerged as relevant from the interviews. However, the analysis also highlights that environmental features per se are not sufficient in explaining patterns of LGs' financial resilience over time.

WHAT DID WE LEARN ABOUT GOVERNMENT FINANCIAL RESILIENCE? CROSS-BOUNDARY FINANCIAL RESILIENCE PATTERNS

Most of the country chapters focused on the fortunes of four local government cases. Using the dimensions of the resilience framework (Barbera et al., 2017), that is financial shocks, vulnerability, anticipatory capacity and coping capacity, the authors provide a vivid picture of how local governments respond to shocks in their financial environment over time. Herein, financial shocks represent any unexpected external event that has significant impact on the finances of a local government. During the investigated period, the most relevant external shocks quoted by the interviewees were mainly related to the financial crisis (and its aftermath), including shrinking revenue bases, significant reductions in transfers/grants, increased demand for social support, etc. Vulnerability is interpreted as the perceived exposure to shocks, that is the level and sources of vulnerability and their development over time. Anticipatory capacities refer to the availability of tools and capabilities that enable organisations to better identify and manage their vulnerabilities and to recognise potential financial shocks before they arise, as well as their nature, likelihood, timing, scale and potential impacts (Barbera et al., 2017). Coping capacities refer to resources and abilities that allow shocks to be faced and vulnerabilities to be managed. The latter comprise abilities to buffer, adapt and transform (see also Béné et al., 2012;

Darnhofer, 2014; Davoudi et al., 2013; Folke et al., 2010), which are not mutually exclusive but can be deployed in conjunction with each other.

The analysis conducted across the 45 local governments (five in Germany and four in the other 10 countries respectively) shows that resilience can take different forms, but that important commonalities can be identified across countries. Indeed, the patterns of resilience identified in the analysis are spread across countries with no single pattern being associated with any one country. Resilience therefore encompasses diversity, while the different paths and patterns associated with it can be thought of as a universal concept. This reveals that there is no one single approach to resilience and that organisations have the choice, based on their latent capacities and how they perceive their vulnerability in the face of a crisis, as to which pathway they follow.

The different patterns of financial resilience that emerge from the analysis are: self-regulative/pro-active adaptation patterns, constrained adaptation patterns, reactive adaptation patterns, and patterns that can be classed as powerlessness and contentedness broadly reflect the typologies proposed by Barbera et al. (2017). These patterns can be interpreted as the result of the dynamic interplay among the dimensions of anticipatory capacity, coping capacity, financial shocks as well as the associated vulnerability to them. Each pattern is described below.

Self-Regulation/Pro-Active Adaptation

The local governments showing this pattern of behaviour are able to look at shocks as opportunities for improvement, and thus appear proactive in responding to them. This includes adopting wide-ranging measures and being ready to adapt or transform to reduce expenditure, reconfigure service delivery and find alternative sources of income. In short, these local governments appear to be able to internally develop, over time, self-regulating capacities that allow them to more successfully react to shocks, employing the full range of coping capacities. Reactions are, thus, based on existing competences and resources as well as exploring new alternatives (e.g. innovation, networking). The nature of these organisations means that they already had good anticipatory and coping capacities in place before the crisis, which in turn resulted in a good understanding of their relative vulnerability leading to lower levels of vulnerability at the start of the period. What differentiates this group from other adaptive types is a belief in their ability to manage not only their internal capacities, but to also their ability to use and shape the external environment to generate opportunities for income creation, demand management, and service delivery. For example, as shown in the case of Municipality D in France and Sesto San Giovanni in Italy, self-regulating/pro-actively adapting local governments put in place strategic processes and took a long-term view across a variety of fronts. In others, this approach was nothing new and had, as was the case for M4 in the United States, Manchester in England and the Swedish S2 and S4, been built up in response to previous crises, allowing these local governments to operate from a position of strength in terms of being able to draw on a range of pre-existing capacities.

Constrained Adaptation

This smaller group differs from the self-regulatory/proactive adaptation group as local governments herein are either unable to control their own destiny or have not yet reached a position where they are able to do so. They are constantly and proactively adapting, but are constrained by external forces, usually exerted by upper levels of government. Even though they do not perceive their environment as being as controllable as their self-regulating peers, this group differs from the reactive adapter group as, in line with the self-regulators, they see shocks as opportunities and have in place, or are able to develop, a range of capacities that allow them to continually change and adapt. Despite this optimistic outlook, there is a danger that under prolonged periods of financial strain, and as perceptions regarding their long-term vulnerability worsen, there could be a tendency to slip into a more fatalistic mode, as shown in the case of Loddonshire in Australia and Wigan in England. Alternatively, this group may try to break free of the constraints and attempt to seek a more self-regulating path in the longer term, something that Derbyshire in England was discussing at the time of the interviews.

Reactive Adaptation

Within this pattern, local governments have learned to deal with austerity largely by adapting to changed circumstances in their environment. The nature of adaptation here appears to be diverse and could extend to both anticipatory and coping capacities, with a consequential impact on respective vulnerabilities. Local governments in this group are characterised by both an acceptance of the need to adapt to changing circumstances as well as the implementation of actions to do so – aspects that clearly distinguish them from more fatalist responses that are sometimes exhibited in the final two groups. Reactive adapters can also be differentiated from the other, constrained or self-regulative/ proactive adaptive types, as they appear to need triggers to activate the deployment or building of capacities. Local governments across this pattern entered the crisis period with varying levels of vulnerability and anticipatory capacity. Rather than having a strong set of anticipatory capacities from the start, the impact of the crisis took some in this group by surprise and as such they did not, at least initially, fully comprehend the extent of their vulnerability. In one case, M3 in the United States, which was temporally closer to the onset of the crisis than other countries, even negated early warnings and did not appreciate the potential magnitude of the crisis. Others, such as Ede and Hengelo in The Netherlands, appear to have had medium anticipatory abilities. In either case, these tend to have been strengthened through investment in the aftermath of the crisis. There is also a propensity to engage in coping capacities that go beyond simple buffering, resulting in either adaptive or possibly moves towards transformative capability. In fact, there are a wide range of coping capacities displayed across this group with some focusing on retrenchment (buffering/ downsizing) (e.g. Brazil 2, US 1, Germany 1) while others seek to reposition themselves in more comprehensive ways (e.g. Austria 2, Brazil 3, B4, France 3, Germany 3, Sweden 3, US 3), possibly putting them in a stronger position should another crisis occur in the near future. This developmental/progression characteristic perhaps also reflects the typical experience of Swedish local governments, which had already been through a major trauma earlier in their life-cycles that left them better prepared to respond to the recent global financial crisis.

Powerlessness

Here, the financial crisis would seemingly exceed the threshold of local governments' existing capacities, leading to a perception of powerlessness and forcing them into a fatalist mode, that is a day-by-day management of emergencies, leaving them highly reliant on buffering capacities, externally driven and constrained by external pressures. Although the anticipatory capacity may be expected to increase over time, such cases (e.g. Rozzano Italy and the French FA and FB) respond with rather passive behaviour, and an orientation towards buffering capacities may prevail. Such local governments may be less willing to take ownership of necessary changes, deflecting issues back onto national governments and postponing solutions. The lack of both anticipatory and coping capacities could lead to such local governments having a poor understanding of their vulnerabilities, leaving them highly vulnerable at the beginning of the crisis and remaining vulnerable at the end. Such an approach is not sustainable against protracted, deep and enduring financial cuts. Indeed, at least one local government that appears to operate under this pattern of resilience (Central Darling Shire in Australia) has come under intense governmental scrutiny and has been placed into an extended period of financial administration. There is a risk therefore that adopting such an approach in the wrong conditions is not merely fatalist, but fatal and could lead to an even higher vulnerability to future shocks.

Contentedness

For this group, we see some local governments that were relatively wealthy and therefore not particularly vulnerable at the onset of the crisis. Such local governments may be expected to have weak anticipatory capacities as their relative wealth has meant they have never had to face a significant financial crisis before, being either immune to shocks, or being able to absorb them comfortably should they occur. Furthermore, their favourable environmental conditions may have encouraged them to downplay emerging and increasing vulnerabilities and to not invest in building anticipatory and coping capacities as their still wealthy conditions and context offset extant anticipatory and coping weaknesses (as was the case for A3/A4 in Austria, GB/GD from Greece, AUS 4 and I4). In short, they would appear to behave like contented organisations, which, resting on their laurels, had not anticipated the crisis, hoping to weather the storm relying on their buffering capacities. In the long term however, this may translate into increased vulnerability and the need to take stronger actions in developing anticipatory coping capacities.

FINAL REMARKS

Looking at 45 local governments across 11 countries, this book provides a testimony on how local governments around the globe are trying hard to keep providing services to their local communities while fighting shocks, austerity and difficulties. The authors of the country chapters offer us a picture that is at the same time worrying and reassuring. Providing public services to local communities, far from being an ordinary task, is becoming an increasingly extraordinary challenge, the more so under the strain caused by rising unemployment and migration, continuously changing national policies, hard central constraints, and cutting back of resources. Seen from the outside, and coupled with mere figures of debt, deficits, and financial cuts, or aseptic descriptions of the local government field, this may sound discouraging. But it would also be too simplistic. The authors of the chapters in this book have not stopped at the door of the local governments they are describing. They have fully engaged with them, talking with people and listening to their perceptions about the everyday challenges they face, but also of the ways in which day-by-day they try to anticipate and cope with them. This allowed them to offer us a richer, nuanced and probably more encouraging picture. Their accounts show that many local governments either had already in place capacities to anticipate and cope with the crises, or were prompted by the crisis to put in place measures to strengthen them. The crisis has surely put them to the test, but has also triggered paths of development of internal capacities and reflections on how to improve the status quo. Thus, financial resilience is not an alien concept to local government. Rather it is a way of being and behaving that needs to be better understood, explored and highlighted, so as to share possible lessons to learn for the future, or for other local governments that are struggling against similar challenges. Indeed, the study also highlighted cases of limited aware-ness of the importance of investing on internal capacities, or awareness of diffi-culties coupled with a pessimistic disposition towards fatalism. In this respect, we hope that this book will help to raise stronger awareness of the importance not only of a conducive institutional and economic environment, but also of nurturing, maintaining and leveraging capacities for anticipation, adaptation, and transformation.

It would be unfair and naïve to reduce the richness and variety that emerges from each country chapter to a number of abstract and aseptic tables and graphs, or a list of lessons to learn. As such, the reader will need to read the accounts presented in each chapter to capture the whole spectrum and depth of the experiences that we are pleased to host in this book. Nevertheless, while each chapter tells us a rich and unique story about each country and the selected municipalities, as editors of the book we are required to draw a few concluding remarks, referring to the main messages that have emerged.

As we suggested above, financial resilience proved a useful concept to cap-ture ways of being and behaving of local governments in the face of difficult times, for several reasons.

First, it allows for a more integrative view of local public finances that focuses not only on pressures and stimuli coming from the external environ-ment, and on financial data, but also a view more focused on organisational pre-conditions and capacities. As such, financial resilience requires us to jointly consider external and internal factors, as well as their interaction. It is not enough to focus solely on traditional financial measures to analyse and predict organisational success or failure in response to crises, but it is also necessary to get underneath the internal capacities and capabilities that act as shaping forces within organisations.

Second, it pointed to the need to recognise that capacities and organisational contingencies are continuously in flux, and interact with each other and with external factors over time. It is thus necessary to avoid simplistic and determin-istic views on cause-effect relationships (such as the crisis will cause cuts in ser-vices, or will translate into the development of coping capacities), while being aware that a number of possible paths of developments are available, depend-ing on the interactions of a number of factors. In sum, the analysis points to the importance of the evolutionary and dynamic perspective of resilience and hence of looking at configurations of capacities over time, rather than statically focusing on some of them at a specific point in time. Financial resilience must therefore be seen as a dynamic concept.

Third, and following on from the above, there is not a single type of resil-ience. The analysis shows that there may be different ways of being financially resilient, resulting from different combinations of anticipatory, buffering, adapting and transforming capacities, perceived sources and levels of vulnerability, and the external environment. Interestingly, a central role in 'mediating' among the different dimensions is represented by the processes through which people in the organisations filter and interpret internal and external conditions, and how they make sense of them (Weick, 1988; Weick & Sutcliffe, 2007). In this respect, the type of path of progress or regression in internal capacities in the face of crises will also depend on how people see and interpret the crises, existing conditions, and the future possibilities of actions. Crises cannot only be seen as triggers for change, but also as mirrors, which prompt organisations to reveal their capacities and attitudes. Along these lines, the stories told in this book tell us that local governments continuously struggle to find an equilibrium between financial and non-financial goals, pressures from the external environment and organisational resources, capacities and responses. For some, this resulted in more active and adaptive paths of resilience, whereas for others they were, at least initially, passive and non-adaptive.

The findings also have some broader implications for both regulators and local authorities. The analysis shows that local authorities' approaches to financial resilience are significantly affected by central government's policies. Thus, policy makers have a strong responsibility in affecting responses to crises. In some of the cases analysed, legislative uncertainty and the current re-centralisation of funding and decision making processes appear to seriously restrict and jeopardise variety in municipal responses, and at the same time provide scapegoats for local authorities to elude and postpone the solutions of problems. Thus, relatively stable and at the same time empowering financial policies may be desirable to ensure self-responsible behaviours of local authorities. In this regard, the analysis shows that research is also needed to determine what characteristics of accounting, control and reporting systems may enhance financial resilience.

There are a number of ways in which the reflection suggested in this book could be enriched in the future. This book focused on 11 countries across Europe, the American continent and Oceania, with a predominance of the former, but we may need to know more about other continents (Asia, Africa), or countries (e.g. other South American countries, or Eastern European ones). Also, it looked at resilience at the local government level, but it would be interesting to expand the analysis to other levels of governments, including intermediate, central or even supra-national ones, and to the interrelationships among them. Another possible way to further develop the analysis is to complement it by adopting different methods, such as surveys or more generally quantitative analyses. Moreover, while we focused on financial resilience, it would be important to better explore the complex links between financial and non-financial resilience, and between governmental and community resilience. While this book specifically focused on the global financial crisis and the related austerity context, it would be interesting to see to what extent and how the lessons learned there can be extended to new shocks and difficulties looming ahead for governments, including migration movements, populism and the unexpected results of elections and referenda, as well as terrorist attacks.

REFERENCES

Baker, D. L. (2011). Local government cutback budgeting. *The Public Manager, 40*(1), 9−11.

Barbera, C., Jones, M., Korac, S., Saliterer, I., & Steccolini, I. (2017). Governmental financial resilience under austerity in Austria, England and Italy: How do local governments cope with financial shocks? Public Administration, forthcoming.

Bozeman, B. (2010). Hard lessons from hard times: Reconsidering and reorienting the "Management Decline" literature. *Public Administration Review, 70*(4), 557−563.

Cepiku, D., & Bonomi Savignon, A. (2012). Governing cutback management: Is there a global.

Darnhofer, I. (2014). Resilience and why it matters for farm management. *European Review of Agricultural Economics, 41*(3), 461−484. doi:10.1093/erae/jbu012

Davoudi, S., Brooks, E., & Mehmood, A. (2013). Evolutionary resilience and strategies for climate adaptation. *Planning Practice and Research, 28*(3), 307−322.

Dougherty, M. J., & Klase, K. A. (2009). Fiscal retrenchment in state budgeting: Revisiting cutback management in a new era. *International Journal of Public Administration, 32*(7), 593−619.

Folke, C., Carpenter, S. R., Walker, B., Scheffer, M., Chapin, T., & Rockström, J. (2010). Resilience thinking: Integrating resilience, adaptability and transformability. *Ecology and Society, 15*(4), 20. [online]. Retrieved from http://www.ecologyandsociety.org/vol15/iss4/art20/

Hendrick, R. (2004). Assessing and measuring the fiscal health of local governments: Focus on Chicago suburban municipalities. *Urban Affairs Review, 40*(1), 78−114.

Hendrick, R. (2011). *Managing the fiscal metropolis: The financial policies, practices, and health of suburban municipalities*. Washington, DC: Georgetown University Press.

Klase, K. A. (2011). The intersection of flexible budgeting and cutback management: Factors affecting the responses of selected states to recent economic recessions. *Public Finance and Management, 11*(2), 197−230.

Kloha, P., Weissert, C. S., & Kleine, R. (2005). Developing and testing a composite model to predict local fiscal distress. *Public Administration Review, 65*(3), 313−323.

Lodge, M., & Hood, C. (2012). Into an age of multiple austerities? Public management and public service bargains across OECD countries. *Governance: An International Journal of Policy, Administration, and Institutions, 25*(1), 79−101.

Maher, C. S., & Deller, S. C. (2010). Measuring municipal fiscal condition: Do objective measures of fiscal health relate to subjective measures? *Journal of Public Budgeting, Accounting & Financial Management, 23*(3), 427−450.

Meyer, R. E., & Hammerschmid, G. (2010). The degree of decentralization and individual decision making in central government human resource management: A European comparative perspective. *Public Administration, 88*(2), 455–478.

Pandey, S. K. (2010). Cutback management and the paradox of publicness. *Public Administration Review, 70*(3), 564−571.

Peters, B. G. (2011). Governance responses to the fiscal crisis – Comparative perspectives. *Public Money and Management, 31*(1), 75−80.

Pollitt, C., & Bouckaert, G. (2011). Public management reform: A comparative analysis – New public management, governance, and the neo−Weberian state. *International Review of Administrative Sciences, 78*(1), 180−182.

Raudla, R., Savi, R., & Randma-Liiv, T. (2013). *Literature review on cutback management.* COCOPS deliverable 7.1. Retrieved from http://www.cocops.eu/wp-content/uploads/2013/03/COCOPS_Deliverable_7_1.pdf. Accessed on December 12, 2014.

Scorsone, E. A., & Plerhoples, C. (2010). Fiscal stress and cutback management amongst state and local governments: What have we learned and what remains to be learned? *State and Local Government Review, 42*(2), 176–187.

Sutcliffe, K. M., & Vogus, T. J. (2003). Organizing for resilience. In K. S. Cameron, J. E. Dutton, & R. E. Quinn (Eds.), *Positive organizational scholarship: Foundations of a new discipline.* San Francisco, CA: Berrett-Koehler.

Trussel, J. M., & Patrick, P. A. (2009). A predictive model of fiscal distress in local governments. *Journal of Public Budgeting, Accounting & Financial Management, 21*(4), 578–616.

Weick, K. E. (1988). Enacted sensemaking in crisis situations. *Journal of Management Studies, 25*(4), 305–317.

Weick, K. E., & Sutcliffe, K. M. (2007). *Managing the unexpected: Resilient performance in an age of uncertainty.* San Francisco, CA: Jossey-Bass.

West, J. P., & Condrey, S. E. (2011). Municipal government strategies for controlling personnel costs during the fiscal storm. *Journal of Public Budgeting, Accounting and Financial Management, 23*(3), 395–426.

Wolman, H. (2014). National fiscal policy and local government during the economic crisis. Urban Policy Paper Series, the German Marshall Fund of the United States, Washington, DC.

INDEX

www.ingramcontent.com/pod-product-compliance
Lightning Source LLC
Chambersburg PA
CBHW050348270326
41926CB00016B/3651